About Island Press

Since 1984, the nonprofit Island Press has been stimulating, shaping, and communicating the ideas that are essential for solving environmental problems worldwide. With more than 800 titles in print and some 40 new releases each year, we are the nation's leading publisher on environmental issues. We identify innovative thinkers and emerging trends in the environmental field. We work with world-renowned experts and authors to develop cross-disciplinary solutions to environmental challenges.

Island Press designs and implements coordinated book publication campaigns in order to communicate our critical messages in print, in person, and online using the latest technologies, programs, and the media. Our goal: to reach targeted audiences—scientists, policymakers, environmental advocates, the media, and concerned citizens—who can and will take action to protect the plants and animals that enrich our world, the ecosystems we need to survive, the water we drink, and the air we breathe.

Island Press gratefully acknowledges the support of its work by the Agua Fund, Inc., Annenberg Foundation, The Christensen Fund, The Nathan Cummings Foundation, The Geraldine R. Dodge Foundation, Doris Duke Charitable Foundation, The Educational Foundation of America, Betsy and Jesse Fink Foundation, The William and Flora Hewlett Foundation, The Kendeda Fund, The Andrew W. Mellon Foundation, The Curtis and Edith Munson Foundation, Oak Foundation, The Overbrook Foundation, the David and Lucile Packard Foundation, The Summit Fund of Washington, Trust for Architectural Easements, Wallace Global Fund, The Winslow Foundation, and other generous donors.

The opinions expressed in this book are those of the author(s) and do not necessarily reflect the views of our donors.

Taking Back Eden

Taking Back Eden

Eight Environmental Cases that Changed the World

Oliver A. Houck

ISLANDPRESS

Washington | Covelo | London

Copyright © 2010 Oliver A. Houck

All rights reserved under International and Pan-American Copyright Conventions. No part of this book may be reproduced in any form or by any means without permission in writing from the publisher: Island Press, 1718 Connecticut Ave., NW, Suite 300, Washington, DC 20009.

ISLAND PRESS is a trademark of the Center for Resource Economics.

Library of Congress Cataloging-in-Publication Data

Houck, Oliver A.
 Taking back Eden : eight environmental cases that changed the world / Oliver Houck.
    p. cm.
 Includes bibliographical references and index.
 ISBN-13: 978-1-59726-647-5 (cloth : alk. paper)
 ISBN-10: 1-59726-647-7 (cloth : alk. paper) 1. Environmental law—Cases.
I. Title.
 K3585.H68 2010
 344.04′6—dc22

                                                    2009020226

Printed on recycled, acid-free paper

Manufactured in the United States of America
10 9 8 7 6 5 4 3 2 1

Contents

Prologue

In the early 1960s, I found myself landing in New York City too late to make the connecting flight home. I called a friend from college with whom I had dreamed about writing the great American novel. Instead, I'd joined the Army and he had become a lawyer. He said to come on over, he had a couch.

I arrived after midnight. Al's wife had gone to bed, but he was up and as disheveled as I'd remembered, his shirt tails hanging like a nightgown and a hairstyle from Morgus the Magnificent. One light was on in a tiny study, and spread over the desk were sheets of yellow paper covered with his meticulous handwriting. The notepad showed a series of sentences begun and crossed out a half a dozen times. He had just started his next try. He was composing a brief, he told me. I had been in transit for nearly thirty hours, but I felt too keyed up to go to bed. And so, moving the cat to sit down on a low chair, I asked him about the case.

In his low, understated voice Al began telling me about a complicated proceeding before the Federal Power Commission, whatever that was. I started to yawn. His clients opposed the construction of a power plant on top of a mountain. Apparently they didn't like the look of the thing, and there was something else in there about fish. The more he talked, the more abstract it seemed. Al, I thought, they are at each other's throats in Korea and you are worried about what? Instead, I tried to follow him through the difficulties of getting a court to hear his case in the first place. His clients didn't deal in power and they didn't own the mountain. So what business did they have contesting a power license? At which point the long trip must have caught up with me because I next remember waking up in the morning to the cat on my stomach and the smell of coffee.

When I walked out of the bathroom and into Al's office, he was already back in there writing. He hadn't shaved yet. He had moved a few pages past the sentences that had been giving him trouble, and looked to be on a roll. We talked about the case again, which was clearly weighing him down. It seems that the fish were called striped bass, and people who tried to catch them cared a great deal about them. I don't remember much more, except leaving later that day and thinking, poor Al, he seems to have gotten stuck in a rut.

A few years following, with a law degree now and a turn as a federal prosecutor behind me, I fell into the natural world. The move was completely fortuitous, but environmental protection became the pole star of my life. Slowly, over time, it dawned on me that much of what I was doing and that the entire field of environmental law was doing had been jump-started by the sentences on the yellow pad on Al's desk in his apartment in New York City those many years before. It was like being present at The Creation. Al was writing the briefs in a case called *Storm King Mountain*, which opened the courthouse doors to a new kind of lawsuit and shook the pillars of government and industry. A revolution that, having swept the United States, is now traveling the globe.

This book is about that phenomenon.

Oliver A. Houck
October 2008

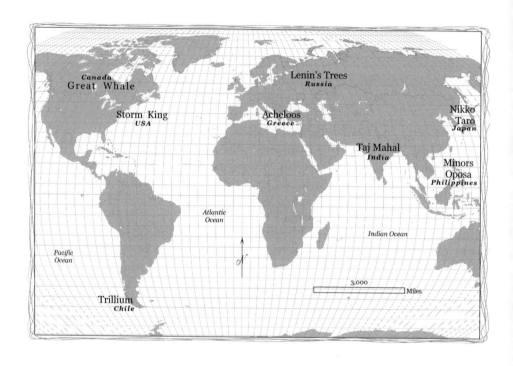

Canada
Great Whale

Storm King
USA

Trillium
Chile

Pacific
Ocean

Atlantic
Ocean

Lenin's Trees
Russia

Acheloos
Greece

Taj Mahal
India

Nikko
Taro
Japan

Minors
Oposa
Philippines

Indian Ocean

N

3,000 ⌐────────────┐ Miles

The Awakening

In no other political or social movement has litigation played such an important and dominant role. Not even close.

David Sive, 1988

WHERE DID it come from?

Growing up in the late 1940s, we all knew how the world was going to end. First came the big flash, then the roar of the bomb, and we disappeared into thin air. Unless of course we took refuge under our school desks as government films told us to do. Those drills seemed a little questionable to those of us who sat in the back row, but we did them anyway. Talking among ourselves, asking around, few were confident that we would live to old age.

Two decades later along came news of a poisoned landscape, the death of Lake Erie, rivers that caught fire and smogs that killed people in London and then shut down Pittsburgh for weeks at a stretch. The bald eagle was on the brink of extinction. Pesticides had eliminated Louisiana's state symbol, the brown pelican, two separate times. Oil coated the beaches of Santa Barbara, and barrels of old chemicals were turning up near where deformed newborns were beginning to die. There seemed to be a new kind of end game coming, and it would not require a bomb after all. You could see it in the paper and smell it from the front door. All we had to do was to keep on trucking.

And then, on a bright weekend day in April 1970, as if by magic, a half a million people appeared on the National Mall in Washington, D.C. They came alone and in families, regular Fourth of July Americans who had never protested a thing in their lives, men wearing Bermudas, mothers pushing strollers, women old enough to be *their* mothers, hippies and straights, the committed and the curious, until they were a sea of faces and homemade signs stretching from the Washington Monument to the far end of the reflecting pool saying that they were fed up with what was happening to the world around them, and they wanted it to stop. The government was asleep at the wheel.

Earth Day caught everyone by surprise. The FBI, certain that the demonstration was inspired by communists, went around the Mall taking names. Similar protests, however, were rising all around the country, which was already reeling from riots over civil rights and the Vietnam War. American youngsters coined a new word, *ecotage*, and set out looking for likely targets. It could have become ugly here too, all over again.

Then another unusual thing happened. Instead of calling out more troops, the country came up with a different answer. It allowed the very people who were protesting pollution to take their government to court. They were the ones with the most at stake. Ordinary people, anyone on the Mall that day, would be able to go toe to toe with the most powerful forces in America to protect the environment by legal process. The idea was revolutionary.

There was precedent here, but very little. Legal aid societies and the NAACP had sued government agencies on behalf of their clients, and more recently urban homeowners were beginning to challenge highways that bulldozed through their neighborhoods. Even federal prosecutors were getting into the act, filing actions against polluters in New York City and Washington, D.C. Things were beginning to perk. But the idea that everyday citizens could sue to protect the environment that none of them owned but that they all shared was startlingly new. Within a wink, new litigating groups such as the Environmental Defense Fund and the Natural Resources Defense Council sprang up to represent them. And they started winning.

The government and its allies in industry were as shocked by these developments as they had been by Earth Day. Major monies were on the line. The prestige of institutions as powerful as the Atomic Energy Commission and the Army Corps of Engineers was at stake as well, to say nothing of the politicians who backed them. And so in the fall of that same year, without prior warning, and with whatever prompting, the secretary of the treasury proposed to eliminate the charitable status of groups that brought environmental lawsuits. It was a bold move. Without tax exempt contributions, these groups would dry up, and, with them, the nascent environmental docket. The groups fought back. They found allies in Congress. New York's Senator Javits declared that these lawsuits, the ability of citizens to sue for the public good, were the nation's answer to "those kids out there in the streets who had little avenue for protest beyond tearing things down." The secretary backed down.

Looking back, environmental litigation was by no means preordained. To begin with, you couldn't go to court. In the early 1960s, when all of this began to break, most people had no right to sue the government, and that included all those people on the Washington Mall who felt this new kind of injury from a wasted and diminishing world. Until finally, in 1965, a court ruled otherwise. They too could file. That case starts this book, Storm King. Then an even more unusual thing happened. Storm King started traveling abroad.

There was no grand strategy. There was no plan at all. Instead, a few deeply committed individuals in Canada, Russia, the Far East, and as far south as Tierra del Fuego began to advance this same notion, that citizens could sue to protect the environment. They had no expectations of getting paid. The money was on the other side. They had even less law to work with than their American counterparts, and they faced real-world repercussions as well. Some had already been arrested for promoting civil rights. A brilliant advocate in Moscow would be put out of business. One attorney featured in this book raided a renegade logging ship at sea to document a complaint. A few years later one of his closest colleagues was assassinated on the doorstep of his home. These are not ordinary challenges.

This book, then, is in part their story. It is also the story of how environmental protection came to some of the most unexpected venues on Earth. It begins with Storm King, a power plant on the Hudson Highlands that ushered in the field. It then goes to Japan where, shortly thereafter, the defenders of ancient trees at a sacred shrine were challenging an invincible construction machine, and from there to the Philippines and Minors Oposa, one man, his children, and the disappearing rain forest. It moves next to Canada where a trio of water projects, each one an agony, established federal authority to protect the environment, then to India and the Taj Mahal, to Russia and Lenin's Trees, and Greece, with its horns still locked over the fate of the Acheloos River. The journey ends in Chile with the case of Trillium and the most unlikely venue yet, a forest at the end of the world.

I have chosen to tell the stories of these cases because they opened the way, and because they involved extraordinary places and things. But I am also writing to celebrate their actors who had the courage to speak truth to power and then to take it on, for pieces of our natural world whose adequate description is difficult and whose value is beyond measure. After them, there is no turning back.

CHAPTER ONE

Storm King

To those who know it, the Hudson River is the most beautiful, messed up, productive, ignored, and surprising piece of water on the face of the earth. There is no other river quite like it, and for some persons, myself included, no other river will do. The Hudson is the river.

    Robert Boyle, Founder, Hudson River Fisherman's Association

IN THE EARLY 1960s, Consolidated Edison of New York City, the most powerful utility company in America, announced its intention to build the world's largest pump storage power plant on Storm King Mountain. It would run into opposition from residents who loved the Hudson River Highlands, and from others for whom fishing the Hudson River was a reason to live. That those two parties got together at all was something of an only-in-America miracle. That they could win was unthinkable.

𝔇

THE HUDSON River rises in the northern Adirondacks and runs more than three hundred miles to the island of Manhattan and the sea. Halfway through this journey it emerges from the mountains near Albany, already level with the ocean, creating a 150-mile estuary above New York Harbor and one of the great inland waterways of the world. For two centuries, the Hudson marked the route of commerce for the American colonies and their principal line of defense. British and American armies would fight, fortify, and attack the length of it, and the very mention of Hudson River names—White Plains, Saratoga, Ticonderoga, and the treason of Benedict Arnold at West Point—is to recount much of the Revolutionary War. Dutch family dynasties as imposing as the Van Cortlands and the Schuylers settled along the Hudson and marked society with their order. In 1825, the Erie Canal finally connected the Hudson to the Great Lakes and Ohio, routing trade through New York City to every continent on the globe. There are larger rivers in America than this one, but none was so present at its birth.

There has always been more to the Hudson, however, than commerce. Ninety miles below Albany it sweeps by Storm King Mountain, guarding the entrance to the Hudson Highlands and one of the most spectacular vistas in the world. Here the river twists through a series of wide gorges flanked by bluffs and ridges that turn green in summer and gold and red with fall, backed by rolling country as far as the eye can see. Early European travelers recorded the scene in wonder. To the German globe-trotter Baedeker, it was "grander and more inspiring than the Rhine." It gave birth to its own movement in painting, whose lead artists, Cole and Church, made raw nature the principal of the play. Humans, where they appeared at all, were tiny and off to the side, marveling at the scenery as if they were seeing the life hereafter.

Marvel they did. The celebrated British actress Fanny Kemble, visiting the Hudson Highlands in the 1830s, wrote in her diary of "the shadow of a huge mountain, frowning over the height on which I stood." "Suddenly," she continued, "a shadow moved down its steep sunny side, threw a deep blackness over the sparkling river, and then climbed the opposite mountain on the far side," followed by a blaze of noonday sun. "I could have stretched out my arms and shouted aloud—I could have fallen on my knees and worshipped—I could have committed any extravagance that ecstasy could suggest." She was seeing Storm King.

The experience was sublime. The Hudson's first explorers, quartered with shipmates who rarely bathed and on ships that reeked with their own wastes, were overcome by the scent of nature that Verrazano called an "exhale" of the "sweetest odors." An early Dutch traveler to Manhattan described encountering "such a sweet smell in the air that we stood still, because we did not know what it was we were meeting." They were not simply seeing the Garden, they were *in* the Garden, and it seems more than coincidence that this region would produce America's first book on gardening and its foremost landscape architect, Frederick Law Olmsted, whose basic operating principle was that of the Hudson River painters: the more natural the landscape, the better.

All of this, then, was in the genes and the mindset of those who went into the lists to oppose the power plant on Storm King Mountain. They had little law behind them, and they faced a daunting adversary.

The Cornwall Hydroelectric Project: Power and Beauty for Tomorrow!
[Consolidated Edison brochure for Storm King power plant]

THE CON ED PROPOSAL was, to its managers, logical and benign. The company supplied electricity for the New York City region, and faced soaring demands from residential growth, air conditioning, and rate schedules that charged less per unit the more one used, a recipe for consumption. Proud to provide the power that heated, cooled, and illuminated this giant megalopolis, Con Ed named its headquarters building in downtown Manhattan the Tower of Light. Rather than build a new coal plant or run the gauntlet of approvals for a new nuclear reactor, the company's answer was a pumped storage facility on Storm King Mountain.

The mechanism was simple. The company would take power from the grid at times of low demand, pump water from the river, and push it two miles up a tunnel to a storage reservoir on the mountaintop. At peak demand the stored water would rush back down the tunnel to a powerhouse that converted the force to electricity. Three kilowatts of juice from conventional plants would be needed to provide only two kilowatts from Storm King, but the three were cheap and the two were worth real money. To Con Ed's engineers, the Hudson Highlands were an ideal location for pump storage power, and Storm King on size alone was the pick of the litter.

They anticipated little opposition. Here was a project that produced no pollution and no risk of nuclear meltdown, and it increased service for its voracious customer base. The only regulatory obstacle was the Federal Power Commission, which licensed these kinds of plants, but over the years the Commission had become indistinguishable from the utilities it was supposed to supervise. The attitude was deferential. "We're dealing with top officials in industry," a federal official said of his agency's lackluster enforcement record, "you just don't treat these people like that." The trigger for the fight to come was a sketch by a Con Ed employee of the project that showed Storm King Mountain with a bite out of one side to house an enormous powerhouse, and transmission lines spreading like tentacles from the scene. It was a perfectly sensible engineering drawing. One look at it was all it took to push Hudson Highland residents, already nervous about rumors of the proposal, over the edge.

The residents didn't see what they were in for either. It just grew. A handful of neighbors banded together as the Scenic Hudson Preservation Conference and did what they knew how to do: they hired a public relations firm. They had the means. The Highlands had harbored some of the iconic families in America, J. Pierpont Morgan, Jay Gould, William Averell Harriman, John Jacob Astor and Cornelius Vanderbilt, and John J. Rockefeller. Have we left anyone out? Before long Scenic Hudson and Con Ed began trading slogans, taunt for taunt. The company literature would announce, "Dig We Must!," and Scenic Hudson would reply, "Dig They Must Not!" The public relations firm took shots at Con Ed, in the words of *Fortune* magazine, "the company everyone loved to hate," which in turn labeled its critics "misinformed bird watchers, nature fakers, land grabbers and militant adversaries of progress." One opponent rose at a public hearing to declare himself a bird watcher but that all he saw from Con Ed was "buzzards and vultures." Insults, however, only travel so far.

Scenic Hudson also hired a lawyer. They chose well, a former federal power commissioner named Dale Doty who had since represented the utilities themselves before the agency. Doty was credible. His problem was that, as deep as the social connections and financial resources of his clients might be, they had very little law on their side. The Commission was authorized to approve power projects, which Congress had already determined to be important to the development of the country, whenever, "in its judgment," it found them to be "in the public interest" for commerce, water power, and "other beneficial purposes." A more deferential, do-whatever-you-want standard would be hard to imagine. To be sure, Congress had since added language about considering recreational interests, but that was about it. Congress had not spoken at all to the question of whether Scenic Hudson or any other citizens could even participate in Commission proceedings, much less appeal the agency's decision to a court of law.

At bottom, all that Doty and his clients had was that they didn't like the look of the Storm King project, which had some emotional appeal but very small legs. Then they received a gift from God.

I think no American river per mile is deeper in history, art, and perhaps literature than the Hudson, and some of its varied richness shows in the lore of the toponyms thereabouts. The river itself has been, to name a few, Cahohatatea, Shattemuck, Muhheakunnuk, Mahicanittuck, Mohegan, Grande Rivière, Angóleme, Rio San Antonio, Rio de Gomez, Rio de Montaigne, Norumbega, Manhattan, Mauritius, River of the Prince, Nassau, Grotte, Noordt, River of the Mountains, and (even today) the North. Along its banks no name is richer than Storm King, which Henry Hudson knew as Klinkersberg but Dutch settlers called Butter Hill, a description the local nineteenth-century "dude poet" N. P. Willis found not at all befitting its dominance of the lower river. He, according to one journalist, "bestowed in cold blood" the name of Storm King.

William Least Heat-Moon

THERE IS another Hudson River with its own set of legends. It is a 13,500 square mile nursery supporting shad, sturgeon, herring, alewives, blue crab, and menhaden, the commercial catch of the Atlantic seaboard. As in all estuaries, this zone of fresh water and salt, stoked with nutrients upstream and mixed by the tides, makes for some of the richest production on Earth. What was different about the Hudson estuary was that the zone stretched so far inland, bringing to the Highlands ocean creatures as rare as electric moonfish and Caribbean sea horses, and exporting trophy catches as far away as Maine and the Carolinas. The Hudson had been a fishery for millennia. Dutch explorers found middens of discarded oyster shells twelve feet deep. As one traveler noted of the Indian tribes along the river, "famine they do not fear."

This is before we come to the striped bass, a fish with the body of a bomb shell, the stamina of a boxer, and a staggering abundance. The Indians caught them in purse seines woven from the stems of marsh plants and weighted down with stones. It was said to be their favorite for taste and for the reputation they carried, as reported by the observant Dutch, for making "their women lascivious." When the men returned from fishing, the report continued, they gave this particular species to the women, "who look for them anxiously." While one does not find reports today of fishermen dropping dead stripers on longing wives, their ardor for this fish, in this place, has scarcely diminished. Many a Northeastern home holds striped bass widows, she alone with a book or the television, he out on some rocks or a deserted beach, it may be raining, trying to catch a big one, the prize.

The striped bass connection to Storm King was made by a freelance writer named Robert Boyle who set out to cover the Hudson for *Sports Illustrated* magazine. Not much was expected here. New York Harbor was widely regarded as a cesspool from which sea life had long been extinguished. To Boyle's surprise, he discovered fish. He also discovered commercial fishermen as far south as the George Washington Bridge. Better magazine copy yet, he found anglers in downtown Manhattan, fishing for stripers at the outfalls of sewers to the river. They talked nostalgically about the big runs at Seventy-Second Street that would attract up to forty men with rods at a time. They changed Boyle's life.

Before long Boyle was writing pieces on commercial fishers operating a few hundred feet from Sing Sing prison and holding their catch alive in abandoned mine pits. He uncovered a disheartening string of illegal dumps and toxic discharges that were poisoning the river. He dug out data on fish numbers and productivity, particularly at the mouth of the Hudson Highlands at Storm King Mountain. Boyle had heard about the power plant and the opposition to it, and he had a few concerns of his own. Among other things Con Ed's pumps were going to pull some six billion gallons of water out of the Hudson a day. A lot of fish would enter those tubes and never return.

In early 1964, ready for action, Boyle walked into the offices of Scenic Hudson. A former Marine, he was gruff, passionate, and loaded with facts. The group had no idea, he said, who the real losers were in this deal: the fishermen. The staff heard him out, jaws dropping, at the end of which one rose to her feet with a gleeful smile: "They're going to kill the fish! They're going to kill the fish!" It was, Boyle said later, like "Churchill hearing that Pearl Harbor had been bombed." Scenic Hudson had a second front, and an entirely new army to carry it.

SCENIC HUDSON needed all the help it could get. The hearings before the Federal Power Commission had not gone well. Con Ed objected to Scenic Hudson being present in the first place, an argument that the Commission rejected in all probability because the group's counsel, Dale Doty, had been one of their own. In these and subsequent proceedings, Doty would emphasize the aesthetic force of Storm King. A Yale University witness described the mountain as rising "like a Brown Bear out of the river, a dome of living granite, swelling with animal power," and went on to parallels in Greek mythology. To Con Ed's attorney, this line of testimony was as irrelevant as Scenic Hudson's very presence in the hearings. "Why waste time hearing people tell us this is an historic area?" he asked. Nonetheless, Scenic Hudson's witnesses were allowed to testify. The area *was* historic and it *was* beautiful. For whatever that meant.

In May 1965, the Commission did what everyone expected and approved the license. The benefits were tangible. The notion of beauty was classically the opposite, and seemed here to be only slightly impaired. Indeed, Con Ed produced a landscape architect of its own who testified that the size of the storage reservoir on top of Storm King would be an adornment to the mountain because "any large lake is handsomer than a small lake." As for the fishery, such issues were up to fish experts, and the company had hired one to claim that the effects would be minimal, particularly with the screens Con Ed promised to install to keep fish out of the tunnel. The decision did not even seem to be a close call.

So Scenic Hudson turned to the political arena. It motivated a committee of the state legislature to hold its own hearings on the matter. At which point Boyle made an amazing discovery. The winter months that year had been hard, and fish seeking warmer water had come to the huge intake structures of Con Ed's Indian Point Nuclear Reactor, only fifteen miles below Storm King. To deflect the fish from their pumps, the company had put in screens similar to those proposed at the Storm King plant, which turned out to be killing machines. Boyle had heard rumors of fish kills at Indian Point and went down to investigate. He was given photos of tons of dead fish piled up and shoveled out of the way in an effort to keep the plant's intakes open. Worse yet, there were striped bass in those rotting piles, the king fish of the Atlantic Seaboard. Armed with reports and photographs, Boyle and the newly formed Hudson River Fisherman's Association asked the Commission to reopen its hearings. Their request was denied, but their evidence in the record provided one more arrow on appeal.

No sooner had the Commission approved the license than Scenic Hudson, who knew the approval was coming, appealed to federal circuit in New York City. A wealthy patron of the Highlands offered to fund the appeal on the condition that it be handled by a lawyer in whom he had great confidence, Lloyd K. Garrison, a founding partner of one of the City's silk stocking law firms. Garrison had strong record in civil service. He was a leader in public education and often represented clients at odds with the US government. He had defended Robert Oppenheimer before the Atomic Energy Commission and Congress. He was also, according to a junior associate who would go on to handle the Storm King case after him for more than a decade, one of the most brilliant writers in the field. The case would ride in on a lion. It would also ride in on a law brief that took a very bold position.

Al Butzel had been with Garrison's law firm for only a few months when he was tapped to assist on the Storm King appeal. A recent Harvard law graduate, he had been floundering without distinction in the corporate department, increasingly nervous about his work and beginning to smoke cigarettes by the pack. Now he was facing litigation. "It was my worst dream," he later recalled, "to be involved in something that could lead to my having to appear in court." Even worse, he and Garrison knew that they were terribly short on precedent here. So

Garrison sent his young associate to find some. After sifting fruitlessly through the books for weeks and weekends, Butzel finally struck a speck of gold, a case that seemed to say that the Commission had a duty to examine issues on its own. This meant that it was not up to Scenic Hudson to prove irreparable damage to the Hudson Highlands or the Striped Bass fishery. Once these problems were flagged, the Commission had to go beyond Con Ed's evidence and investigate them. Such would be the thrust of the appeal. Not that the Commission was wrong, but that it hadn't done its homework.

Garrison was pleased. Getting a court to overrule the Commission's decision as just plain wrong would have been close to impossible, but rejecting the decision for failure to follow proper procedure was at least a possibility. Garrison was also a realist, however. He gave the appeal a "ten percent chance of winning, at best."

𝕯

APPELLATE ARGUMENTS are tactical. There is no time to raise all the issues in the case. The Garrison team's choice was whether to emphasize the technical flaws in the Commission's proceedings, which could amount to legal errors, or to leave those to the brief and argue more broadly that its decision was not in the "public interest." The public interest argument was high risk because it did not seem to be a legal standard at all. Who was a court to tell the Commission, or anyone else, what the public interest might be? But this approach would give Garrison the chance to sell the court on the history, beauty, and significance of the Hudson Highlands.

Garrison took the gamble. If he won the heart of the court and then gave them some technical hooks, they just might rule in his favor. Con Ed's lawyer, for his part, played his strongest cards, emphasizing the Commission's legal authority to make exactly this kind of decision, while the Commission chose to defend the reasonableness of its decision itself. The bench was skeptical. Asked at one point about her agency's position that the powerhouse would actually be an adornment to Storm King, the company's attorney replied that, yes, it would be, because that is what the Commission had found. The judges traded looks. Butzel glanced over at Garrison, but his expression didn't change. After the argument, Garrison upped the odds of winning to one-in-three. "Don't get your hopes up," he said.

The appellate decision came down three months later. Early in the opinion the court described the setting of the project as "an area of unique beauty and major historical significance . . . one of the finest pieces of river scenery in the world." Garrison had sold his message. The court then took him the rest of the way, each of its findings a body blow to Con Ed and the Commission, and the harbinger of a branch of law not yet born.

It began by finding that Scenic Hudson, which had no economic or property interests at stake, nonetheless had standing to challenge the Commission. Rejecting the agency's insistence that government would be "seriously undermined" if "any interested person or group" could challenge its decisions, the court held that neither the Constitution nor the Federal Power Act required that a litigant have a financial stake in the outcome. Those who "by their activities and conduct" have exhibited a "special interest" in the area would be recognized. The public itself could protect public interests. In this one kick, the courtroom door was opened to an entirely new kind of plaintiff. Environmentalists would rush in.

Turning to the merits, the court breathed life into the "public interest" standard by finding that the Commission, in making such a call, had to consider alternative ways of serving that interest. The agency might well decide that a power plant at Storm King was the best way to go, but only after considering other options. This duty would become another tenet of environmental law, alternatives to wetland development, alternative pollution controls, driving old agencies toward new decisions.

In a similar vein, the court scolded the Commission for taking at face value the claims of its friends at Consolidated Edison, while summarily rejecting testimony from the opponents that would give reason for a pause. Such as, the court pointed out, unresolved fisheries issues. The Commission could not act like "an umpire, calling balls and strikes" in the game before it. Its obligation was to dig in and ferret out the facts on its own. A few short years later this language, including the umpire metaphor, would be taken verbatim by the federal appeals court for the District of Columbia in a case called *Calvert Cliffs*, making environmental protection a mandate for the entire US government.

THE VICTORY for Scenic Hudson was short-lived. On remand for a new decision, Con Ed conducted elaborate studies of power production alternatives and empanelled a policy committee on fisheries impacts. To no one's surprise, Con Ed found alternatives to its project infeasible, and the impacts on the fisheries to be negligible. It would accommodate public concerns, nonetheless, by placing the powerhouse below ground, routing the transmission lines away from protesting neighborhoods, redesigning the fish screens, and dedicating on-site recreational facilities. The Commission seemed impressed. "Well, Lloyd," the Commission's attorney greeted Garrison at the opening of the new proceedings; "you have come along on your white charger and forced the bastards underground. Shouldn't you ride off and let them build their project?" The attitude had hardly changed.

Of course, the Commission reapproved the license and of course Scenic Hudson, joined this time by the City of New York, the Palisades Interstate Parks Commission, several national environmental organizations, and Boyle's Hudson River fishermen, appealed. This time they lost. A split panel held that the Commission had dotted its i's and crossed its t's; the Federal Power Act required no more. The judges did not allow themselves to be blinded by aesthetics again. The "preservation of scenic beauty" (from "the slightest intrusion"), wrote the majority, was a policy call that, whatever their personal views, they "could not impose" on the Commission. The dissenting judge wrote with obvious displeasure that Storm King Mountain might "swallow" the project as Con Ed contended, "but the concrete tailrace and abutments, as long as a good-sized football stadium—over an eighth of a mile—and three stories high will surely be stuck in its craw." The Supreme Court declined review.

Which might have ended the matter, but for other Con Ed plans that went awry. Over the course of the Storm King proceeding, the utility was also asking another federal agency, the Atomic Energy Commission, to license a second nuclear reactor at Indian Point. The Hudson River Fisherman's Association intervened to oppose, with evidence of massive fish entrainment at the existing unit and high mortality in juveniles that were sucked through the screens. Sensitized by the decision in *Calvert Cliffs*, the Atomic Energy regulators took a hard look at the allegations. They discovered yet another bombshell. The mortality from the Indian Point project was serious. Worse yet for Con Ed's license upriver, the Atomic Energy staff found that the assumptions underlying the previous predictions of negligible impacts were off. Way off.

The error was basic, if it was an error at all. The Hudson River was tidal, a point lost on the Federal Power Commission and the earlier court decisions. In fact, the estuary did not have a single tide each day, it had two, which meant that small fish and the juvenile stages of all fish were carried back and forth by the ebb and flow of the estuary all day long, across the powerful intake structures at both Indian Point and Storm King. These fish would be exposed to the intakes at ten times the rate previously calculated, with overall kill rates projected not at 3 percent, but at closer to 40 percent. The Atomic Energy staff also found that the Hudson River produced up to half of the East Coast striped bass population, whose number would drop by one third within the first ten years of the nuclear plant's operation. Based on these findings, the nuclear regulators proposed to require Con Ed to recycle its cooling water at Indian Point rather than take new water continuously from the river. Con Ed was appalled. Closed cycle cooling, applied to all Con Ed nuclear units, cost it an extra $500 million in construction and $180 million a year to run. And this was not the end of it. The Storm King intakes were twice the size of those at Indian Point.

Armed with the Indian Point findings, Scenic Hudson and the Fisherman's Association wasted no time returning to the Federal Power Commission to reopen the Storm King license. Scenic Hudson asked for an entirely new proceeding while the Fisherman's Association, presenting a tactical alternative, petitioned only to introduce new evidence on the fishery. The Commission denied both requests, and the parties, once again, appealed. In May 1974 the review court split the baby, refusing to require that the proceedings be reopened in full, but requiring new proceedings on the fishery.

Con Ed and the FPC were now approaching gridlock. With $25 million already sunk into construction, the utility was also facing a number of collateral challenges over water quality approvals, a federal dredge and fill permit, and compliance with the newly minted National Environmental Policy Act. For their part, Scenic Hudson and the Fisherman's Association et al. were experiencing the combat fatigue that comes from a decade of butting heads against the legal and public relations machinery of a major utility and an entrenched government agency. It was time to make a deal. Into this space came another prominent New Yorker, Russell Train, former head of the federal Council on Environmental Quality under President Nixon. Train, trusted by all sides, was recruited by Laurence Rockefeller to mediate the dispute. Twenty months of hard negotiation among federal regulators, four state agencies, several utilities, and the litigating environmental groups followed. In December 1980, the "Hudson River Peace Treaty" was signed at, appropriately, given many of the players involved, a ceremony in the Hotel Roosevelt on Madison Avenue in midtown Manhattan. Russell Train called it "one of the most satisfying moments" of his career.

For Con Ed, the settlement was close to a full retreat. It surrendered its Storm King license and donated the property for public, recreational use. In return, the company would not—and this was the chip it took from the table—be required to install closed system cooling towers on its nuclear plants. On the other hand, it and other utilities agreed to mitigating measures that included partial shutdowns during the summer spawning season, a $12 million endowment for Hudson River research, and a hatchery to restock the river with more than half a million striped bass fingerlings over the next eight years. After the signing, Charles F. Luce, Chairman of the Board of Con Ed, said, "We lost the fight." Robert Boyle said, "We raked in most of the chips and they got cab fare home."

✵

THE FALLOUT from Storm King was even more remarkable. The court ruling had opened the way for citizen standing and announced a set of environmental principles soon captured in legislation that, if in some quarters still heartily disliked, became a part of the country's daily life. It also defined a new strategy for environmental protection that used litigation—as had the civil rights movement—as part of a larger educational and political process. The founders of Scenic Hudson went on to form the Natural Resources Defense Council, a blue-chip public interest law firm, and began buying lands for the Hudson River Valley Greenway, a 150-mile-long corridor of natural areas from Albany to New York City. Al Butzel, who as Garrison's protégè soldiered the proceedings to their conclusion, was then approached by other New Yorkers opposed to a new expressway along the west side of Manhattan, which, once again, carried promises of billions in benefits and the endorsement of every politician in the state. Butzel went to court, and then back to the same federal court of appeals, and prevailed twice, after the government was caught suppressing information, twice, about the impacts of the project on, of all things, the striped bass. The lower west riverside is now being redeveloped, with the support of the governor and the mayor, not as a corridor for automobiles but as an urban park.

The ripples widen. A Hudson River research foundation, originally funded by the Storm King settlement, now spearheads Hudson fisheries restoration. The folksinger Pete Seeger launched his sloop *Clearwater* to patrol the waters, which spun off the Hudson Riverkeeper, a pollution control watchdog supported by a new law clinic at Pace Law School. Boyle's Hudson River Fisherman's Association has continued to play its own brand of sportsman-cum-science hardball, taking on General Electric's legacy of PCB contamination on the Hudson that had limited the recreational fishery, closed the commercial fishery altogether, and remained buried in cleanup negotiations for more than a decade. Boyle even wrote his own book, an ode to his river, and it is a wonderful read.

Perhaps the most unmeasurable impact of the litigation was psychological. Passions as strong as fishing and as elusive as scenic beauty were given legal protection, side by side with the nation's commerce. Injury to these interests not only walked environmentalists into the courtroom, they carried weight in the decision itself. The environment, as a matter of law, mattered.

As early as 1986, the Hudson River, even at the latitude of New York City, was already "cleaner and more inviting, its fisheries more productive," than it had been in memory. Long stretches of the river as far south as Yonkers have since been reopened for swimming. On weekends, sailboats dot the estuary under the Tappan Zee Bridge in clusters that look from a distance like a migration of butterflies. The striped bass numbers are up and steady. There is talk of resuming a limited commercial fishery. The fish remain tainted with PCBs, and there are still some chronic dischargers who have yet to catch the wave, but the river itself is winning. The Hudson Highlands are beautiful. At their entrance stands Storm King Mountain.

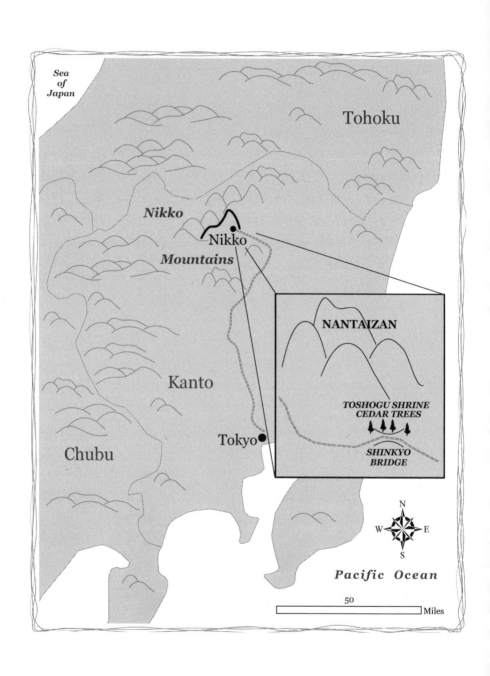

CHAPTER TWO

Nikko Taro

Build a small shrine in Nikko and enshrine me as the God. I will be the guardian of peacekeeping in Japan.

    Tokugawa Ieyasu, Shogun

THE PLAINS above Tokyo stretch for nearly a hundred miles to a series of volcanic mountains that hang like a screen from the sky. These are the Nikko, and their highest peak, Nantaizan ("manly form") is itself a place of worship in the Shinto diaspora. At the foot of the peak is a forest of six-hundred-year-old cypress trees lightly ribboned with streams, a classic location for a shrine. The shrine is called the Nikko Toshogu. Beyond it lies the town.

Nikko is a historic center, heavily visited, and in 1964 it was about to be overwhelmed by crowds coming to Japan for the Olympic Games. The problem was that the road from Tokyo squeezed down to two narrow lanes as it passed through the cedar grove, already scarred by passing automobiles. The traffic jams from the Olympics would be appalling. The decision to widen the road seemed sensible, indeed inevitable.

But for another fact. The cedars here were the most historic trees in the country, and guarded the shrine of its most legendary Shogun. And so, on the road to Nikko, two thousand years of tradition stood in the way of the most powerful government machine in modern Japan. No one said no to the Japanese Ministry of Construction. Indeed, nobody said no to the Japanese Ministry of Anything. Saying no was not in the vocabulary, not of the legislature, not of the courts, and not of people who happened to be in the way. Which is why the Nikko Taro case is so stunning in its place and time.

THE HERO of this story died four hundred years ago. The Nikko Toshogu shrine is dedicated to the most influential man in the story of Japan, which is saying a great deal. Indeed, it commemorates three men who, together, left a Bismarck-like legacy, conquering and consolidating the country, ending its civil wars, controlling the feudal lords and their samurai, centralizing the government, reducing the emperor to a figurehead, and imposing moral and social order. The last of the three was Tokugawa Ieyasu, who seized power in 1598 and never looked back.

Some lives are almost too large to imagine, even amidst the surreal violence and turmoil of warlord-driven, sixteenth-century Japan. Tokugawa Ieyasu was born into a family whose internal feuds murdered both his father and his grandfather. By the time he was six Ieyasu had been sent off as a hostage to a wary ally, only to be kidnapped by yet another rival who threatened to put him to death unless his father agreed to forsake his alliances and change sides. His father refused, saying that the sacrifice of his son would only confirm his existing loyalties. The bluff worked. Ieyasu was freed, and by the time he was a teenager he was joining a cavalcade of battles, sieges, pacts, betrayals, and political shifts that he prosecuted with luck (his armor was penetrated by a bullet in one battle), high ritual (he is said to have sealed a pact with a rival warlord by, together, urinating on it), and tactical cunning (a Japanese proverb has it that "Ieyasu won the Empire by retreating").

Along the way Ieyasu had executed his first wife, forced his eldest son to commit suicide, and slaughtered his enemies and their families. After his final siege of the Osaka castle he ordered the death of every defending soldier that could be found. A visitor soon after described the sight of "tens of thousands of samurai," their heads "stuck up on planks of wood which lined the road from Kyoto all the way to Fushimi." When the smoke had cleared, only Tokugawa Ieyasu remained standing. And he brought peace.

The Ieyasu legacy includes a castle to end all castles, now the Imperial Palace in downtown Tokyo, and books (the best-seller *Shogun*, among others), films, and video games in which he appears as, among other things, heroic warrior, magical leader, and the embodiment of evil. More indelibly, however, it also includes the organization of Japanese society around a rigid caste system in which obedience was supreme and social movement impossible. Economic development came in second as well; Japan maintained an extensive road network, but in order to prevent its use by insurgents wheeled wagons were not allowed. As might be expected from a leader who had risen from chaos, the primary principle was self-preservation and preservation of the existing order.

It worked for a very long time. Within these confines, under Ieyasu and his successor shoguns, Japan experienced a remarkable 250 years of calm and prosperity, for part of which it flirted in trade with the early-adventuring Portuguese and Dutch, and with Christian missionaries as well. These affairs ended, however, with Japan turning inward and becoming self-sufficient in agriculture, commerce, religion, and culture. It was a country unto itself, and that sufficed. Few civilizations anno domino could say the same.

Sensing the approach of death, Ieyasu ordered the construction of a small shrine at the base of the Nikko Mountains, in the cypress groves. Nothing important stays small for long, however, and within years his successors were building a megashrine that has lasted to this day, a compound of more than fifty elaborate, baroque-looking structures adorned with carved monkeys, bears, owls, and animals of all description set among sculpted shrubs and trees. The road from Nikko city to the Toshogu shrine runs thirty-seven kilometers through two lines of towering cypress, fifteen thousand trees, planted in the 1600s. Leaving the shrine one crosses the Shinkyo, the Sacred Bridge, built in

1636 for the exclusive use of the Shogun and his emissaries to cross the Daiya-
gawa River. This bridge too would play its role in the Cedar Tree lawsuit. Across
the bridge, in the precinct of the shrine, stands a venerable giant named the Taro
Cedar, over one hundred and fifty feet tall and nearly twenty feet around. It has
been there for six hundred years. In Japanese it is called the Nikko Taro.

*The most impressive sight repeated in every place throughout the breadth of this coun-
try is nothing other than union of forest and shrine . . . the most compressed architectural expression of the forest as the home of the sacred.*

Civilization of the Divine Forest

SHINTO SHRINES are not churches where one goes to pray to the gods. They
are way stations for the deities themselves, who spend most of their time at
home in their natural precincts but are not above paying a visit to the people at
these select locations. Where possible, the shrines are set apart from the town.
They are visited for official festivities and, more frequently, by individuals seeking a moment of peace. They are built within groves of trees. The roads to them
are lined by trees. Even in the most congested cities, the shrines are surrounded
by trees. These are not sacred buildings; they are sacred places in a long tradition
only recently abandoned by Western civilization.

Millennia before the time of temples and churches, the deities who ruled
the earth were found out of doors, in the most striking places humans knew. In
extreme climates they might be found at a blowhole in the ice or a tropical cave,
but in more temperate zones they inhabited deep stands of trees, the "first temples of the Gods," wrote Pliny the Elder. The Romans marked these sites with
stones and protected them from the axe, from even the gathering of firewood
and leaves. The Greeks carried soil up the barren rock of the Acropolis to grow
cypress trees. So it was in the Baltics where deities guarded oak groves and pun-
ished those who dared to whistle or shout within them. So it was in Africa
where, even now, there remain two thousand sacred forests in Ghana alone. A
European visitor, viewing a rock ledge framed by tall trees and a cascading wa-

terfall, asked, "How do you know God is here? Can you see the figure of God?" His guide replied, "I cannot see the figure of God. But I know God is here." The forest-God story is similar across the cultures of the East, as well. It reached its zenith, however, in Japan.

The Japanese islands may qualify, acre per acre, as the most beautiful landscape on Earth. Certainly the Japanese think so. An eighteenth-century poet wrote, "Our country, as a special mark of favor from the heavenly gods, was begotten by them, and there is thus so immense a difference between Japan and all the other countries of the world as to defy comparison." The *Nihonshoki, Chronicles of Japan*, explain how it came to be that way. One day, Susanoo-no-mikoto, the deity who founded Japanese culture, plucked off a hair from his beard and made a cedar tree. Hairs from his eyebrow, breast, and buttocks soon followed, and before long there were laurel and cypress and black pine, a woods, and then a country of trees. Which may help explain why two-thirds of one of the most densely populated nations in the world remains covered in forest. That, and the fact that the Tokugawa shoguns imposed a massive reforestation program which has been maintained, through war and peace, to this day. In the isolation of the Japanese islands, daily contact with the forests and a sense of human limits prompted a mix of beliefs based on animism, shamanism, and the worship of natural things, above all, the trees. Gradually, a few centuries after Christ, these beliefs would coalesce into Shinto, the dominant religion of Japan.

Shinto confounds the Western mind. It has no defining text, no powerful God, no set of commandments, no fixed prayers, not even an afterlife to inspire faith or fear. It is focused entirely on the here and now, on living a good life, for which there are but four guiding principles: tradition and family, cleanliness, ancestors, and a respect for nature. Every description of Shinto available emphasizes the role of nature as the "manifestation of divine power." To be in touch with nature is to be in touch with kami, the divine spirits of Shinto. These beliefs remained pervasive but informal until, in the sixth century, Japan experienced its first great confrontation with the outside world: China. Japan's response is worth noting for what would come centuries after and lead, among other things, to World War II and, later still, to the confrontation between the highway industry and the shrine for Tokugawa Ieyasu at the foot of the Nikko mountain range. Japan would incorporate the invading influence. Then it would pour incredible energies into going it one better. Absorb and conquer.

And so at a time when Rome was dying, Constantinople was rising, and packs of Goths roamed the woods of Europe, the Japanese were absorbing everything Chinese from city planning to silk robes, writing, painting, and song. Not to be outdone by Confucian texts, they wrote their own books of Shinto and in them reasserted Japanese primacy over the world they knew. The very name *Shinto* was taken from the Chinese "shin tao," meaning "the way of the Gods." They absorbed Buddhism as well, with which, particularly in its view of the natural order, Shinto was handily compatible. They blended Chinese beliefs with their own to the point that Shinto covered the current world, as in marriages, while Buddhism covered the next, as in funerals, a win-win accommodation. All of which is reflected in the Shinto shrine.

It was not until more than one thousand years later that an entirely different set of beliefs based on a vengeful God, only one deity and jealous of all others, with no sacred groves and an agenda to correct sinning mortals and conquer the natural world would confront Japan for a second, earth-shaking time with the tools of war and material progress. The outcome of that confrontation is still in play.

෩

Asphalt blanketing the mountains and valleys . . . a splendid Utopia.
Japan Ministry of Construction, *Utopia Song*, 2001

AS HIGHWAY ideas go, the Nikko road had its merits. Even by the late 1950s the town of Nikko was one of the most visited tourist attractions in Japan. Its historic buildings, set against the mountains and the Nikko National Park and close to the famous Toshogu shrine, provided a sort of Williamsburg-cum-Colorado Rockies experience, only a two-hour drive from Tokyo. The main road was inadequate for the traffic, however, and was pinched into an unsupportable bottleneck—from over fifty feet to less than twenty feet—near the shrine. To one side of the bottleneck was the historic Shinkyo Bridge and to the other a line of ancient trees, including the Taro Cedar. A solution was urgent. Japan was preparing to host its first Olympic Games, and its international face was on the line. Foreign press and visitors were going to pour up to Nikko and nobody wanted them stuck in traffic and blaming the Japanese.

To its credit, the Ministry of Construction did consider alternative routes. Basically, it could blow through the bottleneck, tunnel under it, or build a new road around the Shrine valley. According to its analysis, new routes would cost up to $1.3 billion yen (approximately $10 million), whereas the straight shot, Plan A, cost only $43 million yen (below $500,000), or less than one-twentieth of the price tag. On any scale of economic rationality, taking a few trees made sense. Even the National Park Council, a governmental body with jurisdiction to protect the natural resources of the area, concurred with Plan A. In the national interest, the Taro Cedar and fourteen other trees slightly less imposing would have to go. In one sense, that is all this case was about.

In another sense, it was not what this case was about at all. Below the surface, it was about Japan accommodating itself to a new intrusion of foreign culture, and how far that accommodation would go. The reign of the Tokugawa shoguns had been an irritation to the Western sea powers and their market agendas. Finally, in 1854, US Admiral Perry sailed into Tokyo harbor with four warships and announced, quite unilaterally, an "open door" policy for Japan. In what passed for diplomacy at the time, Perry gave Tokyo some time to think about it and returned the next year with more gunships and an ultimatum.

Faced with open-door-or-else, and enticed by the prospect of American technology and weaponry, Japan signed a number of trade treaties that, among other things, brought down the Tokugawa regime and restored the Emperor to power. Once more, Japan's absorb and conquer response, so successful with China, kicked in, this time to meet the mercantile culture of the West. It launched a boom in manufacture, science, and technology rarely seen for speed and success. Within a few decades, Japan had beaten the Soviet Union in head-to-head sea battles, was rivaling the Western powers throughout the Pacific, and was headed full tilt toward World War II. Japan had created a miraculous machine. The problem was it had no brakes, and it crashed.

The lessons of World War II were several, but near the top of the list was the realization that Japan had been outproduced on the assembly line, and then trumped on the technology front by the atomic bomb. Back to the drawing board; absorb and conquer. Within a few decades more, Japan was leading the world in the design and manufacture of electronic instruments and automobiles, and in the construction of highways. It had adopted more than a US-style Constitution. It bought the US recipe for economic development: massive public works construction. In 1955 America began an interstate highway program that would become the largest construction project on Earth. Over time, highway money, political power, and construction jobs became their own rationale. The program had few checks and even less balance. It was seen as an American success story, however, and for Japan it afforded a model to be as pursued as vigorously as rock music and fast food. Japan had the knack of absorbing, and then going one better.

✒

IN HIS MINOR classic on modern Japan, Alex Kerr writes with love and despair of what he terms the Japanese Construction State. Its chief actor is the Ministry of Construction, and its chief projects are highways and dams. Kerr's data are impressive. At eighty trillion yen, the Japanese construction market is the largest in the world, nearly 20 percent of the country's gross national product (GNP), compared to about 8 percent in the United States. Forty percent of the national budget goes to public works, versus less than 10 percent in America. The numbers on the consumption of concrete alone are staggering; in 1994 Japan outproduced the United States by thirteen million tons. On a square-foot basis, Japan was paving at a rate thirty times that of their American counterparts. In roads, followed soon by automobiles, the Japanese were beating the Americans at their own game. And they were not stopping here. In 1996 the Shimuzu Corporation, one of the country's largest construction firms, announced a new process for making cement on the moon. The general manager of its Space Division affirmed: "It won't be cheap to produce small amounts of concrete on the moon, but if we make large amounts of concrete, it will be very cheap."

The buy-in was pervasive. Kerr writes of the construction syndrome:

Bureaucrats educated in the best universities plan them, consulting with the most respected professors; the finest engineers and landscape artists design them; architects draft far-reaching civil engineering schemes for the future; companies in the forefront of industry build them; leading politicians profit from them; opinion journals run ads in their pages in support of them; and civic leaders across the nation beg for more. Building these works and monuments consumes the mental energies of Japan's elite.

Another observer writes of the money and politics involved:

Almost all of the major highways are toll roads, and some make money. Many do not and some are incredible money losers. There have been cases of bridges costing billions and billions of yen, but hardly have ten vehicles passing over them per day. . . . There is strong economic logic for these highway investments, overwhelming in rural areas, for two groups. One of course is the construction companies, which build these highways, and the other is the politicians of the long-ruling Liberal Democratic Party. The relationship of the construction companies and the party is incestuous.

The physical impacts were massive: valleys paved for roads, mountain passes leveled, hillsides covered with asphalt to prevent erosion, tourist sites dwarfed by overhead lanes, neighborhoods bisected by traffic, each a tangible symbol of the modern way. Highway construction was bankrolled by revenues from the Japanese postal service, whose "bulging coffers" made it the world's largest financial institution. There were no brakes. Save, just perhaps, on the margins, at some unforeseeable point in the future, the restraints of environmental law.

What happened, one might ask, to the commitments of Shinto, the sacred forests and the Way of the Gods? At one level, the same submission to Western values that substituted TV dinners for rice and sake and the music of the Dead Presidents for haiku. Speaking of the need for a questionable transportation project in his district, a local mayor explained its purpose: "so that people can feel they have become rich." They were joining the modern world.

Another answer to the same question, however, is found in poetry, Shinto, and a different face of Japanese culture. Nature, in Japan, was never "red in tooth and claw." That kind of nature was feared and propitiated, part of the dark side. It was the enemy. Over time, Shinto and a myriad of traditions from bonsai tree sculpture to the tea ceremony, floral arrangements, and white stone lawns—the very definition of the Japanese garden—evolved to put nature under detailed order. Shinto's goal was harmony, and harmony required control.

These roots had important consequences for the Nikko highway. One was the subordination of nature. Local highway departments cut the limbs of trees on city streets—not dead limbs but live ones, not partially but the whole limb— because they drop leaves on the ground. The leaves are seen as messy, a loss of control. Local residents complain of the disorderly croaking of frogs in parks and woodlands. Highways surmount these anxieties quite neatly; you can drive anywhere and look at nature from the health and safety of your car.

Another consequence was obedience. Japanese education teaches conformity from early childhood, moving in unison, following the leader. "When the Japanese talk about harmony, it means a denial of differences and an embrace of sameness," says Dr Miyanoto Masao, formerly of the Ministry of Health and Welfare. The saying is learned: "The blade of grass that raises its head feels the sickle." In such a circumstance what type of soul would raise a head to oppose a Ministry of Construction project or, for that matter, any government action affecting the environment?

The culture of obedience, in the context of the Nikko highway, was reinforced by yet a third force, the culture of the bureaucracy, an institution of impregnable power. Throughout Japanese history, the emperor was the offspring of the chief deity, the sun itself of the land of the sun. Warlords of one vein or another were absolute monarchs for more than a millennium. Their officials were ranking Samurai: feared, respected, and above all obeyed. With modernization, Japanese government agencies inherited their mantle. They were a closed aristocracy. Japanese ministries recruited at the bottom, and employment was for life. The judicial process was also at their disposal, and judicial review of their actions was unheard of. Even today it is rather difficult to hear. Government ministries, which of course knew best, were reinforced by a cadre of retired employees now working for their allies in engineering and construction. The name given to this cadre in Japan is rather unique: They are called "amakudari," which means "descended from heaven."

Whatever the adherence to Shinto, then, the Construction State and its highway program reflected a cultural commitment to the control of nature, obedience to superiors, and the conviction that a tight concert of industry and government ruled. These precepts presented an obvious challenge to the development of environmental law.

🐦

IT MAY BE surprising for a Westerner to learn that Japan's experience with environmental issues was not new, nor was recourse to the courts to address them. With limited success. No sooner had Admiral Perry "opened" Japan in the late 1800s than the new Mejii government embarked on full-court industrialization (working slogan: "increase of industrial products"). It was a "Copernican changing time," and in the frenzy feudal lords and local governments caught the wave by destroying their old castles (new allegiance ran to the Emperor only) and Buddhist temples (Shinto was declared the exclusive state religion). Only later did the Emperor decree the protection of shrines and historic sites.

The price for this all-at-once industrialization was massive, uncontrolled pollution on a people that had never experienced it. The first case arose in the late 1880s over contamination from the Furukawa Mining Company, which was exploiting a huge copper deposit on the Watarase River, upstream from the village of Yanaka. With their fish poisoned and their fields dying, Yanaka villagers petitioned the government for a cleanup. In so doing they were challenging a plant responsible for 48 percent of the country's copper production, the nation's third most important export. They didn't stand a chance. The legislature refused to act. When the villagers marched in protest, they were arrested and tried on criminal charges. Their leader, a member of the House of Representatives at the time, tried to appeal to the emperor, for which he was imprisoned for blasphemy. Provoked by the public uproar, the government finally came up with a bizarre, if pragmatic, solution: it condemned the contaminated lands and then flooded them for a reservoir. The villagers were evicted with "little compensation, or none at all." The outcome was hardly just, but the first alarm bell of an environmental problem had sounded.

A series of similar cases followed, most notably one in 1916 against a copper refining company, Osaka Alkali. Local farmers sought damages for heavy crop losses. The Supreme Court, setting a new stage, eventually held the company liable. The path was now cleared for a limited class of lawsuits, not challenging industrial development but providing compensation to its victims.

Following World War II, Japan launched its second great industrialization offensive. It was not long before people suffering strange illnesses, in great numbers, started going to court. All pollution has its price, but the price tags in these cases were horrific. One case was called "Toyama itai-itai," as the victims of cadmium poisoning cried out "it hurts, it hurts!" The responses to these complaints by government and industry set a mold of their own, in turn: flat denial, concealed evidence, science-for-hire, blame-the-victims, and most reliably, stall-the-case-until-the-victims-die. All the maneuvers later seen in US litigation over industrial asbestos, contraceptive devices, cotton dust, tobacco, and automobile safety played out here in Japanese courts, facing similar issues of great complexity and social impact.

Among the many such lawsuits filed, four reached notoriety and are known as the Big Four in Japanese legal history. The first was prompted by the discovery of Minamata disease in families ingesting methyl mercury from the discharge of the Chisso Chemical Company in the Kumamoto Prefecture. In 1967, the courts convicted Chisso of knowing endangerment and of active concealment of its data on the disease. Petitions for damages, however, dragged on for twenty years without resolution. Two more of the Big Four cases stemmed from pollution around Yokkiachi City, a Louisiana-scale complex of oil refineries and petrochemical and power plants. People became sick, then they started dying. The government would not act. The companies would not act. In the same year as the Minimata case, shortly after one of the Yokkiachi victims committed suicide, twelve others filed suit. Meanwhile, the fourth action was rising from villagers who had ingested cadmium discharged into the Jintsu River by the Mitsui Mining and Smelting plant. Company doctors insisted that the illnesses were simply nutritional problems. The government agreed. In 1968 a suite of victims filed suit. By the time the case was decided twenty-one of them had died.

The Big Four litigation was long, drawn out, and in the end, for the plaintiffs, unsatisfactory. They sought damages, because damage actions were all that were available to them, and damages for dead relatives are hardly anyone's first choice. In no case did the courts seek to enjoin or abate the pollution; that would have required more from courts than they were ready to deliver. On the positive side, however, these cases drew wide media attention and public sympathy, educating, changing a mindset: there was a problem, the government and industry were not gods, they had acted badly, they needed to deliver better answers. These cases, further, thrust the courts, willing or not, right into the mix, examining on their own the environmental impacts of industrial, and, indirectly, governmental actions. The prevailing culture of harmony and obedience had failed; the machine was malfunctioning. There was a judicial role.

As the Big Four cases were gestating, responding to terrible injuries with de minimis payoffs, the Nikko highway came along. Here was a different kind of injury. While the Japanese people were still in the price-of-pollution, blame-the-victim, and pray-to-the-gods mindset when it came to industrial growth, here was a proposal to destroy the surroundings of the sacred Toshugo shrine. The shrine would sue, and it was not asking for money damages. It wanted to stop the road. In 1964, its case reached the High Court of Tokyo.

STRIPPED OF its factual findings, the Court's opinion is quite short. Six paragraphs of no more than thirty lines each, packed with as much meaning as a haiku poem. It affirmed a trial court decision that was long on facts but almost blank on the law. For good reason. There was no law. On appeal, the Tokyo High Court was acting on a new sheet of paper. The only environmental agencies involved in the project, the Ministry of Health and Welfare and the National Park Council, had, albeit with reluctance, agreed to the highway plan. Nonetheless, the High Court reached conclusions that have since been captured as principles of national law in the United States and elsewhere, even international law. It looked at the Ministry of Construction, the Colossus of Japan's domestic government, and saw feet of clay. It enjoined the project.

The first notable thing about the Nikko Taro opinion is the court's reach for law to apply. There was no environmental law at the time. The Land Expropriation Law allowed government ministries to condemn lands, such as the trees adjoining the Toshugawa shrine, provided that the project was an "appropriate and reasonable use of land." A more permissive legal standard would be hard to find. The Ministry of Construction had been building highways and appropriating their rights of way for decades. To be sure, it had to pay compensation, but it had the right to take the land. Public roads were, furthermore, by definition "appropriate and reasonable" uses of land. Indeed, they were national priorities. Even without this opposing momentum, a legal standard such as "appropriate and reasonable" would be extremely difficult to apply. Courts, it is widely said, do not exist to decide what is best for society. Particularly so for the courts of Japan arising from a strong civil law tradition the mantra of which is: all-we-do-is-apply-the-written-word. Deciding what is "appropriate" is for the other two branches of government.

And yet, the Court held the Ministry's decision to be inappropriate, unreasonable, and unlawful. How could it do that? For one, because it very much wanted to. The saying goes in environmental litigation, "give me the facts, I'll give you the law," and the facts here dominate the opinion from the start. The early sentences of the opinion read:

> The land in question is situated at the entrance to the Nikko National Park. It is an awesome composition of man-made beauty with the Sinkyo Bridge painted in red, shrines, the natural beauty of the surrounding forest of huge cedars, and the crystal stream of the Otani River.

Clearly, this was, in the words of the trade, an "educated court." It was looking for a hook to save the trees.

It found what it needed in, of all places, the Land Expropriation Act. In its view, the requirement that the highway be "appropriate" meant more than that the Ministry could "identify some public benefits" derived from it such as accommodating increased traffic. The Ministry had also to find the highway "necessary" and "worth the cost of such environmental deterioration and destruction." Here then we have two new standards, neither of them written in the statute, both of tremendous potential. The key to what is *necessary*, the court wrote, was the availability of alternatives. In this case, the Ministry had other routes, and if they were more expensive to build then they might be operated as toll roads. What emerges is a standard very similar to that of US law, prohibiting highway projects from taking parks and cultural sites unless there is "no feasible and prudent alternative." Only there was nothing remotely similar to this provision in Japanese law. From the Expropriation Act, the Tokyo High Court invented one of the most powerful protections on the books. And that was only the beginning.

Addressing its "worth the cost" standard, the High Court also found that the Ministry erred in concluding that the highway's benefits were decisive. "We wonder," the Court mused, if a route that avoided the valley completely would be more economical "if the benefits of the preservation of the cultural value of the area were considered." The Court did not "wonder" for long. It went on to say that the preservation of these values "should be given the highest importance." Had preservation of the environment been given proper consideration, it concluded, preservation would have prevailed. Indeed, a decision to take all automobiles away from this road and convert it into a "pedestrian walk" might prevail. Second-guessing an administrative decision doesn't get any closer to the administrator's shoulder than this.

The court was not yet done. The Nikko highway was apparently being upgraded in conjunction with the construction of other roads in the Nikko area. Construction agencies like to build incrementally—you cannot construct a system all at once—and they are loath to reveal the full impact of their plans. Revelations only bring questions. The Tokyo High Court was onto this tactic as well. It required review as well of whether "other roads should be constructed in the near future for industrial development or tourism in the undeveloped area behind Nikko." And so the Court also solved one of the most chronic issues in the yet-to-be-born environmental review process, dealing with the whole project up front.

At bottom, this one court, at this prenatal moment in public environmental law, exhibited the independence of mind that separates real judicial review from a rubber stamp. It took nobody's word for it. Not that of the Ministry of Construction, which ended up arguing the urgency of the Olympics to defend a must-build decision. Nor would it take the word of the National Park Council, which had approved the project in part on the basis that some trees had been blown down by a storm and so the destruction had already occurred. This appellate court, as the US panel in Storm King, was willing to make up its own mind. Convergent evolution, a half a world away.

Suffice it to say, the Nikko Taro opinion was years ahead of its time. The question remained whether it would blaze a new trail within Japan or wander about, in the words of US Chief Justice Vinson, "derelict on the waters of the law." The answer is very Japanese in its accommodation of ambiguity. The answer to both questions is: yes.

恕

BY THE LATE 1960s there was a widespread perception in Japan that industry was out of control, massively so, and that government wasn't safeguarding the public interest. Japanese courts, in the absence of statutory law, addressed horrible injuries by, after years of delay, basically paying off the victims. It was a way of having your industrial cake and eating it too. The solution to pollution was not stopping it; it was compensation.

Environmental cases like Nikko Taro, however, involve public, not private, injuries. When Japanese plaintiffs sought to prevent harm to public values, they fell into a Kafkaesque labyrinth of dead ends. Lawsuits would be tried all the way to the Supreme Court only to discover that they had been pled in the wrong form. Were this hurdle cleared, they faced another, standing to sue, which in Japanese law required physical or personal injury. Under rules like these, few environmental cases reached the courthouse door. The ministries remained untouched, like gods.

And so, even following Nikko Taro, Japanese citizens seeking judicial review of badly sited waste dumps, industrial outfalls, airports, urban renewal projects, and other questionable decisions have been turned away. Most of their cases were never heard. The ones that were heard received money damages, when what they wanted instead was a safer location for the dump, or noise abatement at the airport. So why did Nikko Taro fare differently?

One explanation is the importance of the plaintiff, the most revered shrine in Japan. The public and the media strongly protested the location of the highway and, say what you will, courts read newspapers. Since the shrine owned the property, it also had the requisite legal standing. This said, the language of the presiding magistrate, Kenzo Shiraizi, spoke in broader terms: "Although the plaintiff has private ownership of the land," he wrote, the bridge, trees and shrine also had values that "should be shared and preserved for all the people as their common cultural heritage." Judge Shiraizi was more than a member of the Tokyo High Court. He was an administrative law scholar in the vein of US appellate judges of the same era who were making similar advances. He is known in Japan not only for this opinion but for several others, at least two pitting individuals against transportation decisions, staking new ground for judicial review. In a 1966 lecture, as the Nikko Taro case was winding its way toward his appellate court, he addressed the Tokyo Bar Association on "The Way of Administrative Litigation." Reviewing recent developments in the United States, England, and Germany, he concluded that while, as judge, he would not interfere with the substantive decisions of state ministries, he would intervene to ensure proper procedure.

True, but not the whole truth. Because the Nikko Taro opinion did not stop with proper procedure, it went beyond to the very merits of a decision that Judge Shiraizi had told the Tokyo Bar was beyond his domain. There is no way, reading Nikko Taro, that, whatever procedural hoops the Ministry of Construction might jump through to justify taking those cedar trees, the Tokyo High Court was going to let it happen. To people who care about the sanctity of courts, this was a cardinal sin. To those who care about the sanctity of sacred places, it was a triumph.

There is one last shoe from Nikko Taro yet to drop. One wonders what would have happened had the Toshugawa shrine accepted a payout from the Ministry of Construction for the removal of those historic cedars. Such a scenario is more than imaginable. Could anyone else have defended the trees?

The jury remains out. Unlike the United States, which adopted the safeguard of judicial review over government actions within a few years of its founding and professes its faith in the "rule of law," Japan did neither. No Far Eastern society did. Rather, they developed systems in which the government made public decisions and in which grievances, including those arising from government action, were to be tolerated as long as possible and then conciliated. Not litigated. "Traditional philosophy," writes a Japanese scholar, "sees the law as a makeshift technique good only for disciplining barbarians."

This perspective goes a long way to explain the resistance to citizen enforcement of environmental laws in Japan. After all, we are supposed to be working together. Lawsuits against the government assault a fabric that has bound the country together for centuries, and, who knows?, may in the long run turn out to produce significant environmental results. America was born in confrontation, teaches the adversary process as Rule One in its schools of law, and has developed a highly adversarial process for protecting the environment. Perhaps Japan can squeeze more juice out of conciliation than the United States can from confrontation.

But probably not. The phenomenon of high-handed, mistake-prone, and politically manipulated government decisions is common to the world. Government institutions are not evil, but they are very human and they resist change. Game plans for reconciling conflicts like those at the Nikko Taro bridge by good faith and reason are based more on hope than reality. Unless members of the public can challenge unreasonable government decisions before an impartial body, public values lose. There is simply too much weight on the other side. Judge Shiraizi's language in Nikko Taro would allow public challenges to protect broad public values in Japan. But they have not happened yet.

Highway Approved Near Sacred Site: Ireland approved a highway yesterday that will pass near the Hill of Tara, an ancient site at the mythological heart of the country.
                                                                    Times Picayune, May 2005

THE ISSUE will not sleep. The Japanese highway program, like its godfather in the United States and the ones coming in India and China, rolls on. Japan's immediate problem seems to be that it has laid so much pavement already that the costs of maintaining it have produced a forty-four trillion yen shortfall. Nonetheless, yet more roads, largely in rural areas, remain the holy grail. More Nikko Taro cases are almost certainly in the wings. Where else can new highways go?

One wonders what Shogun Tokugawa Ieyasu would make of all this. Here he was, the ultimate, authoritarian chief of state. Along comes a challenge to one of his ministries. It is hard to imagine anyone even dreaming of such a challenge in his time. It is impossible to imagine anyone surviving it. And yet, the Toshogu shrine is his memorial, and according to Judge Shiraizi it belongs to all of the Japanese people. As do fresh air and clean water. Tokugawa Ieyasu, meet Kenzo Shiraizi.

The Nikko Taro road still winds through a bottleneck at the Toshogu shrine. Two narrow lanes curve toward the Sacred Bridge, thick with automobiles on weekends and flanked by tall cedars that reach out into the road and remain scarred by contact with moving fenders. Which would be a misery, except that the Ministry of Construction, rather than try to rehabilitate its decision to widen this stretch of road, decided to build a bypass beyond the valley instead. The Olympics came and went, and were by all report a success. The personnel of the shrine, the judges and the lawyers involved in the litigation have gone on as well. What remains is a remarkable judicial opinion, whose full promise remains yet to be fulfilled.

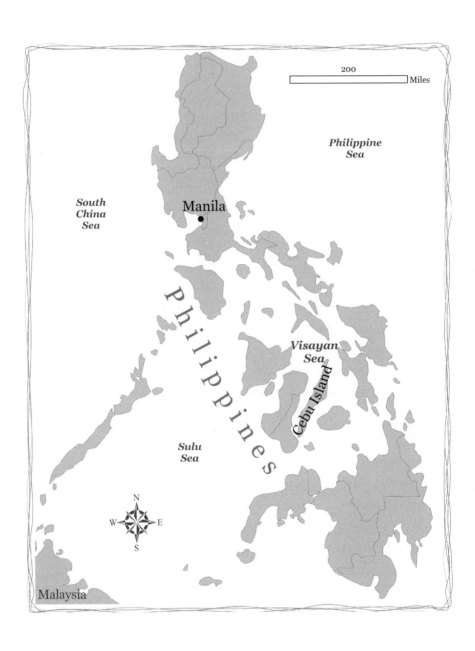

CHAPTER THREE

Minors Oposa

It looks like the threats against me have not been empty.

Antonio Oposa, 2006

IN THE EARLY 1990s, an unflagged freighter pulled out from the island of Luzan, the largest of more than seven thousand pieces of the Philippine archipelago spread over half a million square miles of water, each with its own jagged coastline, impossible to police. On deck, in open view, was yet another illegal harvest of the last remaining virgin timber from a country so vast in forests that it had until recently supplied the world—and was now reduced to importing its wood from abroad. While local mills and foreign corporations stole the rest.

Suddenly, out of the air, came the sound of a military helicopter, louder and louder, hovering over the ship, lowering a line to the deck, on which some tiny figures could be seen shimmying down. Surprisingly, perhaps fortunately, there was no one in view. One of the men who boarded, a lawyer from Manila, opened up his computer and typed out a warrant. The captain and the ship owner were arrested. Meet Antonio Oposa.

Oposa had launched an all-out assault on illegal logging. He created a multiagency task force to enforce the law, enlisted the help of local communities who had long believed (with good reason) that the government was part of the problem, and then went in with the troopers. His team seized a raft of recently cut logs floating alongside a company dock, held a hearing on the spot, and six hours later the owner and operators were in jail. They made an amphibious assault against another timber operator in Isabela. On the island of Butuan, they broke down doors. They brought in the press, the cameras, and the reporters, raid by raid, sending the message: this is a new day. Oposa's enforcement philosophy was very simple: "swift, painful, and public."

Pieces of a larger frame. Within the next few years, Antonio Oposa would author the first compendium of Philippine environmental law and compose a book entitled *The Laws of Nature and Other Stories*, which captures environmental policy with elegant simplicity. He would bring lawsuits, start nongovernmental organizations, form collaborative working groups on intractable problems, teach law to school children, teach ecology to lawyers, speak, cajole, listen, raise hell, and seek peace. He is not driven by the law. Rather, he is driven by what he sees as a beautiful and imperiled planet, and the hope, as he wrote in a recent dedication of his book, that the young, "in their time . . . will do better than we do in ours." In his way he is a reluctant lawyer.

Yet the one thing above all else for which Antonio Oposa will be remembered, around the world, is a lawsuit that he brought on behalf of his children and children yet unborn to save the rapidly vanishing forests of the Philippines. The case is known as *Minors Oposa*.

THE FORESTS that moved Oposa had been the dominant feature of the Philippine landscape for all of recorded time. They contained an astonishing variety of living things; on a plot smaller than a city block you could find over a thousand different species, the most impressive of which was a bird the size of a Great Dane and topped by a cowl of yellow feathers, which glided effortlessly over the landscape and then slashed down through the trees at speeds beyond fifty miles an hour to snatch small animals from the canopy, the ultimate nightmare of terrestrial beings, the Philippine monkey-eating eagle. Legend has it that, long ago, the sky was so near the sea that you could reach up and touch it. But he, the eagle, the bird king, pecked off parts of the sky and used them to make his nest. Provoked by this assault, the sky rained down rocks on him, the largest that could be found. The rocks missed, and fell into the sea, which is how the Philippine archipelago was formed. This is not, then, your usual bird, and it is completely dependent on the carpet of tropical and subtropical forests that covered the islands. As the carpet was destroyed, the eagle would follow.

It happened so quickly. At the close of the nineteenth century, despite the inroads of Spanish rule, nine-tenths of the Philippines retained its original tree cover and an estimated ten thousand of its prized eagles, the symbol of the nation. Before European contact the forests were managed by the datu, tribal chiefs who set harvest limits for each community and in turn supported a brisk commerce in wood products with oared sloops and lateen rigs from Arabia, China, and India. The Spanish who came next were also traders and only incidentally occupied the land. Forest management was the province of the Roman Catholic Church, exercised by a ruling "friarocracy" by granting concessions to converted chieftains. Forests for political favor became the pattern, but it did not lead to aggressive timber cutting. Spain needed long-term supplies of lumber for its ships and fleet. It banned commercial logging outright.

Then came the Americans.

ᴅ

The wood of the Philippines can supply the furniture of the world for a century to come. . . . And the wood and other products of the Philippines supply what we need and cannot ourselves produce.

Alfred Beveridge, United States Senator, 1900

IN 1898, THE AMERICANS invaded, ostensibly to defeat the Spanish, and went on to prosecute a war against Philippine independence that would cost as many Filipino lives as the Second World War. From the American occupation arose many familiar-looking traditions, including a constitution and the wholesale exploitation of natural resources. It was about this time that President Theodore

Roosevelt, battling to save forests in the United States from wildcat logging, commented that "the American had but one thought about a tree, and that was to cut it down." To the incoming Americans, the Philippine forests were the prize, what would be called today a "strategic resource," and reason enough for military occupation and control. The trees began to fall in staggering numbers and, despite the lofty principles of American forestry, virtually out of control. It is true that the United States promoted forest mapping, inventories, timber processing, and even a new school of scientific forestry, all the trappings of modern management, but the basic message was simple: get out the cut. The Philippine government took it to heart. By 1934, only fifty million acres, less than half the original inventory, remained. The only thing that stopped the party was the war.

It would not stop for long. With the postwar came a housing boom, and the Philippines were soon supplying one-third of the world's lumber, much of it en masse, some as rare and costly as Philippine mahogany, and none of it sustainable. The United States was the largest importer in the West, while its newfound ally, Japan, was the largest in the East. Ironically, the Pacific theater's two mortal enemies had joined forces to consume the forests of the Philippines. Not that the Filipinos were unwilling. They saw the same thing everyone else saw, a ready source of foreign currency, apparently without end. Timber concessions went to friends of the president in a pattern set by the Spanish two centuries before. By the mid-1950s, the Philippines had become the world's largest exporter of timber. On islands large and small, the forests continued to fall.

The slaughter was too big to ignore. In 1969, President Ferdinand Marcos, in response to the newfangled but apparently popular notion of environmental protection, announced the suspension of new timber concessions. After his re-election, however, the suspension was quietly reduced to one year and then disappeared altogether. The cutting continued. In 1975, a new forestry law imitated the multiple-use, sustained-yield policies of US forest management, restricted log exports, and even tried to involve indigenous communities in forest protection. It all sounded good. President Marcos, by the late 1970s a ruler of virtually unlimited powers, even declared:

> If necessary, I will cancel all licenses to protect the forest. . . . I have seen fortunes
> made overnight from the forest, and the wastage, and it makes my skin crawl to

realize that there are many Filipinos who just don't care about the future genera-tions' legacy in the way of forest resources.

At the same time, however, Marcos was handing out new concessions to po-litical allies on the order of 100,000 acres of forestland a piece, more than double the typical commercial allotments. Marcos family members also dotted the Philippine timber landscape. The president's mother was the chairman of the board of one major wood processing company, and a major shareholder and board member of a competitor. In 1971, a handful of concessionaires controlled some thirty million acres of the remaining Philippine commercial forests, from which they earned an average of US $300 million a year in exports alone. Against odds like these, the trees didn't stand a chance.

By the late 1980s, only 4 percent of the Philippines remained in native cover, hiding as if in exile in steep ravines and on remote islands like Palawan. In-evitably, the big money in timber was playing out, and the environmental bills were coming due in eroded hillsides, dead rivers, dying reefs, water shortages, and wasting floods. A different momentum was building. By 1987 Marcos was gone and the Philippines was under new management. A new constitution de-clared a right to a "balanced and healthful ecology." President Corazon Aquino created a Department of Environment and Natural Resources in whose name and mandate the word *environment* was added, the word *exploit* was deleted, and new phrases like "sustainable use" and "enhancement of the quality of the environment" appeared. Still, the cutting continued. More than one hundred major timber leases were in force, fifty-year contracts with decades left on them, and the loggers were moving on last places like Palawan, the remaining habitat of the Philippine monkey-eating eagle. The question was whether the new laws and phrases had any meaning. Enter Tony Oposa.

"Somehow when we are in the presence of a large tree or in a grove of trees, especially when we are inside a forest, we feel a certain sense of exhilaration and surge of seem-ing spiritual energy. . . . After all, we are each other's counterparts—both being climax species of our respective kingdoms."

Antonio Oposa, 2003

NOBODY KNOWS how the fire broke out. Young Tony Oposa, home from law school on Christmas break, woke up in the night to the smoke and roar of his house in flames. He had been sleeping upstairs. Between him and the front door was a solid field of fire. He says that he thought to himself, "[i]f I die, I'd like people to know I died fighting," so he ran downstairs into the heat, the front door that was supposed to be locked simply opened for him, and he went out. His head and arms were on fire, and his skin was "dripping like wax." Two other people did not make it. From then on, Tony Oposa was a little more serious, a little more focused, but still unprepared for the fight ahead.

It was hardly preordained that Oposa would be an environmentalist, a lawyer, or anyone of note. Hyperactive as a child, trouble-making in a mischievous sort of way, he seemed headed for the life of a lightweight among the cream of conservative, staunchly Catholic Philippine society. His father was a well-known surgeon, and when his mother developed early signs of cancer they went to the United States, leaving young Oposa with wealthy grandparents in Manila, where he enjoyed every attention a boy could want. He drifted into a degree in business administration, following which, his countercultural strain appearing, he went to Bantayan Island off of Cebu and lived "like a Robinson Crusoe," complete with manservant, cooking fish and rice on an open fire and sleeping on a bare floor. It is hardly surprising, then, that on returning to Manila, he tried and quit jobs in trade and banking. He did not want to spend his life "counting the money of other people." Instead, he took up speed reading. He wanted to learn how to "understand and enjoy words."

These impulses led Oposa to law school, again for no visible purpose, graduating in 1982. His only environmental accomplishment to that point had been to persuade fraternities to plant trees in front of the school. In itself a modest tactical plan, it signaled his ability to enlist the energies of others and foreshadowed larger strategies to come. Oposa married, but he became restless to the point that his wife, an accountant by profession, finally told him, one senses with no small frustration, to "find a specialty." Unfortunately the only thing he really cared about was nature and there was no such specialty for lawyers. As he was wont to say, "Who will pay me my fees, the fish?"

He consulted with his law professors, one of whom went on to become a member of the Supreme Court, and found an interest in environmental law but no opportunity to learn it. So he took a scholarship to study in Norway and returned with a novel notion, large but still unformed: the idea of environmental protection was not to benefit him, nor even his children, but for children yet to come. He went back to the island of Cebu and was shocked to find that the trees were gone. "I walked up in the mountains one day," he later wrote, "and did not see a single hectare of forest." It was not just Cebu. He saw satellite photographs of the Philippine rainforest, before and now, only fragments of canopy remaining. The images fell on a ready mind. The more he looked into it, the worse it appeared. If there was a defining moment, this was it. Antonio Oposa had found his purpose. He "uprooted" his family from Cebu to Manila. He did not know how, but he would save the trees.

For Oposa, it was never just about the trees. He saw an entire history collapsing. These same forests hosted indigenous people who spoke more than sixty different languages. Forest roads were cutting into their sanctuaries and hunting grounds like Panzer movements, destroying the natural capital of the country and sending the profits abroad. A very special universe of humans, plants, and animals was on the brink. It made no sense. Oposa would later explain: "The liquidation of more than 90% of the Philippines' primary forests from the mid-1960s made a few hundred families US $42 billion dollars richer; but it left 18 million upland dwellers economically, and the rest of the country, ecologically, much poorer." It was about justice.

A few years out of law school, Oposa formed the Philippine Ecological Network, one of the early environmental organizations in the country and the first dedicated to the use of law. The timing was propitious. The country had just adopted some fine-sounding legal principles and launched its new department to carry them out. As the Network's president, Oposa wrote to the incoming department secretary, Fulgencio Factoran, protesting the continuing deforestation. The letter was a bit strong. It demanded that all logging concessions be terminated within fifteen days. To the young attorney's surprise, the secretary, who was also an attorney, not only replied to his letter in person but arranged a personal meeting as well.

The meeting introduced Oposa to the realpolitik of environmental policy. Secretary Factoran was quite sympathetic to his objectives and expressed his own desire to change forest policy. His problem was that he had little support in the legislature and less in the administration. Fine-sounding language on the law books was one thing, but no one wanted an "environmental coup." The secretary's hands were further tied because the department's budget was subject to legislative approval and could be cut in a heartbeat. Factoran would provide Oposa the necessary information. But Oposa would have to sue.

Anthony Oposa was only a few years out of law school. This would be his first environmental case; in fact it would be his first case of any kind. And, so, he brought it.

THE THRESHOLD question was whom to sue. The most obvious targets were the logging companies, who, after all, were the ones cutting down the trees. The difficulty here was that the companies held signed and sealed government permits allowing them to log for decades into the future. They also had at their disposal stables of the country's best lawyers ready to swamp their opponents in paperwork, supported by hot-and-cold-running politicians on tap where needed. The Philippines ranked high among the politically corrupt countries of the world, and its judiciary, historically, followed suit. All it would take was a few quiet phone calls from the timber industry to who knows whom and the case could simply disappear. As a legal and practical matter, then, the only feasible defendant was the Department of Environment and Natural Resources, a friend or otherwise in the affair.

To the Philippine Ecological Network, the facts behind *Minors Oposa* were overwhelming. The department had ninety-two long-term concessions outstanding for over ten million acres of virgin timber, and was under pressure to issue yet more. That was already five times the amount of original forest left in the entire country. It seemed crazy, but then again many things seem crazy but they are not against the law. The trick was to prove that logging on this scale was also illegal and that its real victims, harkening back to the idea Oposa had returned with from Norway, were the children who would inherit a wasted country, children yet unborn. What he saw wrong here was an attack on posterity. He also saw a way to frame his case to capture the attention of the courts and the media. The children would sue.

There remained, however, the matter of who would dare to bring such a lawsuit against the government in their own names. Oposa recruited a few friends and family members to join him, with their children, but none had the appetite to go first. He later explained, "one can imagine how skeptical and afraid they were, who the heck would sue the Government?" Their fears were understandable. One logging boss out of the ninety-two concessions at issue, he mused, "could simply hire someone to have me shot and killed." And so Oposa's friends and relatives insisted that, because the suit was his idea, Oposa's children would go first. His oldest was three and one-half years old, his youngest just nine months. And so the case was captioned *Minors Oposa*.

The suit was filed on behalf of Anthony Oposa and his children, other children and their parents, unnamed children of the future, and the Philippine Ecological Network against Secretary Factoran who, whatever his personal feelings, was represented by state attorneys sworn to defend government actions. Originally styled as a "taxpayers' action" on behalf of all Filipinos, and with a rhetorical extravagance that few American lawyers would dare—"the unabated hemorrhage of the country's vital life-support systems and continued rape of Mother Earth"—the complaint alleged violations of the environmental provisions of the Constitution. It sought nothing less than the cancellation of all existing timber concessions and an injunction against processing new ones. Oposa was shooting for the moon.

He lost. The government filed a motion to dismiss, and the case sat for nearly a year. Finally, without hearing oral arguments, the trial court found the complaint short on facts—"replete with vague assumptions and vague conclusions based on unverified data"—and shorter on law. It failed to allege with "sufficient definiteness" either a "specific legal right they are seeking to enforce" or a "specific legal wrong they are seeking to prevent." Nothing in the law, you could hear the court thinking, prohibited logging. Furthermore, the concessions in dispute were so impressed with "political color" and "public policy" that judicial review of them would do violence to the constitutional separation of powers. This was politics, and these were executive decisions. Were this not enough, the court added, whatever platitudes the Constitution may offer about a healthy environment, it also explicitly guaranteed that contracts would be free of impairment. Relief of the kind sought by Oposa would require more than impairment of the timber licenses; it would eliminate them. Three large strikes for the home team. A fourth was yet to come.

When Oposa appealed to the Supreme Court, the solicitor general had a new defense. He questioned Oposa's right to represent entities as diffuse as all Filipinos, to say nothing of children yet unborn. It had no basis in law and sounded more based in hubris instead. Who could claim to represent people who didn't know him, who didn't even know of the lawsuit, who weren't even people yet? Unwilling to abandon his theory, Oposa came across writings by an American scholar who spoke in terms of "intergenerational equity," the duty one generation owed to the ones to follow, and the phrase captured his vision. He had never heard the term before, but the generations to come were at the center of his thinking since his return from Norway, and what he was convinced the new Philippine Constitution meant by the right to a healthy environment. He had no legal precedent for this point, from any country, not even a body of scholarship, which usually precedes advances in the law. He was on his own, and from here on it would be up to his argument and the judges. Which turned out to be enough. The Philippine Supreme Court, astonishingly, ruled for Oposa on every argument.

The opinion was written by Justice Hilario G. Davide Jr., the Court's most newly appointed member, joined by ten other justices of the Court. His opinion reads in part like poetry; in other parts it reads like Oposa had written it himself. Turning first to the issue of the unborn children, Davide found that Oposa had the right to represent his generation's interest in environmental quality, as well as that of succeeding generations. This right flowed naturally, in the Court's mind, from the Constitution's own language, which referenced "the rhythm and harmony of nature." The maintenance of "rhythm and harmony" included the "management, renewal and conservation" of the country's resources, so that they would be "equitably accessible to the present as well as future generations." Each generation, therefore, held a "responsibility to the next" to preserve nature. That obligation was the basis for standing to sue, for this generation's own sake and for those to come.

So far so good, but at this point Oposa et al. were only inside the courthouse door. The next step of the opinion was equally bold. The Constitution, Justice Davide declared, not only accorded the right to litigate but also granted a right to protection as well. This protection was so fundamental that it had been required all along, in the way of natural law, even had the Constitution said nothing of the kind. The principle was "assumed to exist from the inception of mankind" he wrote, a sort of ecological right to self-defense, and were such a right not implied, "the day would not be too far when all else would be lost not only for the present generation, but also for those to come—generations which stand to inherit nothing but parched earth incapable of sustaining life."

Having rolled this far, the Court was not about to let the impairment of the Constitution's contracts provision stand in the way. It found the timber concessions not to be contracts at all in the legal sense, but rather licenses that were capable of being withdrawn for the public welfare. Even viewed as contracts, the Court continued, their cancellation would be justified on the facts at hand as a valid exercise of the police power. The Court turned last to leave-it-to-the-political-process argument. The case did not concern politics or "policy formation." What was involved, rather, was the enforcement of a right expressed in law. Further, even if the case touched on politics, the Constitution had expanded judicial power to determine whether there had been a "grave abuse of discretion" by any branch of government. These are your concessions to issue, Department of Environment and Natural Resources, but it is our duty to review them.

Of the eleven justices sitting, this was the opinion of ten. It would be hard to imagine ten of eleven votes in favor of any of the four conclusions just described from any court of appeals in the United States, much less the Supreme Court, at any time in history. The decision was a bombshell. Not just one bomb, but several. Where in the world, one might ask, did it come from? From no single source, doubtless, but one may reasonably postulate several contributors.

The judges in this case, like their country, were coming off decades of quasi-dictatorial rule, the antithesis of law, and were reasserting their role. At the same time, during the late 1980s, the Filipinos were catching their first heady wave of the environmental enthusiasm that had swept the United States a decade before. New ink was barely dry on the far-reaching and aspirational declarations of its Constitution. The politicians may not have been ready for them, but the courts—in many countries the most educated and the least politicized branch of government—were less shackled to the past and more free to change course. Justice Davide, who, one has the sense, grew into environmental literacy with the experience of their case, went on to lecture to international audiences on the importance of an independent judiciary in environmental protection, and the need for support in legal and public education. Pure Antonio Oposa.

At the end of the day, however, this case was decided by the towering, remorseless assertion of facts from which there was no escape. The Court's detailed recitation of Oposa's allegations—a parade of horribles—shows that it understood them and was impressed. The Philippines had taken its greatest natural treasure and turned it into a liability, impoverishing everyone. There seemed no other way to stop the train. At times, hard cases make great law.

AT FIRST glance, life after *Minors Oposa* appears very similar to life before it. The sun still rises and then it sets, and in between the battle between exploiting the planet for short-term gain and holding onto it for long-term survival continues on every island of the Philippines, as it does on every continent of the globe. The great trees that moved this case continue to fall, much less rapidly, but then again there are fewer left to cut. After the Court's ruling, the case went back to the trial court for examination of the individual logging concessions . . . where it disappeared. Oposa and the children did not have the means to pursue it. In 1991, a tropical storm swept the Philippines and brought a recently logged mountainside down on lowland villages. Thousands died. In 1999, another heavy rainstorm hit a denuded hillside and did exactly the same thing. In 2006, it happened yet again. Hundreds more died. You could look at *Minors Oposa* and conclude: nothing happened. Some, in fact, have. They miss the forest for the trees.

The Supreme Court opinion dealt timber concessions on native forests in the Philippines a legal and psychological blow from which they will never recover. During the proceedings of the case, Secretary Factoran issued an administrative order that prohibited new logging on the remaining virgin stands. The case gave him the political cover he needed to act: environmentalists were pressing, the media were in full cry, and the courts had his program under review. There were 142 logging concessions outstanding when the issue came to Oposa's attention, ninety-two when he filed suit, forty-one when the case was decided, and nineteen remaining in 2001. By 2006 there were only three timber leases still in effect, one more inactive, and one under review, all set to expire within the next five years. The annual rate of deforestation had fallen to about 2 percent. Clearly, none of these reductions were ordered by the Court. But the results were foreordained, and a vehicle now existed to compel them if the government failed to act.

In place of the timber concessions, however, illegal logging boomed. There is major money in virgin timber, the forests are remote, surveillance is rudimentary, and big trees continue to fall. Gigged forward by Tony Oposa, the Philippine government has attempted to crack down on illegal loggers, securing nearly two hundred convictions since 1995 when its program began, up from virtually zero a few years before. It has tried export bans, manifests to track timber shipments like hazardous waste, and repeated enforcement raids, but the headlines tell a sad story: "DENR cancels 8,000 timber permits due to illegal logging," "14 draw prison terms for illegal logging," "Ban on illegal activities in Shilan forest sought," "Group says Sierra Madre rape goes on," "Rebel group claims collusion in Caroga log sector," and "DENR Quezon head axed over logging." For more than twenty million Filipinos living in the interior, many of them indigenous peoples, and for many timber-short countries willing to pay whatever is necessary, the lure of illegal logging is irresistible.

And so the fight rages on, beyond the Philippines to Russia, Indonesia, Brazil, and wherever virgin trees remain. In Liberia wildcat logging funded the bloody regime of Charles Taylor. The last native forests of Borneo, home to the red orangutan, a close relative of *Homo sapiens*, are expected to disappear within the next ten years. Brave voices emerge. The Brazilian ecologist Chico Mendes spoke out against illegal logging in the Amazon and was assassinated. The Liberian Silas Kpanan' Ayuning Siakor, recently honored for opposing the theft of

West African forests at considerable risk to his life and family, explained, "our struggle for the environment is not about trees. It is a campaign for social justice and respect for human rights." He sounds like Antonio Oposa.

Meanwhile, the *Minors Oposa* opinion continues to echo through the Philippines in support of environmentally protective decisions. It has been cited in eight reported cases, each with favor, usually on the procedural question of standing to sue. Although it is true that the cast of environmental plaintiffs always includes members presently living, recognition of future generations as stakeholders casts their issues in an entirely new light. It challenges a host of assumptions concerning the nature of gross national wealth, and whether sustainable development is a nice idea or a legal command. According to the opinion, it is the latter. Which is a bombshell all of its own.

Perhaps the most noted affirmation of *Minors Oposa* to date has been a recent pollution-control case pitting a group called Concerned Residents of Manila Bay against a dozen Philippine government and private entities, each of which could legitimately contend that the Bay's pollution problem was really caused by somebody else. The complaint was bold and sweeping in its parade of facts (the most polluted water body in the country), its public visibility (at the edge of Manila City itself), the array of its defendants (which included malfunctioning sewage treatment plants, port authorities, agriculture and fishery agencies, several private septic companies, and industrial dischargers), and the boldness of the relief requested. It wanted the court to do nothing less than direct the defendants to clean up Manila Bay. Few courts would rise to such bait. This one did, stating: "The modern trend is to invoke the judiciary in the protection and preservation of the environment. The role of courts at present is to act as guardians of alive and future generations. They have trustee duties towards nature." Citing *Minors Oposa*, the court then proceeded to issue a series of orders, one per defendant, outlining its cleanup responsibilities, be they to install a sewage treatment facility, to treat ship discharges, or to provide a sanitary landfill. The orders sound as if they were written by the plaintiffs' attorney. The plaintiffs' attorney was Antonio Oposa.

At the end of the day, *Minors Oposa* is perhaps most important precisely because of its aspiration. The language is biblical. It sets out a goal as necessary in our time as the ever-elusive concepts of justice and peace. Like a prophet it leaves to others the job of figuring out how. Jurists and scholars wrestle with it. Quotations from it have begun to appear in statutes, treaties, and the popular press. These kinds of opinions reverberate for a very long time. We live by their signals. The most important one from *Minors Oposa* is that the environment not only matters, it really matters.

TONY OPOSA moved from the forests back to the oceans, which were his first draw to the environment from the days he camped on Bantayan Island and cooked fish he caught from the shore. One of the most productive bodies of water in the world is the Visayan Sea, a triangle of ocean running from the Philippines south to Borneo and Indonesia. Called "the Amazon of the Pacific," it is so rich in life that a square kilometer of reef contains more kinds of coral than are found in the entire Caribbean and over twelve thousand species of fish. Until blast fishing, cyanide fishing, and just plain overfishing took out most of its marine life and nearly all of its reefs. It was the Philippine forests debacle all over again, only this time under water, off shore, and much less visible to the public eye.

Oposa made it his debacle and began in typical fashion with "swift, painful, and public" enforcement raids like the one described at the beginning of this chapter. He persuaded the government to empower local communities to manage their nearby waters, creating a Visayan Sea Squadron of more than a hundred local vessels to patrol the reefs, inspect fishing boats, and clamp down on illegal take. One of Oposa's closest colleagues was the spokesman for the Squadron, a local fisher by the name of Elpidio de la Victoria, familiarly known as Jojo. Organizing enforcement actions against people who are willing to use dynamite and cyanide to kill fish makes enemies, and both Oposa and Jojo received death threats, which is not uncommon for environmental activists in many parts of the world. Only these were more than threats. On April 12, 2006, Elpidio "Jojo" de la Victoria was shot four times in front of his home in San Roque, Talisay City. He died the next day. The triggerman turned out to be a policeman. As of this writing, the people behind the killing have yet to be identified.

Tony Oposa is an optimist. In *The Laws of Nature* he points out that the Chinese word for *crisis* combines the characters for *danger* and *opportunity*. Immediately following the assassination of Jojo de la Victoria, he wrote to environmental colleagues around the world. He was not afraid, he said, to admit that he was afraid. But, he went on: "We can turn this crisis into an opportunity not only for us that work together but more important, for the tide to turn in the Philippine marine conservation movement." As it had for the forests.

Meanwhile, the action for which he is best known, *Minors Oposa*, hangs out there on the legal horizon like a mirage. Like a dare. Whether human beings can attain the norm of living with the "rhythm and harmony of nature" that the Philippine Constitution prescribes and its Supreme Court relied on is one of the unanswerable questions of our time. For the moment it seems way out of reach. And yet, there is this beacon. It is terribly attractive. Everything else is meanwhile, and in the trying.

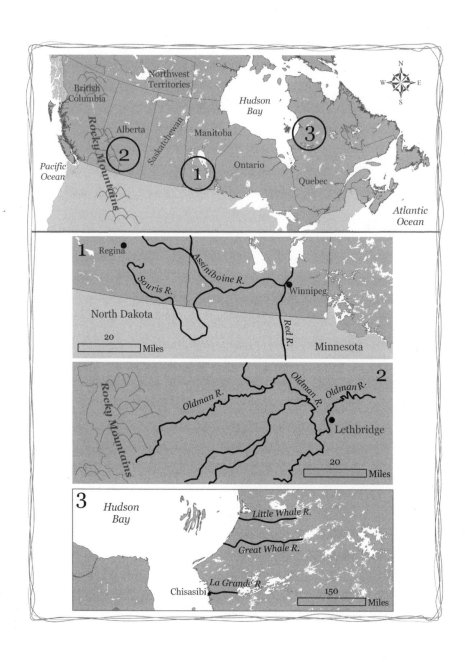

CHAPTER FOUR

Great Whale

When the dams are built where will the animals go? The caribou won't know which way to go.

Samson Nahacappa, hunter, Cree Nation

IN THE SUMMER of 1981 an unusual group of tourists wandered the streets of Quebec City, marveling at the tall buildings, the crush of traffic, and the pervasive curbside trash. They were dressed in an assortment of store-bought clothes, blankets, and feathers. Some wore animal skins. They spoke neither English nor French but in dialects at times unintelligible even to each other. They looked out of their element, indeed out of their century, and they were. They were hunting and fishing families of the Cree Indian Nation, some eight hundred miles from their home base on the Canadian Shield, and they were not here on vacation. They were here to speak in yet another terribly strange environment, a federal court of law, hoping to get a non-Indian judge to understand them. They were trying to protect land on which their Nation had been living for five thousand years and was about to go under water. They would be in court for ten years.

The Cree cases capped a trilogy of lawsuits that brought environmental law to Canada and shook the government to its core. They were surrounded by fierce politics and the passions of people so thoroughly convinced they were in the right that they did not need to explain. Opponents took to the streets; crown and provincial ministers traded verbal abuse; people went to jail. Canadians then and since use words like "fiasco," "an embarrassment," and "a long litany of screwups" to describe the action. The objects of these cases were water projects, each more massive than the one before, and they reached their apex on the Great Whale River, avidly sought by Quebec City and defended by the Cree. But the rumblings began years earlier with the Rafferty and Oldman dams, out on the western plains.

⌘

WHILE THOSE who came to settle North America did not find easy pickings anywhere, some particularly harsh scenarios played out east of the Rocky Mountains. Lured on by railroad promotions that combined fantasy with out-right fraud, the prairie settlers broke the earth, buried native grasses, planted wheat, lived in sod houses, endured unimaginable winters, and prospered or failed by the rains. "Rainfall follows the plough" declared the agronomists of the day, theorizing that the release of moisture from cultivated soil would seed the atmosphere and prompt an ever-increasing cycle of precipitation. As we know, the opposite happened.

By the time of the Great Dust Bowl prairie farmers had stripped the land of its cover. The winds rose, and storms of snow and dirt blackened the skies and buried telephone poles as far east as Chicago and Albany. A Canadian who lived through it recalls a joke about the Saskatchewan farmer who went out to culti-vate his land and ended up finding it in Manitoba. When the winds finally died, the answer was: more water projects. One of the first out of the box was the Raf-ferty Dam.

George Hood lived the saga of the Rafferty project. A public planner with no engineering background, he was brought in by the province of Saskatchewan to make Rafferty happen. He arrived to see a region living marginally on oil field jacks and small canals designed to convert the feast-or-famine waters of the Souris River to human use. To Hood, and to the entire political establishment of Saskatchewan, this was a place that could use a dam. It was simply a matter of jumping through the hoops. A headline in the *Toronto Star* reading "Rafferty-Alameda Dams Could Reduce Bird Populations by 30,000" caused them no alarm. It should have. They had no idea of what they were getting into.

THE HIGHEST hoop seemed at the time the most unlikely, a group of hunters and fishermen in the Saskatchewan Wildlife Federation. Sportsman's organizations had been an engine of conservation long before the word *environment* was born. In the wake of the Dust Bowl, American waterfowlers promoted the purchase of wetlands, financed by taxes on their own licenses and shotgun shells. Now they saw these same areas threatened by a wave of government engineering. They had their own lobby in Washington, D.C., the National Wildlife Federation, and when environmental litigation appeared on the scene in the early 1970s, the Federation followed suit. Within a few months it was suing the Army Corps of Engineers over dams.

Meanwhile, north of the border, the Canadian Wildlife Federation, a loose conglomerate of sportsmen with barely the budget to rent an office, was going in no particular direction and in no particular hurry. In 1985 in walked Ken Brynaert, an entrepreneur with ideas to grow the organization to fit the times. He told the Federation board that all he needed was $150,000 in startup money. "It shouldn't take a week," he said. "You've got a week" said its president, Orville Erickson. By coincidence, Orville was upset about the Rafferty Dam. He hunted waterfowl, and thirty thousand ducks was a lot to lose.

With exactly seven days to make his case, Brynaert hopped the next flight south to Washington, D.C., to meet with the National Wildlife Federation chief executive, Tom Kimball. Kimball, who had formerly directed the fish and game departments of both Arizona and Colorado, enjoyed enormous credibility in the outdoors world. A devout Mormon with a flair for the malaprop (he spoke of "our foundling fathers" and "expotential growth"), Kimball had great personal courage and a sense for the right thing to do. He lent Brynaert the money to get started and welcomed him to the family. Where Brynaert met the Federation's lawyers and learned about environmental lawsuits.

At a joint meeting in Quebec in 1987, the Canadian and National Wildlife Federations passed a resolution opposing the Rafferty Dam. They also passed a censure motion against the Canadian environment minister for failing to block it. Brynaert delivered the motion to the minister in person at his hotel room. More aggressive still, they were going to sue the minister. They had one complication. It was not clear that he had any power over the Rafferty project at all.

𝕯

THE GOVERNANCE of Canada is pretty much what Americans thought they were creating two hundred plus years ago, a partnership of states in which the federals were confined to a very small box in Ottawa. The rest was left to provincial capitals. Of course, the United States began to depart from this model when it traded the Articles of Confederation for the Constitution, and has been departing ever since, but Canada had clung to a states-rights model, tested increasingly by modern imperatives. None the least of these would be environmental protection.

There was another governing principle as well, and it concerned the judiciary. Courts were designed to resolve disputes between private parties; they did not set policy, nor did they gainsay the policies of elected officials. The United States broke this mold too, early on, when the Supreme Court declared its authority to find government actions, even laws, unconstitutional. Under that power, American courts gradually became players in racial integration, school prayer, and other social issues. Canadian courts viewed these events with alarm and resisted all initiatives to join the fray. Environmental issues would put this philosophy, as well, to the test.

The root problem was as follows. Neither the delegates to the US Constitutional Convention of 1787 nor the drafters of the Canadian Constitution Act of 1867 had the slightest notion of environmental issues. No language even close to the word *environment* appears in either document. In a government that leaves all matters not federal to the states, then, federal authority to protect the environment would seem to be zero. US courts, over time, found it through an expansive interpretation of the commerce clause. Nobody knew how Canada would slice it when environmental law appeared on the scene.

The Environment Ministry in Ottawa was small, inexperienced, underpowered, and far away from the action in provinces. Both the government and industry feared recent developments south of the border, where environmental groups with names they had never heard of were taking new laws to court—and stopping favored projects in their tracks. On the other hand, the idea of environmental protection had caught public attention as a sensible thing to do. Tentatively then, feeling its way, without explicit statutory support but pressured by the public to do something, the Ministry issued a skeletal directive in the early 1970s establishing an environmental assessment process. It was to be run by a new Federal Environmental Review Office with the unfortunate acronym "FEARO." The process, so written, then went into hiding. Which is where the Rafferty case came in.

𝕯

RAFFERTY CAME in waves. The first case was brought in 1986 by ranchers whose lands were about to be flooded. They lost. When their representative in the provincial parliament complained about the impact of the project on the ranching industry, the prime minister replied, "[H]istory will show what you know and don't know about the stock growers would fill a large room, my boy." My boy. It was the attitude, and it would characterize everything about Rafferty from then on.

Enter the Canadian Federation with a new claim. It wasn't just Saskatchewan that was violating the law; it was the Environment Ministry in Ottawa that had cleared the project without environmental review. With public criticism rising, the Rafferty projects were by this point a hot potato, and the minister wanted no part of them. He argued that FEARO guidelines imposed no duties on the Ministry; they were only suggestions, not law. The trial court disagreed. The guidelines were more than "mere description"; they created enforceable rights. The opinion produced a certain irony: the Environment Ministry had done with its guidelines what it could never have gotten through legislation in Parliament; it had written an enforceable law. Now it was stuck with it.

A scant two months later, the appellate court upheld the ruling. As Ken Brynaert, who was sitting in the audience, tells it, the judges did not even bother to retire to consider the government's case; they whispered among themselves and then ruled—appeal denied. News of the decision hit George Hood's team like the end of the known world. They had fully expected to win. This was their dam, not Ottawa's. A local legislator announced that he was "madder than hell" about getting stopped by people "no more interested in the environment than they are in flying to the moon." Hood ratcheted up the politics. He even made a movie, *Dreams in the Dust*, featuring a widow whose husband keeled over from a heart attack when he learned of the project delays. Hood was on the offense again. His story of the fight that followed is entitled "Getting the Better of Them."

Given a mission it had by no means sought, Environment Canada, as the federal Ministry was now called, had to conduct the dreaded environmental review. Under pressure, it found no significant problems, approved the project, and crossed its fingers that it would go away. Instead, the Canadian Wildlife Federation took it back to court for another spanking. "If there be anyone who ought scrupulously to conform to the official duties which the law casts upon him or her in the role of a high State official, it is a Minister of the Crown," the court admonished. "That is just plainly obvious." Which put poor Environment Canada back on the hot seat. It not only had to redo its environmental assessment, it would have to convene an independent review panel for the job. Enter George Hood and the Rafferty supporters with a very sweet offer. The Ministry would conduct its independent review, but it would allow Hood to go forward with land acquisition and construction. Ottawa would, further, agree to compensate the Saskatchewan authorities up to $10 million for any more project delays. Environment Canada agreed. Hood et al. uncorked the champagne.

The results were absurd. Canada was now conducting an independent review on a project released for construction, for which the government would itself be liable for any delays, to say nothing of the cost of possible alterations or an ultimate decision not to proceed at all. In the dam-building business, poured concrete is nine-tenths of the law. As Hood proudly recalls, the work "rumbled on into the night, unabated, twenty-four hours a day, seven days a week until freeze-up." Locals came out in lawn chairs to watch the action. The Rafferty litigation had brought environmental policy out of hiding, but it did not catch the train.

⟡

THE SECOND chapter of the Great Whale saga also came from the West. The Oldman River rises from snowmelt in the Rockies of Alberta and comes tumbling down to the prairie. The Blackfoot Indians are thought to have entered this region after crossing the Bering Strait, but their own story of Genesis begins otherwise. They were placed at this spot by Naipi, the Old Man, who made the world and everything in it. At which point, after instructing the people how to hunt and live, Naipi is said to have retreated "to the high mountains in the headwaters of the river that now bears his name," the Oldman. They had lived here for up to twelve thousand years.

The Peigan tribe, the largest of the Blackfoot Nation, were buffalo hunters and when first encountered by European fur traders in the early 1800s they controlled the plains from the Canadian Rockies through Alberta and south into Montana. With the arrival of the snows, the Peigan, like Naipi, withdrew to the Oldman valley where they remained until spring. Their central wintering ground was at the confluence of Crow Lodge Creek and the Oldman River as it emerged onto the prairie, lined by a green ribbon of cottonwood trees. The river stages marked the seasons for the Peigan, who timed their sweats and sacred ceremonies by its rise and fall. To Milton Born With A Tooth, the Oldman was a "religious ecosystem." To the oncoming whites, it was a "water resource."

The first white entrepreneurs into the area were American whiskey traders, up from Montana, forcing the Dominion government to send in the Mounties and build the usual forts, the first of which was called Fort Whoop-Up. Settlers soon followed. The Peigan resisted what they saw as an invasion, but they were outgunned from the outset and within a few decades, dying of starvation, they came to terms. In 1877 they surrendered their lands to the Crown in return for a small site on the Oldman where they failed at farming and succumbed to alcohol, smallpox, and other diseases. By the early 1900s they were down to 250 souls. Eighty years later, whatever tangible symbol remained of their religion and culture lay in the Oldman River, where it came out of the mountains to the plains.

So the situation remained until the end of World War II when returning soldiers and new waves of immigrants again looked to the West. The federal government launched several water projects to assist them but soon learned that irrigation on the prairie was a money-losing proposition. As Ottawa maneuvered to get out of the business, however, in stepped Alberta, which was betting its future on expanded agriculture, food processing, and crops like sugar beets with a great thirst for water. Alberta had only two available water sources, and one of them was the Oldman.

In 1984, the Alberta prime minister announced his intention to dam the river. He anticipated, he said, "no environmental concerns." A fledgling group of farmers started asking questions, nonetheless. The answers they received were evasive, if anyone bothered to answer at all, and the battle lines slowly formed. The farmers called on an environmental network for help, and down from Calgary came Martha Kostuch, a veterinarian and expatriate from Minnesota now living in a town called Rocky Mountain House, six hours of hard driving away. Kostuch formed the Friends of the Oldman River Society, "something with a positive ring," she explained. As the issues heated up, the insults flew, followed by intimidation. At one point Kostuch had the Mounties tap her phone to monitor the threats she was receiving. Provincial environment minister Ken Kowalski branded her group "pot smoking social anarchists."

As the battle crystallized, the Peigan tribe was torn. Desperately poor and in need of government aid, they were offered millions of dollars in mitigation for the dam, which translated into schools, education, and the improvement of their lives. But the tribe was tied to the river, root and branch, in every aspect of its physical and spiritual culture. Which way did responsibility lie? Deeply divided, the tribal council voted neither to support nor oppose. A warrior group within the tribe, however, the Lonefighters, maintaining a tradition of young braves that extended back beyond memory, took a more aggressive stance. Their spokesman was Milton Born With A Tooth. They would raise hell.

✥

IT IS HARD for outsiders to understand the intransigence of the players in water resources litigation. Most people who sue other people seek money. What the
people opposing the Rafferty, Oldman, and Great Whale projects wanted, however, was deeper and far less attainable: they wanted the water left alone. Money
doesn't work here. A deal offering them half a loaf doesn't work either. How
does one halve a river? True, you might be able to buy out an acutely poor tribe
for cash in hand, but to the Peigan Lonefighters and to Friends of the Oldman
River these cases were like defending Eden from an invader who is bent on ignoring them, funneling public money to supporters, and breaking the law. An
invader who doesn't understand them at all.

Alberta had strong feelings here too. Projects like these were the future of
the region. Who could farm the plains without water? The projects were, further, planned by duly elected officials. Quite early in the process the officials
adopt these projects like their own children, and quite soon the line between
public good and private ego disappears. Not only is their project on the line,
they are on the line, and so begin the personal attacks, the anger, and the need to
ram things through come hell or high water. In the Oldman Dam case, there was
another driver as well. Deep down, and one does not have to dig too far, Alberta
was defending its right to do what it thought best against an encroaching bureaucracy in Ottawa. To the provincial government, this was a civil war.

Friends of the Oldman River brought a lawsuit that was long on passion but
short on available law. In a rhetorical flourish, Minister Kowalski pronounced
their claims "absurd, nonsensical, and to the point of being ridiculous." Then, in
the midst of the proceedings, as in a miracle, the Rafferty Dam decision came
down from Saskatchewan ordering the environmental minister to obey his own
rules for federal review. Not long following, the Oldman court issued a similar
ruling: the minister would have to conduct a federal review here as well. Alberta,
true to form, appealed to the Canadian Supreme Court and put dam construction into overdrive. Which would simply replay the Saskatchewan scenario, but
for Alberta's brief to the Court. It went very deep. Federal environmental review
was unconstitutional.

⅏

MEANWHILE, the Peigan Lonefighters were about to take matters into their own hands. Their list of grievances against the government went back a hundred years. They viewed the treaties by which they had ceded land to the government as "shams," signed by white Indian agents whose corruption was legendary. As one current tribal leader says, "[W]e didn't know how to read and we didn't know how to write; we were still riding around on horses and shooting Winchesters." In the early 1920s, without so much as a by-your-leave from the tribe, Alberta had cut an irrigation canal across the reservation. The Peigan saw it as a continuing insult. By the late 1960s, as Oldman was percolating along, their suspicions and sense of injury were already high.

Seeing no relief from the court actions and the project rising before their eyes, the Lonefighters announced a "ground breaking" ceremony, rented a bulldozer from a local construction company, and attacked the dam. Milton Born With A Tooth had volunteered for the job. His friend Edwin Small Legs recalls sitting with him at a strategy meeting and deciding that "somebody had to go to jail." Nobody was paying any attention to their protests or even to court decisions. Milton spoke up. "I'll do it," he said. "I'll go to jail." At a press conference in nearby Head-Smashed-In-Buffalo-Jump, Milton explained that the Lonefighters were acting to protect the Peigan way of life. "No more courts for me, no more panels for me," he said "It's time passion is brought back to this country." There is a photo of Milton, his sister, and an unnamed Lonefighter on a dike at the "ground breaking" site. Milton is long haired, broad faced, and naked from the waist up. He is wearing an amulet around his neck, and he is smiling. What followed was a tragedy of mistrust and botched communication.

The Lonefighters began deconstructing the diversion canal for the dam. Their machine sank into the mud. They got it operating again. Alberta went into negotiations with the tribal president and agreed not to invade the reservation. But the Lonefighters, marching to their own drum, went on pecking away at their cut. Then, on September 7, without further warning, the provincial government entered the reservation supported by Royal Mounties, heavily armed. They impounded the bulldozer and then, helicopters overhead, moved on the

Lonefighter camp. No one got hurt, but two shots were fired. The man who fired the shots was Milton Born With A Tooth.

𝔇

MEANWHILE, back in Ottawa, Environment Canada's inertia on Oldman Dam was becoming embarrassing. An Environment Canada official announced that the review panel was "on ice." The construction was going forward rapidly. When asked whether Alberta could actually operate the dam without federal approval, a provincial minister observed, "Of course we can . . . we're doing it now."

All eyes were now on the Supreme Court, grinding its way through the briefs and arguments of Alberta and no fewer than five sister provinces, all of whom saw their turf on the line. Arguing for the environmentalists was Brian Crane, an attorney from Ottawa who had succeeded before these same judges in Rafferty not so very long before. Finally, in February 1992, the court ruled. One can usually tell how a case will turn out within the first few sentences of any opinion. In this case, the opinion began: "The protection of the environment has become one of the major challenges of our time." Crane knew he had won.

The opinion moved through the statutory issues like so much underbrush and then arrived at the main event. In a government of limited powers, and with no express power over the environment, was federal environmental review constitutional? To Alberta and her sisters the review was a "Trojan horse" enabling Ottawa to intrude deeply into provincial affairs. If the provinces were correct, on the other hand, then federal environmental protection for nine-tenths of the country would be history. The Court split the baby. Faced with the disagreeable alternative of invalidating a process the court plainly believed was beneficial, it found that environmental review didn't really intrude on the power of the provinces. Rather, it simply helped federal agencies do their business, where at least a plausible federal business could be found. The provinces would have to get used to this new partnership.

In the meantime, Oldman Dam was winning the race with time.

𝔇

IN MAY 1992, the Oldman review panel issued its report. The dam was a loser, it said, and the best option was to "decommission" it. Reality, however, was otherwise. The dam at this point was 80 percent complete. Always quick with a quote, Alberta Minister Kowalski labeled the report "technically adolescent." The dam would be completed, he said, no matter what the panel did. He was correct. Alberta went forward anyway and finished the project. Fish biologists had predicted that the dam would eliminate the prize species of the region, the bull trout. They also were correct. Three years after the gates closed, a magazine reported that Alberta's remaining bull trout "teetered on the brink of extinction." The province reacted promptly. In May 1995 its legislature proclaimed the bull trout one of the province's "official emblems." The problem was apparently solved.

The Peigan came out a little better. In 2001 they changed their name, rejecting the English version and reverting to their own pronunciation, *Piikan*. Two years later they struck a settlement of their claims against Alberta and the government of Canada for $64 million. Edwin Small Legs says, "I can tell you this. If it hadn't been for Milton and what he did, we would not have that $64 million today."

It was left to Milton Born With A Tooth to pay the piper. His first trial on firearms charges was so patently unfair that he became a First Nation celebrity. He had fired the two shots, however, and at the end of the day he was retried. He was sentenced to sixteen months in jail, served twelve, and moved away from the Oldman forever. He had once said, "I'm going to do it my way . . . they'd better kill me before I get home because I'm willing to die for this." He did not die. At least not physically.

The Province of Alberta had a response of its own to the adverse national press it had received. It planned a big party to inaugurate Oldman Dam. Exercising his talent with words once again, Minister Kowalski christened the event "A Festival of Life: A Celebration of Water," a four-day program featuring water rides, a children's carnival, a 500-seat dinner for dignitaries, a concert by Canada's top country band, and a church service. Martha Kostuch, no slouch for a phrase herself, called it: a "festival of death, the death of three rivers." She called up the scheduled country band and asked, "Do you know what it is you are celebrating?" The band canceled its engagement. The Piikan refused to participate as well, not just the Lonefighters but the entire tribe.

In the end, Minister Kowalski called off his ceremony, alleging a criminal conspiracy. The *Calgary Herald*, questioning the basis of his claim, advised him to "put up or shut up." He did neither. Instead, in lieu of his public celebration, on a July morning he sent a squadron of sixteen flag-bearing horsemen to the top of the dam where they were duly photographed and memorialized. "[A] respectful affirmation," said the *Alberta Report*, "of their support for water management in Southern Alberta." Replied the *Calgary Herald*, it was "more like a public relations attempt at damage control." Martha Kostuch said that she thought it might be better to leave the dam standing after all, as a "monument to government stupidity." The Oldman case was over. Federal environmental protection in Canada had been declared constitutional, but it had also missed the train.

🐋

Quebec is a vast hydro-electric plant in the bud, and every day, millions of potential kilowatt hours flow downhill and out to sea. What a waste.
Robert Bourassa, Premier Quebec Province, 1991

BY THIS TIME, halfway across Canada, the Cree Nation had come to Quebec City to plead their case against the Great Whale project, the biggest of them all. In April 1971, the government of Quebec had announced plans to build one of the most ambitious works in history on the Canadian Shield, a vast complex of lakes, tundra, and forests east of Hudson Bay. The venture would consume twenty wild rivers and cover an area the size of France. Even more spectacular was Quebec's further dream of sealing off the bottom of James Bay with a one hundred-mile dike and selling its waters to the western plains, as far away as California. Designed in three phases, phase one would drain six entire rivers into the La Grande River, doubling its flow and funneling it toward an underground powerhouse more than twice the size of the Notre Dame Cathedral. By comparison, Rafferty and Oldman were mere pretenders. The province stood to make a fortune selling electricity. Better yet, none of these impacts would be felt

by Quebecois. The project was sited on the territory of the Cree Indian Nation.
Only nobody bothered to tell the Cree.

The struggle that followed pitted two passionate antagonists, each with its
history of grievances and struggle for self-determination. In one corner stood
Quebec, whose separate language, culture, and politics fed a near-constant quest
for greater autonomy, if not outright independence from federal Canada.
Emerging from a history of English dominance, Quebecois were the least pre-
pared Canadians then or now to take directions from Ottawa. There were few
better ways than a hydroelectric bonanza to fuel provincial ambitions. These
were Quebec's projects. They would be built and guarded by its alter ego, the
James Bay Development Corporation.

In the opposite corner stood the largest and most functionally independent
Indian nation left in North America. According to the explorer Mackenzie, the
Cree were sharp negotiators but "naturally generous, good-tempered, and honest." Catholic missionaries seconded the compliment, calling them "high in
morality." Depleted elsewhere by white settlements and disease, the James Bay
Cree remained almost entirely on their own in the north woods, protected by its
harsh winters, summer rains, and legendary biting insects, intact and in equilib-
rium with the place they lived.

⬥

THE CREE position was simple. These were their lands. In 1971 they filed suit,
represented by an Indian law expert named James O'Reilly who in fire and elo-
quence was Irish to the bone. The lead attorney for Quebec was Jacques LeBel,
who by coincidence was the brother-in-law of Quebec premier Robert Bourassa, author and champion of the James Bay plan. To the Quebec team it was
no contest, and they treated it that way: Canadian lands belonged to the
provinces and, besides, the impacts of the project would be beneficial to everyone, including the Cree.

The Cree case was a conglomerate of history, religion, and ethics, all cen-
tered on the hunting way. Today, we would use the phrase *the environment* but,
as the trial would reveal, no such word began to convey the meaning of the relationship of the Cree to the land. Frank Speck, an early ethnographer, called Cree

hunting a "religious occupation." A later researcher, Harvey Feit, set out "suspicious," he later wrote, of popular images of these Indians as either "ecological saints" or as "wanton over-exploiters." What he found was a complexity in the order of Catholic or Talmudic doctrine.

Hunting was the organizing principle of Cree life. The word itself had at least five separate meanings ranging from observing to catching to growing and continuing to grow. Every element in nature possessed a spirit, and the closest to humans were animals who, at appropriate times and in appropriate ways, gave themselves up to be killed. Successful hunters demonstrated competence by maintaining that balance with the world in which animals die and continue to grow. Depleted animal populations became "angry" and denied the humans their privilege. These were not just words. For centuries Cree wardens had supervised individual hunting zones of more than a hundred square miles each, monitoring the game, advising the hunters, limiting the take. All of the things that environmentalists would come to say about the interconnectedness of life and its spiritual dimension, the Cree lived. The question was, For how much longer?

To the whites, of course, all of this was incomprehensible. What ensued was a "dialogue of the deaf" for the provincial lawyers, who began the case "without really thinking it was necessary" and only woke up to the fact that the judge was paying attention as the proceedings wore on. Judge Malhouf was respectful to the native witnesses, asking one, whose answers had been cut short in cross-examination, if he had finished his answer. "It's okay," said Billy Diamond, a Cree chief. "It's not okay," the judge replied, "if you have not finished it you will be given the opportunity to finish it. That's why we're here." After a few days of testimony, he rejected the government's motions to dismiss. There were real issues here, he said.

The legal case was of first impression and immense. Was this enormous tract of wilderness really Cree land? To the Cree, of course, the very concept of ownership was countercultural. "It is quite ridiculous," testified Cree hunter Ronnie Jolly, "this idea of the white man that a person can own all of the earth, and everything under it, and everything that moves on it." As was the idea of money, particularly money in compensation for the loss of land. William Rat testified, "When you talk about money I do not really know the value of it. I do not use it very often." Losing the land would be "like losing my life," he added. He meant, of course, a relationship to land as strange to the Quebec attorneys who were questioning him as a relationship with the moon.

O'Reilly's legal argument was that the rights of the Cree and other tribes had been protected from the beginning by the English Crown, and that the settlers were instructed by King George III "not to disturb them in the Possession of such Parts of the said province as they at present occupy or possess." These understandings were subject to change only by later, negotiated treaties, which in this case had not taken place. All of which, to O'Reilly, meant that the Cree held rights to that land.

The government's position, besides saying that the Cree claims were absurd, was that the Cree had abandoned their described lifestyle some time ago. And if they hadn't, it was high time they should. Wasn't it a fact that the Cree used outboard motors now?, asked a government attorney. Yes, a Cree answered, but we also go upriver by canoe. Don't the Cree use snowmobiles? Yes, a Cree witness answered, but when people leave for their trap lines they still go by dogsled and wear snowshoes. What were the Cree witnesses eating in the city, white man's food, no? Answer: "I have come to the stage that I can hardly eat this food." Cree hunter John Kawapit continued, "When I go back home to Great Whale River I'll be able to eat better, because I will be eating the food that I have been eating in the past."

But were they telling the truth? When a Cree hunter was called in to testify about the effects of a James Bay access road across his trapline, he was asked to put his hand on the Bible and swear to tell the truth. A long dialogue with the translator ensued. "He does not know whether he can tell the truth," the translator told the judge. "He can tell only what he knows."

After seventy-eight days of testimony from 167 witnesses and several more months of deliberation, Judge Malhouf dropped a bomb. His 170-page opinion found as a matter of law that England and then Canada had always treated the Indians as sovereigns and undertook to possess their lands by agreements, not by simple appropriation. He credited the Cree witnesses and several supporting scientists who testified to severe disruption of the culture and livelihoods by even the access roads and preliminary construction works proposed. He enjoined them.

☞

QUEBEC'S RESPONSE mirrored that of Saskatchewan and Alberta: disbelief, at first, followed by defiance. It saw itself as the victim of a robbery with catastrophic losses of income, jobs, and security. It accelerated project construction. The weekend following the injunction, with work proceeding on the double, it imposed a news embargo on the area; pilots who flew reporters in to see what was going on would lose their licenses. At the same time, it rushed to file an appeal and stay Judge Malhouf's injunction. Within days the appellate court heard the stay motion. They had questions only for attorney O'Reilly, none for the government, and the tenor was not sympathetic to his cause. They opened with the question, as to a miscreant, "Well, Maitre O'Reilly, what have you got to say?" Within five hours the stay was lifted. The construction continued to roll. Then fate took a hand.

Throughout the winter and in extreme cold, construction stalled at the primary dam site. Two rival unions had a falling out. After a series of minor flare-ups, a group of workers seized some heavy equipment and rammed it into the power plant. Then they set it on fire. The company was forced to fly the entire crew out, fourteen hundred men. The work stopped for months. Asked by a reporter for his reaction to these events, a local Cree said, "If you don't quote me, I'll tell you; it sure as hell beats an injunction."

The respite was short lived. By the next summer the appeals court was ready to hear the case against damming the La Grande River on the merits. This time the government briefs were compendious, and the court swallowed them whole. The Canadian Shield was not the homeland of the Cree Nation, it concluded, but, rather, the Quebec frontier already settled by whites and in need of their improvement. The Cree life described by Judge Malhouf was ancient history. Justice Turgeon, writing the main opinion for the court, noted "the lack of importance of country food in the diet of the Indians," who ate "as do people inhabiting the urban centres." He found that a considerable number of Cree held "interesting jobs" and did not "give themselves over to hunting and fishing except [for] recreation." The James Bay project would provide a "salutary shock" to these people and "help in the elaboration of the necessary policies of transformation." It would be beneficial to the environment, as well. Far from drowning out fish and wildlife, the reservoirs would actually increase wildlife populations and spare them the hazards of uncontrolled nature and flooding. Judgment reversed.

And so, the Cree's first lawsuit failed in court, but its attendant publicity succeeded in prompting the government to negotiate terms for the now inevitable La Grande phase of the James Bay development. With no remaining leverage in law, the Cree were under enormous pressure to take whatever they could get. The government added to the pressure by cutting assistance to the tribe while the negotiations took place. Against this backdrop, it is remarkable that the Cree walked away with anything at all.

What they walked away with was the James Bay Northern Quebec Agreement, ratified by the Cree Nation and the Canadian Parliament, which extinguished native land claims in return for the creation of small, Cree-owned reserves and a $225 million payout. The La Grande project would go forward, but the location of its major power plant would be moved one rapid upstream, saving a historic Cree rendezvous of central religious importance. No other project modifications were obtained. The rivers would be drowned.

And so, the project described by Quebec premier Bourassa as a "conquest" of the Canadian North rolled forward. Twenty years later a brochure of Hydro-Quebec, now operating the facilities, urged the reader to "Follow the Energy Road!," where "You will experience the infinite landscapes and brilliant skies where thousands of Quebec workers built the La Grande complex." Thousands of Quebec workers perhaps, but very few Cree. As of 1991 only five residents of the town of La Grande worked for Hydro-Quebec. Half the town was unemployed, and the entire population suffered from "alarming rates of alcohol abuse, teenage pregnancy, divorce, and suicide." The hydro dams had also converted forms of mercury, harmless in their natural state, into methyl mercury, which is toxic to fish and humans. By 1984, a study of Cree living downstream from the complex found two-thirds of them with levels above the toxic threshold. Hydro-Quebec responded by telling the Cree to eat less fish. Asked about the positive impacts of the project on the community, Sappa Fleming, the former mayor of the Inuit population in Great Whale, said, "Well, my children can choose from six different kinds of potato chips at the Northern [grocery store]. . . . I suppose that is a kind of progress."

The same brand of progress came to the wildlife of the region. When the massive sluices and diversions opened, ten thousand caribou drowned trying to make the crossing in the raging and unfamiliar waters. Migration patterns throughout the region were scrambled. One old-timer said, "The geese have lost their way."

The first Cree lawsuit against the James Bay development had two other impacts not lost on the Cree or anyone else. The first was to politicize a loose grouping of tribes and families into a centralized Cree Council with allies in politics, international assemblies, and the rising environmental community. The second was to underline the need for legal leverage and to find it beyond Indian claims in the emerging field of environmental law. Enter the Great Whale.

ॐ

The central question about the Great Whale Basin is this: Should large parts of it be under water?

Sam Howe Verhovek, *New York Times*, 1992

THE GREAT WHALE is a special river even by Canadian standards, an entire country of special rivers. It inspires poetry from hard-nosed journalists and scientists alike. One reporter writes, "As the Great Whale river rises east out of Hudson Bay in northeastern Canada, its broad sandy shores quickly give way to a carpet of light-green lichen studded with granite outcroppings. Beyond the banks lies a vast expanse of black spruce and tamarack, great coniferous forests, broken here and there by lakes and bogs and kettle ponds." It teems with life in fall and spring, he continued, "when enormous herds of caribous stomp across the earth and millions of migratory birds tarry in the estuaries of James and Hudson bays, some stopping to double their weight as they feast on eelgrass and coastal shrimp before flying as far south as Tierra del Fuego." This much was obvious: "With its many rapids and falls, and its canyons and cliffs, it is a spectacularly beautiful river." It would be erased by the James Bay project, phase two.

The Great Whale project began for the Cree exactly as La Grande had, without notice. But not entirely by surprise, because back from political exile to lead the province of Quebec once again was Robert Bourassa. His passion for the project had not changed. Nor had his attitude toward the Cree. As he explained to the press, "[C]onquerors are not courteous." Nor had the project changed its posture toward the environment. One historian writes: "That the James Bay rivers should be turned to electricity to feed the world's hungriest and greediest energy markets and that James Bay itself should become the continent's water tank" was, in Quebec's view, "rational and inevitable." A consultant for the project company explained, "In my view, nature is awful, and what we do is cure it."

The Cree were not going to take this one lying down any more than they had the last. They elected a new grand chief, Matthew Coon-Come, a young, slim, and passionate man with a flair for oratory and a mandate to stop the development. Quebec professed surprise, arguing that the Cree had in the James Bay Agreement agreed not to oppose the James Bay projects. To which the Cree replied that this surrender of claims applied only to La Grande. And further, that the entire Agreement was void for duress, throw in fraud, misrepresentation, and nonfulfillment by Canada of its part of the bargain. Whatever the merits of these positions, they put all the more weight on the forthcoming environmental review.

Like its sister provinces, Quebec was determined to keep whatever environmental review was necessary at home and firmly under its thumb. The now-familiar question was whether any of this would receive federal review at all. The first answer was yes. Environment Canada minister Lucien Bouchard, a Quebecois as well but one who had been scorched by his ineffectual responses in the previous dam cases, admitted federal jurisdiction. In October 1989, he wrote to his Quebec counterpart that, given the "considerable magnitude of this project," it was "extremely important" that assessment be conducted "as objectively and independently as possible." He offered the province a "cooperative approach." Nothing, of course, was further from Quebec's mind. In the best tradition of the provinces, it did not even reply. Following up, the federal administrator of the

James Bay Development wrote Hydro-Quebec to reiterate that the Great Whale was subject to federal review. As a court later noted, "[a]n extensive period of silence then prevails." After which point the federal administrator appeared to have undergone Miraculous Conversion. In November 1990, he told a Cree audience that there was no need for federal review after all. One might forgive the Cree for feeling, once again, betrayed. They filed suit, this time based on environmental law.

It did not take the court months of testimony to get the point. Its recitation of the facts was a chronicle of government deceit. The Cree claim was that the James Bay Agreement itself required independent environmental review for subsequent projects "if the development is to have any significant impact" on the native people or wildlife resources of the territory. "I doubt," noted Judge Rouleau dryly, "that anyone can suggest that the Great Whale phase of the James Bay project will not result in 'drastic changes to the traditional way of life.'" Of course, Hydro-Quebec was not ready to concede any such impacts, but it had a better defense in mind. It denied the Agreement.

To Quebec, the James Bay Agreement was merely an understanding between two private parties. It was at best a contract, not a statute, and contracts were not enforceable in federal court. Judge Rouleau's anger shines through. "I feel a profound sense of duty," he wrote, to honor the Cree claim. "Any contrary determination would once again provoke, within the native groups, a sense of victimization by white society and its institutions. The Agreement had been signed in good faith for the protection of the Cree and Inuit peoples, not to deprive them of their rights and territories without due consideration." If one were to accept the federal government's sincerity toward native peoples, he observed, "one is at a loss to understand" its refusal to fulfill the Agreement. Quebec, of course, appealed.

The appellate court concurred, and so at long last, embarrassed by the press, castigated by the courts, mocked by the provinces, reeling from the after-effects of its timidity over the Rafferty and Oldman projects, dragged into the Great Whale with its heel marks all the way down the aisle, in July 1991, Environment Canada announced that if Quebec did not want to cooperate the federal government would review the project on its own. Softening its punch, it added that it could not guarantee that Quebec would delay construction until the environmental findings were released. Even this concession was not enough for Quebec's energy minister, who told reporters that the province would "never submit" to Ottawa's procedure. The bluffs and threats continued. But the Cree had purchased some time.

IN SPRING 1990, a strange procession made its way south from the Inuit and Cree villages along James Bay, to Montreal, and then down the Hudson River to New York City. At the suggestion of an American paddler who had fallen in love with the area, it featured a new symbolic kind of boat with the bow of an Indian canoe and the stern of an Eskimo kayak, given the hybrid name Odeyak. On April 20, Earth Day, with press boats following and small planes overhead, the Odeyaks, supporting canoes and sixty Cree and Inuit, reached port near Times Square. The first to speak was Mathew Coon-Come. "Hydroelectric development is flooding the land, destroying wildlife and killing our people," he said. They would change Hydro-Quebec's world.

The long sought environmental review now unfolded on two fronts, each feeding the other and making life increasingly difficult for the James Bay developers. One was in Canada, where Hydro-Quebec hoped to complete the environmental review process within a year. It cobbled together five thousand pages of studies and dumped them on the table. The summer construction season was passing and loans were pending. Time was not on Hydro's side.

The second front was more important, and it could not have been anticipated. The prime market for electricity from the Great Whale project lay south of the border in the United States. Hydro-Quebec had signed power sale contracts with Vermont and Maine, but the prize was an "agreement in principle" for twenty-one years of supply to the New York Power Authority, bringing up to $40 billion in revenue to Hydro-Quebec. The project would cost nearly that much to build. Which is to say that New York held the cards, and its agreement was only "in principle."

Opposition to the Great Whale project along the southern tier began with the arrival of gigantic transmission corridors across the towns and dairy farms of Quebecois near the American border. People feared the power lines—their size, sight, magnetic fields, and the herbicides needed to maintain them. They learned about them not from Hydro-Quebec but from American environmental groups and newspapers. They found the official responses to their questions "arrogant" and "contemptuous," and that the company "tried to mislead." The allegations had a familiar ring. Residents calling themselves PROTECT (Prudent Residents Opposed to Electrical Cable Transmission) formed to oppose a line across the New York countryside. No Thank You Hydro-Quebec campaigned against the lines in Maine and then, in a breakthrough, succeeded in persuading their state legislators to reject the Hydro contract.

Then, in New York, the wheels came off. Organizations of every stripe began to lobby politicians to cancel the New York Power Authority agreement. At one point there were at least thirty anti–Great Whale groups on college campuses throughout the state. To Hydro-Quebec and its supporters, Great Whale electricity was a no-brainer for New Yorkers: clean power, good rates, and long-term stability. But the opponents raised a larger moral question: was this source really clean? or, in the words of a New York commentator, "simply tantamount to exporting environmental and cultural destruction to the taiga"? Hydro-Quebec's campaign featured pictures of its employees "carefully airlifting animals to safety from islands created by the flooding." The photos didn't persuade one Buffalo politician, who spoke for many when he said that New York should avoid becoming "an accomplice to the crime." It was at about this time that Mathew Coon-Come and his Odeyaks appeared in Times Square.

The Hydro-Quebec ball was now no longer in Canada's court. It was in Albany with Governor Mario Cuomo. The New York Power Authority had already flexed its muscles. In a letter to the *New York Times*, the Authority's chairman stated: "Largely at my urging Hydro-Quebec agreed not to begin construction of roads and other ancillary features until the entire project has undergone review." In a single stroke, the power authority of another state in another country had succeeded in accomplishing what neither Environment Canada nor the Canadian courts had been able to do in three tries from Rafferty to Oldman to Great Whale, and it was the most obvious step in the world: stop construction pending environmental review. Then, in late 1992, Governor Cuomo canceled

New York's agreement to buy Hydro-Quebec power, citing lack of future power demands. He had become a believer in demand side management, he said. Energy conservation.

A YEAR and a half later, with the Great Whale project still alive for its sponsors and under Canadian review, yet a third Cree lawsuit came down from the Canadian Supreme Court. Hydro-Quebec not only needed American purchasers, it needed the all-clear from the Canadian National Energy Board to export the electricity. The board's standard was highly permissive, that the sale should be in "the public interest." Vague standards like this are usually a joy to the regulated community, which can then pressure the regulators in the directions they wish. In this case, however, the Energy Board not only required prior completion of the review process but insisted that the review cover more than the power lines. It would cover "future construction of production facilities." Another nightmare for Hydro-Quebec. It appealed, and this case too went all the way up.

In March 1994, a unanimous Supreme Court had little difficulty agreeing that federal review should consider production; it was all part of the package. Lurking beneath this finding, however, was the question that has continued to haunt all of Canadian environmental law: did such a broad reading of the board's authority contravene the basic, decentralized structure of the Canadian Constitution? Here the Court did a lawyerly thing. It said that it would "expressly refrain" from "making any determinations" that interpreted the Constitution in this regard. Next, it proceeded to do so.

"It must be recognized," the Court began with some understatement, that environmental protection was "a constitutionally abstruse matter" that did not "comfortably fit within the existing division of powers without considerable overlap and uncertainty." When judges start using the word *abstruse* they are acknowledging thin ice. The court had to ensure, it went on, that the Board's authority was "truly limited to matters of federal concern." This did not "artificially limit" the scope of environmental review to the power lines alone, a sentence that is up to this point clear, "but it equally does not permit a wholesale review of the entire operational plan." Which at this point is not clear at all.

If federal review could not constitutionally extend to the entire plan, then what was in and what was out? The access roads? The methyl mercury? Without offering an answer, the justices concluded that the Board had "struck an appropriate balance between these two extremes." A constitutional train wreck was postponed.

The Court was even more equivocal when it came to the question of whether to stop project construction while the review took place. Wringing its hands much as Environment Canada had over the same issue, the Court noted that it was "preferable" to treat the environmental concerns before proceeding with construction, but it would go no further. All of which meant that Hydro-Quebec remained free to march forward at its own peril, loading the dice in its favor through contract commitments and sunk costs. It would sink $400 million.

The squishy nature of the opinion notwithstanding, this last ruling complicated matters enormously for Hydro-Quebec. Yet another review, and on a scale larger than any before. The company tried to put on a brave face. "As long as the Supreme Court hasn't canceled any of our contracts, we are satisfied," said its president Armand Couture, but the interest on the borrowed millions was making its product more and more expensive. Then, in mid-November 1994, all three Canadian environmental reviews came in: Hydro-Quebec's hastily assembled environmental assessment did not comply with the federal guidelines. The company would have to go back to square one. That was a very long way.

The next afternoon, Premier Bourassa of Quebec, faced with the loss of his US customers, mounting opposition, and the added obstacle of new environmental reviews, threw in the towel. He announced the abandonment of the Great Whale project. He said he had never been in favor of it anyway.

STORIES LIKE this should have an end, but they never do. Money finds its way like water, and there is no containing it. Perhaps the most destructive phase of all the James Bay projects was yet to come. Phase three planned to divert the Nottoway and Rupert rivers, legendary white waters and historic routes of the fur trade, into seven new reservoirs, passing the flows through eleven powerhouses and transforming the lower portions of "the most magnificent wild rivers in Canada" into dry rock.

The biological impacts would be even more severe. The shallow reservoirs flooded an area about twice that projected for the Great Whale and destroyed warmer and wetter and more productive habitat. They would also release more toxic mercury downstream. There were core fisheries and habitat for moose, caribou, and beaver at stake, on which the Cree depended. The access roads would bring up loggers, miners, trappers, petroleum drillers, and a host of white-run development from the south. The majority of the Cree lived in this zone. Most of their villages and hunting grounds were here. The lands along the Rupert and Nottoway were the "veritable heartland of the Cree way of life."

Cree feelings ran high. When Hydro-Quebec officials came to the mouth of the Rupert River to sell the village of Waskaganish on a joint venture this time, sharing some of the profits, the reaction was so adverse that they were "put into a canoe and hustled out of town." But the money was huge. The Cree were reeling from, by their estimate, the loss of $5 billion a year in lost resources from the La Grande project, for which they were receiving, despite all the promises, next to nothing in return. The interest on their resistance compounded daily.

In October 2001, after more than thirty years of fighting the James Bay projects in total and ten on the Rupert-Nottoway, the Cree capitulated. In a deal hauntingly reminiscent of the James Bay Agreement twenty years before, Quebec and Hydro-Quebec beat them again. It would be hard, indeed impossible, to blame them. Still living on the margins and largely deprived of the benefits of the earlier agreements, they were at the end of their tether. Very few Cree had been employed by the companies. The cash payments proved inadequate. Then these, too, ran out. At the same time more intrusion kept spilling up like wagon trains from the south, from which the Cree were getting no cut at all. As one of the Cree negotiators explained the settlement, "I feel it is about 51 percent a good idea, and 49 percent bad."

This time the Cree received more autonomy and more money. They assumed authority over wildlife management and community development, and an annual cash payment rising to $70 million for the next fifty years. The price was cheap for Hydro-Quebec, which, in the end, as a state monopoly, would not have to pay for it anyway. It was huge money, however, for an entire people on the brink. Which way did responsibility lie?

Quebec left nothing to chance this time. The Cree agreed to drop all lawsuits and not to bring any more lawsuits against the province. They not only gave up their heartland, they gave up their law. A Quebec northern expert, Louis-Edmond Hamelin, later commented: "nothing in this document indicates that each side has understood the culture of the other."

And so, in the end, the Rafferty, Oldman, and La Grande projects were built; the Rupert-Nottoway grinds forward; and the Great Whale is stopped for now, but as a practical matter remains on hold. Ambitions like these rarely die. Were the same projects to resurface tomorrow, the provinces would be back in the lists behind them, and the federal environmental agencies in Ottawa, as in any other country, would be cowering in their tents. It would again be up to the people, and courts of law, to give them a shot at protecting their heritage. The Canadian cases, at great sacrifice, brought them this far.

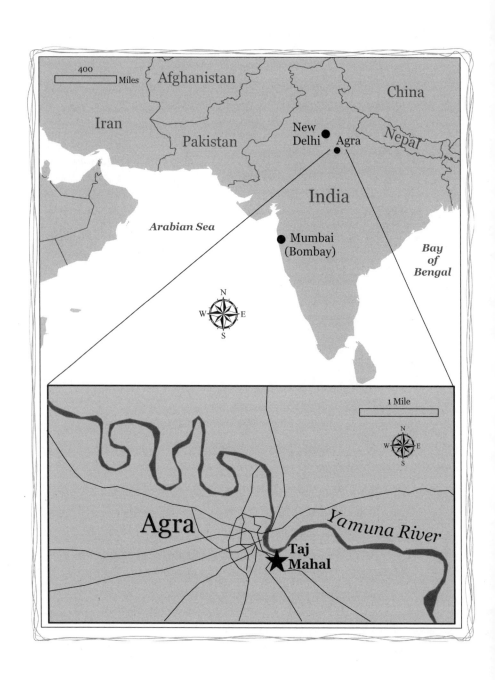

CHAPTER FIVE

Taj Mahal

God directed me to the right path. It was all predestined and based on
circumstance. After the incident, I just started walking, that is all.

M. C. Mehta, 1999

OUR STORY begins in turmoil. By the late 1960s, the newly independent nation of India, having united to throw off three centuries of British rule, was beginning to fall apart. Mahatma Gandhi had died, then Jawaharlal Nehru died, followed by a war of partition with Pakistan, border clashes with China, and a rapid slide toward feudal systems that predated the government by centuries and religious sects that took to the streets at the drop of an insult. In 1975, Prime Minister Indira Gandhi, Nehru's daughter, was back for a second try at leadership and hanging by a thread. Sensing the thread about to snap, she declared a state of emergency and suspended the Constitution, on which the ink was barely dry. Opposition assemblies and organizations were banned.

Over the next eighteen months more than 110,000 people were detained, most for political reasons, some without counsel, often without charges. Private lawyers, many from opposition parties, took their cases to court. The Indian courts had no tradition of hearing such cases nor of reversing government decisions, particularly ones that reeked of politics, but this time was different. The provocations were egregious. The lawyers started winning, and an era of civil rights litigation was born. As in the United States, half a world away, environmental rights would follow.

The story resumes in 1983, at a party for young lawyers in the capital city of Delhi. Several had been engaged in the civil rights struggle, including a newcomer from the country by the name of Mahesh Chander Mehta. As Mehta tells it, a young man came up to him, visibly angry, and declared that lawyers had become "too greedy"; they were not interested in helping the country. When asked what his problem was, the man replied, "the Taj Mahal is dying—the marble cancer. I have gone to so many lawyers and nobody has taken my case." Mehta, curious but no more, and without the slightest instinct for environmental issues, gave the man his card and asked him to send whatever he had, if he indeed had anything, to back up his claim. That moment, Mehta recalls, changed the course of his life. He went home pondering the accusation. It was true, lawyers were a greedy lot. He was a religious man, and he felt the injury. A few days later a packet of information on the Taj Mahal came in the mail.

What followed is one of the most remarkable journeys in the annals of environmental history. Mehta went on to become, by any objective measure, one of the most successful environmental lawyers in the world, and the Supreme Court of India, one of the the most active in environmental protection. As it happened, both were triggered by an achievement with little parallel in human history.

Neither Words nor pencil could give to the most imaginative reader the slightest idea of all the satisfying beauty and purity of this glorious conception. To those who have not seen it, I would say—Go to India; the Taj alone is well worth the journey.
Lord Frederick Sleigh Roberts

THE TAJ Mahal is a capsule of Indian history surrounded by facts, fictions, and mysteries. It defines India in a way that few monuments can emulate. Ask a stranger what image pops to mind upon hearing the word "America" and the Grand Canyon, the Statue of Liberty, or the Marlboro Man could as easily follow, perhaps in reverse order. But when one mentions India, it would be the Taj, which attracts more than three million visitors a year and adorns the covers of more books on world heritage and architecture than any building save, perhaps, the Acropolis. The essence of the Taj is its fusion of two cultures whose mere co-existence seems improbable, to say nothing of their joint contribution to something that, despite the best efforts of writers, photographers, and poets, remains indescribably beautiful. Perhaps this is what makes the Taj so eternal. In a world of perpetual conflict, it conveys hope.

The hope springs from another day. Leaping back in time, past the wars of independence, the British occupation, the rule of Muslims, the rule of Hindus, the time of Christ, and to as many centuries before Christ as we have now lived since, some five thousand years ago, Assyrian herdsmen left the Caspian Sea, scaled the Hindukush mountains, and came down into a fertile basin with rich soil and permanent, snow-fed streams. The first major river they crossed they called the Indus, which would name the country they were occupying, as the mountains named their religion. They resisted, and absorbed, the incursions of Alexander the Great, and then Genghis Kahn, until, in the thirteenth century, another religion and another empire arrived with Mohammed of Ghor. For the next five hundred years, a chain of Islamic dynasties overlay a culture of Hinduism, finally broken in the 1750s, by the armies of the British East India Trading Company. By that time, the Taj Mahal was in its heyday, and the man who built it had been dead for two hundred years.

The birth of the Taj invites wonder and myth. We may take for established that, in 1526, a young prince from Central Asia soldiered into northern India, consolidating it under his command and establishing a ruling lineage whose power, by the time of the British invasion, stretched across the plains from Afghanistan to Burma. The reigns of monarchs are precarious everywhere, however, and the fifth emperor, Shah Jahan, came into power in 1627 through a

bloody coup against his weaker brother, who was supported by his father's powerful widow—a scene equally at home in medieval England or Japan. Legend
has it that Shah Jahan was fond of socializing with his subjects in public places.
On one such occasion, it is said, he spotted a gorgeous young woman selling
silks and glass beads at the market. It was love, he declared, and he soon took Ar-
jumand Banyu Begum to be his second wife with the name Mumtaz Mahal
("Chosen Person"). They were inseparable; she followed him even on his military adventures and died giving birth to their seventeenth son while on campaign with her husband in 1629. Her dying wish was that he erect a memorial in
her honor, one that would endure.

It took twenty-two years. The Taj was set on the banks of the Yamuna River
in the town of Agra, about 150 miles north of New Delhi, the work of twenty
thousand laborers and close to one billion dollars in treasury. The central dome
measures 60 feet in diameter and rises 180 feet into the air, constructed by the
use of a brick scaffold so massive that the construction foremen estimated it
would take two years to dismantle it. Legend, one of many, has it that instead, after completion of the Taj, the Shah decreed that anyone who wished could take
bricks from the scaffold, following which it was dismantled overnight. Legend
also has it that the Shah ordered the hands of skilled craftsmen mutilated so that
they could not repeat their work. Other legend says that the Taj was only phase
one of a structure that would continue on the far side of the Yamuna, the Black
Taj, and yet another that the Shah did not really build the Taj at all but, rather,
expropriated the palace of the local maharaja, which he then converted to a
mausoleum. Others claim that it was formerly a Hindu temple. Still others contend that the Shah was not so much in love with his wife as with power, and the
Taj was simply a status symbol, complete with a fortress-like wall. Beautiful
things, like beautiful people, spawn doubters.

The essential truth about the Taj is that it was designed by Islamic architects, built by Hindu workers, and fused these two traditions in an immortal
way. Starting with a basic Hindu structure that featured flat walls and an abundance of idols, it superimposed an Islamic penchant for rounded domes, spires,
and minarets. It scrapped the idols in favor of elaborate surface decorations—
geometric, arabesque, and calligraphic. The interior space was arranged in

courts for solitude and prayer, garnished with tiny watercourses. The result was both square and rounded, earth and water, exterior and interior, open and secret, secular and religious, frankly Islamic but with enough Hindu to appease, as enigmatic as the smile of the Sphinx.

Built to endure, the Taj lasted for several hundred years without maintenance of any kind. For reasons that are in dispute, the British, who had no qualms about looting the national treasures of Egypt, and who even stripped the brickwork from the famous Red Fort in Delhi for transport back to England, did not dismantle the Taj as well. It is said by some that they tried, but concluded that it would cost more than they could sell it for. All agree, however, that in the early 1900s Lord Curzon, then governor-general of India, was deeply moved by the Taj and ordered its restoration to the complex we see today. But for one development. It wasn't looters that would destroy this great monument to a lost queen. It was something far more insidious, largely invisible, and nearly beyond the capacity of India to stop.

BY THE 1960s, Agra had become a sprawling industrial city of over ten million people; two million cars and diesel trucks and buses; nearly three hundred major industries, including refineries, foundries, glass works, brick kilns, and tanneries; and countless smaller operations with one thing in common: fueled by coke, coal, and petroleum, they all discharged carbons and sulfur into the air, which came to rest on the marble faces of the Taj Mahal. From there, it was basic Introduction to Chemistry in action. Oxides of carbon and sulfur eat marble. The rates are steady, measurable, and visible to anyone trying to decipher the worn inscription on a gravestone in Vermont or a gargoyle on a French cathedral. Air pollution destroys more building stone and statuary than any weathering process in the world, with which the weather, too, conspires. Each layer of carbons leaves its own shield, which would prevent further erosion but for the rains, monsoon rains in this case, that wash the shield away and reopen fresh marble for destruction. In Mehta's words: marble cancer.

It was worse inside. The interior walls gave off a "yellow pallor" that was in places "magnified by ugly brown and black spots." The rot was most aggressive in the inner chamber, where the tombs of Shah Jahan and Mumtaz Mahal were found. It was the ultimate sacrilege.

More than industrial pollution was attacking the Taj. Some six and a half million tons of trans-India truck traffic ran through Agra, not far from the monument grounds. The city of New Delhi and all the smaller towns upstream were dumping nearly 300 million tons of raw sewage into the Yamuna River, which then washed down to the Taj. In fact the river ran under it, squeezing human wastes into the foundations of the mosque. There were also plans to build shopping malls and restaurants on the fringe of the monument to capture more tourist dollars. Indeed, there were concessions sprouting up inside the walls. The state of the Taj reflected forces that were changing India and indeed the world.

As the Second World War showcased the power of industry, India, too, would grab for the ring. True, Indian culture was steeped to the point of reverence in the natural world, but these beliefs were routed by the demands of a seething population with appalling rates of poverty and disease. Mahatma Gandhi, reacting to centralized British rule, had envisioned a country based on village republics and small-scale industries, Jeffersonian democracy abroad. Like Jefferson, however, Gandhi's policies were swept away by those of his successor, Jawaharlal Nehru, who based his "tryst with destiny" on the Western and Soviet models of heavy industry and massive public works. He called his dams the "Temples of Modern India." He offered subsidies for new factories and rich incentives for foreign investment. By the mid-1990s India was even into the hazardous waste disposal business, importing toxics from nearly fifty countries. Mining and manufacturing jumped 160 percent. Other industrial output topped 250 percent. It was working.

Then, in 1972, came a wave of environmental concerns from a first-ever, far-away conference in Stockholm, Sweden, the UN Conference on the Human Environment, a meeting that would rattle the world. India, as many developing countries, viewed the new movement with frank skepticism. It looked as if the developed world, having raped its own resources and profited from rampant industrialization, was now trying to limit the competition. In her address to the conference, Prime Minister Indira Gandhi spoke from the heart:

On the one hand the rich look askance at our continuing poverty—on the other, they warn us against their own methods. We do not wish to impoverish the environment any further and yet we cannot for a moment forget the grim poverty of large numbers of people. Are not poverty and need the greatest polluters? . . . The environmental problems of developing countries are not the side effects of excessive industrialization but reflect the inadequacy of development.

Harmony with nature was well and good, but the first priority was to grow the economy. India genuflected toward the high-sounding declarations of the Stockholm meeting, enacting framework laws for the management of air, water, and forestry, but their provisions were so vague, their sanctions so weak, and their execution so halting that they were laws in name only. The brick kilns, tanneries, refineries, and motor traffic contaminating Agra continued to boom, unabated and uncontrolled, as they did around the entire country. Until a country lawyer newly arrived in Delhi walked up the steps of the Supreme Court to file a petition on behalf of himself and the Taj Mahal.

THIS IS the way history happens. A remarkable man comes along at just the right time. A different individual, at a different time, and nothing changes course.

Mehta's story retells the log-cabin narrative of America a century before. Born into a devout and Hindu family, he grew up in a small village in Kashmir. The public school was five miles away, a journey he trekked daily and in all weather, fording two rivers along the way. He broke from family tradition to leave home for college, working part time, taking ten years to finish his law degree and absorbing new notions about social justice along the way. Odd jobs followed, as an accountant for a shoe store, then public school teacher, then headmaster, and finally an all-in-one newspaper reporter, editor, and publisher. He emerged from these experiences with a farmer's appetite for work, a teacher's sense of human beings, and a journalist's passion for the facts, all of which would mark his approach to the mega-lawsuits ahead. This is where they came from.

The year 1983 turned out to be the pivot point in Mehta's life. He married Radha, a freelance writer and social activist, and moved to the capitol. An aspiring lawyer with a few labor and civil cases under his belt, he had no experience before the Supreme Court, where he was determined to practice. Shortly thereafter, materials on the Taj promised by his chance acquaintance at the civil rights lawyer meeting arrived in the mail. Stung by the accusation against his profession, Mehta dug into them and then went many leagues beyond. He read Mogul history, then books on the Taj itself, then studies on pollution and environmental law. Reading only went so far, however, and so a few months later, accompanied by his wife and a noted environmental scientist, he pilgrimaged to the site. He examined the walls, saw the degradation, felt it with his fingers, toured the city of Agra, smelled the air, smelled the water, saw millions of people living in the same conditions that were corroding the face of the mosque, and was converted to the cause. He began to prepare his brief.

Here we have a second great circumstance. The Supreme Court of India, for the first time in its history, was ready for such a case. Barely so, and certainly not intentionally so, it had been moving on a tangent toward environmental protection for several years. It had started with civil rights and, as had the United States Supreme Court in the infamous *Plessy* and *Dredd Scott* decisions, it got off on the wrong foot by ignoring Indira Gandhi's repressive orders and widespread detentions, declaring them beyond judicial review. The opinion was seen by both academics and the media as cowardly, a capitulation by the one remaining institution that still enjoyed public respect. Smarting from the rebuke, the Court reversed course. Relying on a specific constitutional guarantee that "no person shall be deprived of his life or personal liberty" except by law, the Court expanded the concept of personal liberty to "wider meanings" that included freedom of movement and expression. The Constitution, explained the Court, should be "flexible enough to meet the newly merging problems and challenges." One such new challenge was about to walk in the door.

Having staked out this broader liberty, the Court proceeded to open its door for all the people to use it. Unlike the Supreme Court of the United States, the Indian Court could hear cases of first impression, as a trial court, on matters of "fundamental rights." Moreover, one could petition for the Court to hear such cases by filing a special writ. One of the first things the Court did was to relax the requirements for these writs to virtually anything written on paper. A letter to the justices would suffice. It then reached out to admit the pleas of groups such as unions on behalf of their members, ("to whom a life of basic human dignity ha[d] been denied") and to recognize harms to the public at large ("social justice is due to the people and therefore the people must be able to trigger off jurisdiction vested for their benefit"). It began to conduct its own investigations of government misconduct and to compel government agencies to take remedial actions. It created committees to monitor compliance. The machinery that would handle complex environmental cases was taking shape.

The vision of the Court in these early opinions was revolutionary. In their view these cases were were more like an audit involving "collaborative efforts" by the citizens, government authorities, and the court to secure "legal rights and social justice." The Court would not be deterred by fears that "all and sundry [would] be litigation-happy and waste their time and money and the time of the court" on frivolous cases. Rather, given the power of "lachrymose millionaires" who enjoyed "five star advocacy" to protect their private interests, the "les miserables," too, were entitled to "all procedural indulgence," including active fact-finding by the Court itself, in order to level the playing field. In cases beginning with political rights, then labor rights, then rights to honest government, they found a judicial role. Next in line were environmental rights, and along came M. C. Mehta.

IF THE HAND of destiny was behind Mehta and the Taj Mahal, however, nobody seemed to know it. The petition was filed in the summer of 1984. It was submitted under the Court's newly expanded, anyone-can-apply writ jurisdiction, and it claimed injury both to the Taj buildings and to the people of Agra who were experiencing the same, corrosive pollution every day of their lives. It rested on the constitutional guarantee of life and liberty, the same right invoked in the civil rights cases, but applying this guarantee to air pollution was a stretch. The Court would be moving into unchartered waters with environmental claims. Friends advised Mehta not to bother. The Supreme Court would sit like "statues," one told him. They would not engage in dialogue with him, and they would dismiss his case. It almost happened.

The psychological turning point for this lawsuit, and for all of environmental policy in India, came a few months later with one of the most horrific industrial accidents yet experienced in any country of the world. In the middle of the night in the city of Bohpal, with the population fast asleep, the Union Carbide plant in Bohpal leaked forty tons of deadly gas across the city. No one is sure how many perished. Estimates of deaths directly attributable to the leak range upward of two thousand. Over two hundred thousand people suffered injuries. Businesses closed; crops died; cattle died. The failure of the Indian government to pay attention to industrial risks lay exposed like dead children in the cellar.

With great reluctance, a United States federal judge sent an ensuing lawsuit by victims and their families back to India for trial, knowing that the remedies would be minimal. They were. Union Carbide paid out an average of $1,500 per individual, a result that finally moved India to act. Within a few years it had created an elaborate bureaucracy with authority to regulate, inspect, and enforce controls on all forms of pollution. This done, it pretty much went back to sleep. The pollution of Agra, the contamination of the country, and unbridled development went forward as if nothing had occurred. The bureaucracy, however, was about to experience the jolt of its life.

It may seem hard to ignore the Taj Mahal, but the Court nearly did. Young and inexperienced, attorney Mehta drew a conservative panel of justices that behaved exactly as his friend had predicted. Perhaps his inexperience saved him. He simply would not take "no" for an answer. He had filed his writ, but the Court had to accept it for the case to go forward, and it was apparently in no mood to do so. We do not know what you are doing here, they told him. Even the lawyers who practice here do not know what you are doing, they added. They were ready to vote. Sensing Mehta's desperation, perhaps out of sympathy, one judge was prompted to ask exactly what he expected the Court to do, but, after a minute or two of confusion, the justices were ready to vote again. He was wasting their time.

Mehta became emotional. He had spent more than two hundred hours preparing this case, he told them, and they had a duty to listen. Who are you to tell us about our duties, asked a justice, at which point Mehta—one can hear the passion—replied that as judges they might have legal duties but as citizens of India they had a higher duties to protect the environment and the lives of the people. Indeed, he continued, given the stakes involved here the Court should be taking this case on its own initiative. The Court was not fulfilling its responsibility, he was emboldened to say, nor providing him, the petitioner, justice.

One doubts that a seasoned Supreme Court advocate would have dared go this far. One doubts that the Court would have accorded a seasoned advocate this amount of leeway either, which bordered on disrespect. Instead, however, the Court invited him, once again, to say his piece. And so, Mehta began anew, a third time, to explain his pleadings. He went on for the next half hour. There were no interruptions. When he had done, the justices conferred in whispers on the high bench while Mehta waited below. At last, they smiled at him and said, yes, we will take notice of this matter. They accepted the writ.

The world of environmental policy in India had just made a seismic shift. Indeed, it was about to turn upside down and, as might be expected, Mehta, having tasted a bit of success, would be pushing all the way. He was not the only lawyer to bring environmental cases to the Court, but he would bring his share, some of them so bold they seemed hopeless, others so big that they remain, today, among the most complex legal proceedings in the country. The Taj case had opened the door—two doors really—one to the lifetime marriage of M. C. Mehta to environmental policy and the other, by the simple fact of accepting the writ, to Supreme Court protection of the environment, through the Constitution. The Taj case itself would remain hanging—the writ accepted but untried—for nearly a decade before the Court came to grips with it again. Meanwhile, through the door came other cases involving new environmental and public injuries. These lawsuits, in turn, and the Court's approach to them, would draw the roadmap for the Taj Mahal. The most important of these cases involved the Ganges River and, once again, our mutual friend.

Ganga was sunken, and the limp leaves
Waited for rain, while the black clouds

Gathered far distant, over Himanvant . . .
Datta. Dayadhvam. Damyata.
Shantih shantih shantih.

T. S. Eliot, The Wasteland

THE GANGES is the work of nature and the Taj Mahal is the work of human beings, but they have one thing in common: they are both sacred places. Hindu myth presents the river as a goddess, worshipped as the consort of Shiva. It is said to cleanse the souls of sinners, and every Hindu desires his last rites to be performed on its banks. The ancient texts declare that "impure objects like urine, feces, spit or anything which has these elements, blood or poison" should not be cast into it. M. C. Mehta was a Hindu. "There was a time when milk, incense and flowers were considered to be the moot offerings to such a venerated river," he wrote. Today, he continued, the offerings were "huge quantities of refuse, rubbish and poisonous effluents." It was another sacrilege. In 1985, within a year of the Taj filing, Mehta was back before the Supreme Court asking it to clean up the holy river of India.

The trigger this time was not a stranger at a party for lawyers. In late 1984, the Ganges caught fire. No one could miss the news. A mile-long stretch of the river burned for thirty hours with flames leaping twenty feet into the air. Apparently, the candles of mourners cremating their dead on the river bank had ignited a thick chemical sheen from factories nearby. There was more than religion at stake here. One tenth of all humanity, over a half a billion people, depended on the Ganges for their survival. Into the river poured toxins from over fifty thousand industries, along with sewage from three hundred townships, six million tons of chemical fertilizers, and nine thousand tons of pesticides as notorious as DDT. Fecal coliform counts on the river near the pilgrimage city of Varanasi exceeded World Health Organization limits by ten thousand times. Not surprisingly, one third of all deaths in India rose from waterborne diseases. Compared to the Ganges, coming to grips with Agra and the Taj Mahal would be a picnic.

Its defenses breached by the Taj petition the year before, the Court accepted this one with less cavil and, in the exercise of its original jurisdiction, went directly to trial. Out of caution and to make his case manageable, Mehta had sued only the national government, two industries most directly connected to the fire, and two officials whose negligent performance, in his view, had led to the disaster. Initially, he asked only that the court "regulate the regulator," and force the government environmental agencies to do their job. He based his case, again, on the Constitution, which by that time had been stretched in a case involving stone quarry workers to cover environmental conditions of the workplace. The Ganges would take the Constitution one step further, beyond the conditions of workers, to the general public and the river itself.

To Mehta's surprise, the Court not only followed him but, with his encouragement, was willing to up the ante as well. The pollution of which Mehta complained was hardly restricted to these two factories. Rather, it implicated the discharges from thousands of industrial activities stretched across several hundred townships and eight states. But how, mused the justices, could interests so numerous and dispersed even be served with legal process? Mehta had an answer. He suggested that they use newspapers and television networks, directing all industries to appear. Captured by the magic, propelled by the momentum of their prior cases, the Court bought this novel procedure as well, and soon hundreds of factories and manufacturing plants of all shape and size began coming to Court to respond. At one point there were more than twelve hundred lawyers for the defense. The only petitioner was Mehta. As it evolved, the case was no longer about forcing the regulators to do their duty. Facing their continuing failure, the Court was about to do it instead.

What followed was a litigation program more reminiscent of mass tort actions than constitutional law. The Court grouped the defendants geographically, separated out the cases against agencies and townships, and then focused on tanneries, distilleries, and other industrial sectors, nineteen categories by journey's end. Every step of the way, aided and abetted by Mehta, the Court was innovating procedures, evidence, and substantive law. It accepted data on pollution of the Ganges from open sources, magazines, and academic reports. It took industry reports to establish that pollution control technologies were available, and then required them. It conducted no cost–benefit analysis; the financial

capacity of industries was "irrelevant." Just as all enterprises had to pay the minimum wage in order to exist, reasoned the Court, so they should have to pay to
treat their wastes.

As a test category, the tanneries came first and provided what Mehta would
later call the "turning point." Those that did not adopt control technologies,
within a short and specified period of time, were ordered to close and forbidden
to reopen until they complied. Tanneries on the Ganges began to close. No discretion was left to government agencies. Instead, they too had their orders to
monitor compliance and report their findings to the Court. The Court retained
jurisdiction over the case, and over the next ten years it ordered the closure of
eighty-four plants in Uttar Pradesh and thirty more in West Bengal.

The Court's language was equally strong. "We are conscious," wrote Justice
Singh in one of the early Ganges opinions, "that the closure of tanneries may
bring unemployment, loss of revenue but the life, health and ecology have
greater importance." Armed with the Constitution, a hellish set of facts, and a
government in default, the Supreme Court of India was striking out on its own.
The Taj Mahal had forced the opening. The Ganges rushed in. And, in turn,
marked the way for a final decision on the Taj Mahal.

ॐ

It is too pure, too holy to be the work of human hands. Angels must have brought it
from heaven and a glass case should be thrown over it to preserve it from each breath
of air.

M. C. Mehta v. Union of India

ANY JUDICIAL opinion that begins with an ode to the subject of the case, followed by three paragraphs of its celebration in poetry and prose, rather tips its
hand. This judgment, however, was a long time coming.

It took more than a decade. It took thirteen years, in fact, if one counts from
the time Mehta first learned of the plight of the Taj Mahal, and twelve from the
time he took his first walk up the steps of the Supreme Court to argue his way
past the gatekeepers and onto the docket. The Court was sufficiently sympathetic to keep the case around, but its jurisprudence had not yet ripened to the

point that it could deal with the case. Nor, in 1984, was Mehta ready for the challenge. It took the Ganges litigation and several others of considerable magnitude to forge new mechanisms and a judicial attitude that, by God, it was time to make things happen. The Taj opinion, like the structure itself, is the culmination of these things.

The Court began hearing testimony in 1992, based on the allegations in Mehta's petition. Perhaps lectured by the Ganges, it did not jump into the business of law enforcement with both feet. It tried, instead, a regulate-the-regulator approach, relying on studies unearthed by Mehta going back fifteen years on the degradation of the monument. In January 1993, it ordered the national Pollution Control Board to survey the area, inventory the polluting sources, take measures to ensure that necessary antipollution measures have been undertaken, and report back to the court by May. Given the state of the Taj and its surrounding air pollution, the Court may have been a bit naive about having the antipollution measures in place. Of course, they were nowhere near in place. On May 3 the Board reported that it had identified 511 industries in the area, some as large as the Mathura oil refinery, as well as 168 foundries, 20 rubber factories, and 55 chemical plants. It stated that 507 of these industries, a whopping 99 percent, had no air pollution controls at all. Indeed, 212 did not even respond to the notice. At which point, it seemed clear that India's fine-sounding environmental programs and their accompanying bureaucracy were not operating on a full tank of gas.

The Court took over, and for the next three years issued a series of commands to state agencies and directly to individual industries that more resembled battle orders from general headquarters than judicial opinions. The major pollution sources were industrial, and the problem was their use of coke and coal. So the Court got into the energy business, inquiring about the availability of propane and natural gas, weighing their costs, directing the location and rapid construction of a new gas pipeline, summoning the responsible agency heads and CEOs of the oil and gas companies directly—with the quaint observation: "With a view to save time and Red-Tape we are of the view that it would be useful to have direct talk with the highest authorities who can take instant decision in the matter." It was a forced march. The deadlines were tight, three days from today, a week from today, but the Court's focus was still investigative, hoping that the government would take charge. It was the "primary duty," it continued to say, of the Indian government and its Ministry of Environment to "safeguard" the monument.

In 1995, with more hope than optimism, it ordered the Ministry to review the latest information and "indicate in positive terms the measures which the Ministry is intending to take to preserve the Taj Mahal." The Court made clear that, in its view, the relocation of polluting industries was essential, and that it could not be done without the "positive assistance" of the Ministry, the national government, and the state of Uttar Pradesh. It had "personally requested" the minister himself to examine the matter and present a scheme for relocation. However, "nothing positive has come before us." One can sense the exasperation. Still, it deferred to the regulators to take action. "It is of utmost importance that the pollution in the Taj Trapezium be controlled," the Court reiterated. "We want [a] positive response from the Ministry." One last chance for an administrative solution.

It didn't work. Whether by intention or simple paralysis, there was "no helpful response from the government of India." It is important to remember, when assessing the Supreme Court of India's actions in this case and in environmental cases more generally, what it was facing here. The situation was urgent. When pushed, hard, the responsible government agencies would collect information. But they would not act.

Finally, in its opinion of December 30, 1996, the Court put the hammer down. Citing several articles of the Constitution, three statutes and three principles of international law, the justices declared that the pollution affecting the Taj should be "eliminated at any cost." Not even a "one percent chance" could be taken when—human life aside—"the preservation of a prestigious monument like the Taj is involved." It ordered the conversion of some 292 industrial plants to natural gas, or their relocation from the area. It ordered government assistance for the relocation, and the creation of a new agency to facilitate the process. It ordered the construction of a bypass to funnel traffic away from the area, a green belt of protection around the monument, the removal of intruding concessions, and first steps to clean up the Yamuna River.

Turning to the social impacts and at Mehta's suggestion, the Court also looked to the employees affected by plant closures and relocations and directed that they continue to receive wages and benefits during the transition. The workers would even receive an additional "shifting bonus" of one year's salary to help them resettle. The Court had already put a new public drinking water supply project in motion and on schedule. Now it went on to require that the Mathura refinery set up a fifty-bed hospital and two mobile units to provide medical treatment for residents within breathing distance of the plant. This was the whole package—abatement, new fuels, relocation, government assistance, worker assistance, and public health. It might not work, but no one could blame these justices for not taking their best shot. Until later, when they would be blamed for shooting at all.

ONE LONGS for a final chapter. But these cases are simply too big and too human. The Court's running battle orders on the Taj have, indeed, closed many polluting facilities, relocated others, established a green belt, removed the most invasive of the souvenir shops, brought natural gas into the city, and accelerated construction of a heavy vehicle bypass. It has required new reports, engaged itself in decisions as minute as monitoring stations and parking lots, directed an allocation of Taj entrance fees to the city for its improvement, and issued contempt citations against actors it believed were responding too slowly, or not at all.

And yet, the air of Agra remains toxic, the Yanuma still stinks, and the marble faces continue to erode. The Archaeological Survey of India has begun applying packs of brown mud to the Taj walls in an attempt to save them. Having rid itself of small concessions, the monument has been turned over for management to the Tata Group, which climbed its way to the top of the Indian business world by manufacturing automobiles. In a word, much remains to be done, and there is reason to worry about what is being done. There is also reason to worry about who is doing it, and who is not doing it, and how long this scenario can last.

As the Court itself stated in its Taj opinions, its Ganges opinions, and others not described, this is a job for the government of India, not the judiciary. Time and again, the Court gathered the information and then asked the government to act. Time and again, it received excuses for inaction in return. In another Mehta case treating chronic air pollution in the capitol city of Delhi, at levels so unhealthy that they killed—not injured, killed—an estimated ten thousand people a year, the Delhi Health Minister's response to the Court's inquires was that these pollutants did not increase the risks of heart or lung disease. Each time, the Court has had to move from government denial of the problem, to grudging acceptance, to the performance of routine, step-and-fetch-it duties. A news report on the Ganges litigation captures the problem:

> There are limits to what a gung ho court can do in the face of an indifferent bureaucracy. The boards in the Ganga states appear resigned to doing no work except for a knee-jerk response to judicial orders. Besides, the word on the street is that the Supreme Court's orders are misused by dishonest board officials to line their own pockets. Unless a bribe is paid, an unfavorable report is made to the court.

To some, and to the Court itself as it was wading into these cases, this depressing scenario is exactly the reason it had to act. Either it waded in or ten thousand more people in Delhi died each year, countless more from contact with the Ganges, which continued to catch fire while the Taj Mahal corroded slowly into a lump of stone. To others, however, the depth and complexity of the job were exactly why the Court should never have taken the plunge.

The arguments against "judicial activism" are the same anywhere. In India, they are only more acute. It is said that courts lack the technical capacity to control pollution, which is true. On the other hand and as revealed in this case, the obstacles to pollution control are more institutional than technical. Where expertise is required, this Court proved that it could come up to speed in a hurry.

It is also said that as an unelected institution, court actions of this type are undemocratic and should be best left to elected officials, and this view has its merits. On the other hand, the laws and the constitution itself on which this Court relied were passed through democratic processes; what this and other courts see themselves as doing is backing up these processes with action.

It is further said that, by plunging so deeply into the management of issues that carry large social and economic price tags—relocation, jobs—the Court risks losing the popular support on which its credibility depends, a risk the Court itself has acknowledged. On the other hand, there is strong public support for cleaning up the Taj, the Ganges and the airshed of Delhi, and the social and economic costs of the victims are equally as real.

It is said as well—and this appears to be the bottom line for many critics—that the Court's preoccupation with environmental rights is misplaced, and that the justices should instead facilitate economic development from which social justice will then flow. Indira Gandhi made the same statement to the Stockholm Convention in 1972, and it is a seductive one. On the other hand, the world has come to realize that the latent price of uncontrolled development is terribly steep, and the damages are often irreversible. Ten thousand deaths a year are not insignificant. You lose the Taj, you do not get anything like it back again. In this regard, this one complex may be the world's most visible "canary in the coal mine." Written on its walls, beyond the calligraphy, is the message that things are very wrong.

For his part, M. C. Mehta walks on, continuing a journey that spans a quarter of a century and has only broadened with time. In a case involving a gas leak he introduced the principle of strict liability for hazardous activities. In another treating a back-room transfer of a park reserve for the construction of a hotel, Mehta argued successfully that this was a violation of the public trust, setting another foundation stone for environmental protection. He went on to win punitive damages against the offending government official. In one of Mehta's more imaginative petitions, he persuaded the Court to require that all children be educated on the need for environmental protection. In furtherance, the Court directed the broadcast of environmental messages in the media, environmental education in schools and colleges, and the production of documentaries on stewardship, pollution, and the natural world.

Perhaps with an eye toward public support for its own environmental initiatives, the Court explained that "if the laws are to be enforced" and the "malaise" of the public addressed, it was necessary that "people be aware of the vice of pollution and its evil consequences." It continued, "We are in a democratic polity where dissemination of information is the foundation of the system. Keeping citizens informed is an obligation of the government." Judicial activism? Surely so. But in a world where government information seems so largely directed to self-promotional ends, perhaps refreshingly so.

Mehta is a deeply religious man. He made his mark with litigation, but he takes teaching as a mission. He has started his own environmental education center, lectures at the university level, and has trained a small but steady stream of environmental advocates. He continues with the seemingly endless proceedings on the Taj Mahal, the Ganges, and the air pollution in Delhi, any one of which would exhaust most mortal beings. He has his own legends, not all of good will. Public success breeds jealousies. Then again, there are ill-willed legends of the Taj Mahal as well. They are both still standing, however, Mehta and the Taj, and despite the corrosion of a world hell-bent on other objectives, they remain in their own ways surprisingly resilient. The fusion of beautiful things.

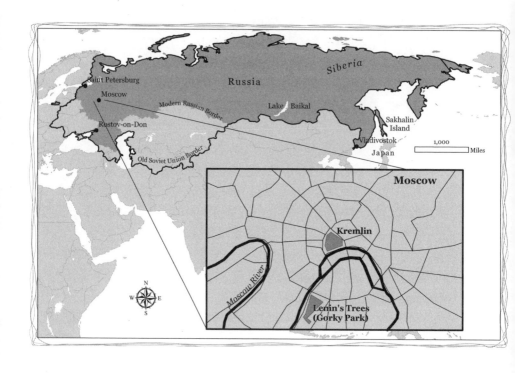

CHAPTER SIX

Lenin's Trees

We were the first who acquainted judges and other officials with the Constitutional right to a favorable environment and unlimited guarantee of protecting this right in court. It was a revelation for them.

Vera Mischenko, President of Ecojuris, 2001

O N A COLD April day in 1997, in a narrow corridor of a gray building on one of the grayest streets in Moscow, a remarkable pageant was unfolding, new to the people who came to participate, new to the media who were out in force, and new to the Supreme Court of Russia, where it took place. Many of the onlookers were from the Moscow oblast. Others had traveled from as far away as Khabarovsk in the Far East. They were filing their lawsuit.

Inside the building, Vera Mischenko, the head of a small environmental organization called Ecojuris, and Tamara Zlotnikova, chair of the Environment Committee of the Russian Parliament, pushed their complaint through a barred window where it was duly stamped and received by functionaries who were clearly uncomfortable with this kind of attention. Television cameras whirred. Journalists snapped photos. Mischenko and Zlotnikova made statements. Outside, it was barely twenty degrees Fahrenheit, but the crowd was laughing and cheering. The lawsuit accused the Russian Forest Ministry of giving away the public's most cherished parks to private developers. The practice was not new. They had complained before, about this and other government actions, but with no definitive result. This case, however, would go all the way, and it would make Russian legal history.

✼

THE RUSSIAN forests are as enormous as a dream. Setting aside the oceans—some oceans, not all—they are the largest natural feature on Earth, stretching across twelve time zones with a monotony that can numb the mind and a seeming endlessness that invites the axe, the bulldozer, and the plough. Here is, at last, the inexhaustible natural resource. In one sense, then, it is a wonder that the Russians have managed to destroy so much forested landscape. At the same time it is also a wonder that so much remains standing. Russia is full of such contradictions. It has never been certain whether its compass pointed east or west, whether it would mark the years by the Gregorian or Julian calendar, and whether it would conquer or retreat from the world. Or what it would do with its greatest natural asset, nearly one-quarter of the forests of the entire planet.

The tap root that forests provide for all of Russian culture is hard to appreciate in a country like America, which is still so young that it has no tap roots, and little reverence for any but a few set pieces like the Grand Canyon, now, too, under siege. Months of the old Russian calendar were named by forest practices; January was the cutting time and March the burning season, when birch groves were reduced to ashes for the fields. The Russians distinguished between black forests, their leafless silhouettes against the snow, and red forests of spruce and cedar, red in the core and in the old sense of "beautiful," as in Red Square. They had distinct words for forest types—*pine bogs, spruce bogs, thickets covered by lichen*—with as many nuances as the Inuit vocabulary for ice and snow.

They had conflicting emotions as well. Russian folklore painted the deep woods in dark colors; bad accidents happened here, and the spirits that haunted them were not good neighbors, yet these same woods supplied food, firewood, and virtually everything needed for survival, including faith. With the adoption of Christianity, the Russians dedicated certain forests for protection with "a procession of icons, holy banners, and prayers," the investiture of a church. Here, too, as in Nikko Tarro, the idea of sacred forests dates back a long way.

In the seventeenth century, the state secularized the process. Peter the Great brought in professional foresters, planted reserves as a defensive wall along his western border, and protected still more as stock for the Russian fleet. "I know you think that I will not be alive to see these oaks mature," Peter told a skeptic. "It is true. But you are a fool. I do it so that future generations will build ships from these trees. I do not labor for myself, but for the future of the country." He was quite serious about it. Unauthorized cutting brought death.

With Peter's own death, however, came the first of several policy reversals, and forest management gave way to a century of privatization and "merciless logging." The high-end reserves were the first to go. By the turn of the century, about 10 percent of all Russian forests had been eliminated. Finally, in 1802, appalled by the damage, the government adopted a new charter that—nearly a century before management principles came to the United States—called for a "precise relationship between harvesting and reforestation," in today's parlance "sustained yield." The new code also required the preservation of special "conservation forests" in their natural state. They formed green belts along coasts, rivers, and transportation corridors; they formed parks in populated areas, where they were called "the lungs of the city." Then came a second, sweeping policy reversal, the Russian Revolution, and more contradictions.

Initially, the revolution brought chaos. The needs of Russian peasants for forest materials could not be contained and, with the tsar and his guards deposed, the woods were again up for grabs. The Bolsheviks, committed to the egalitarian idea of "localism," transferred all state forests to the control of community land committees, at which point there was no order at all. Finally, reversing course, Vladimir Lenin signed a decree abolishing private forests and calling for professional management based on "planned resource renewal" of the state domain. Which could have returned Russia to the policies of Peter the Great but for the fact that Lenin also put management on a quota system that depended on massive logging to "serve the goal of building socialism." The people's commissar for forest industry declared it "imperative" to expose "opportunistic, kulak-capitalist, damaging theories and practices stemming from the 'principle of sustainability.' The main principle of forest exploitation, he continued, must be "concentrated clear-cutting."

To the communist mind, the pillage of resources was the hallmark of rampant capitalism, the enemy of the people. Output quotas were the answer. As high quotas become unsustainable, the response was not to change the numbers but, rather, the bureaucracy, and so Russian forest policy became a game of musical chairs. In the nineteenth century, forest management was reorganized four times. In the twentieth century the forest ministries would be shuffled twenty times. Three times they were "liquidated" altogether. Meanwhile, the pendulum was stuck on clear-cut and no one could move it.

THE STORY goes like this. The winter of 1919, one of the coldest on record, was a Valley Forge moment for the Russian Revolution. The White Army was on the attack and pressing at the gates of Moscow while the Bolshevik loyalists, without fuel or shelter, were freezing to death inside. Wood was at a premium, and the city's last remaining stock was in the trees of a city park. The pressure to cut them down was enormous. It would save lives. It might save the Revolution. Lenin forbade the cut. The park was the heritage of the Russian people, he said, it was part of what the Reds were fighting for. The trees remained. They and their offspring are to this day called Lenin's Trees. Whether the story is true is immaterial. It is believed. Lenin's Trees became the symbol of forest reserves.

Remarkably, the notion of protecting these special preserves survived the long years of communist management. In 1943, a special decree divided all Russian forests into three groups by economic and ecological value. Groups Two and Three, which constituted the lion's share, allowed varied amounts of harvest. Group One was off limits, its woods consecrated for clean air, water purification, flood control, biological research, public recreation, and the indefinable, know-it-when-you-see-it sense of beauty that trees provide. Group One forests had, at that time, no counterpart for protective management in the world.

We need to pause here for a historical pulse-check. In Russia, the year 1943 was the nightmare year of World War II, one of the most wasting wars in human history. In less than four years, the country would lose twenty-seven million people, more than seven million a year. The same year saw the desperate and prolonged battles of Stalingrad and Kursk that determined the eastern front and, over time, the outcome of the war. Yet, extraordinarily, in the midst of all this, the Soviet government attended to its forests, including the heightened protections for Group One. Whatever else would die with the collapse of the communist regime decades later, the notion of protecting Group Ones remained.

In 1991, the Soviet Union dissolved and the nation of Russia emerged with half of its population, three quarters of the land mass, and over 90 percent of the forest cover. Domestic and foreign timber companies swarmed in, gold-rush style, to convert the trees to cash. The Russian Duma reacted quickly, vesting forest management in a new ministry—no longer called Forest Industry—under a Code that included all the buzzwords of modern management: *sustained yield*, *conservation*, *ecological services*, and *biological diversity*. More particularly, it expanded the Group One reserves.

The words of the Code sounded reassuring. As towns and cities expanded, however, the temptation to use Group One reserves for highway corridors, condominium developments, waste dumps, and weekend dachas for local officials was irresistible. There was no process for public protest, and the bureaucracy in Moscow was often great distances away. The path of least resistance was to approve. Whatever the law said, the government began giving Group One forests away.

𝔇

THE SOVIET Union came to environmental law in its own unique way—as a science like any other in the Rational State. Even during the darkest years of the Soviet regime, the Academy of Sciences Institute exercised a quasi-independent right to advocate environmental policy from within and is credited, among

other things, with protecting Lake Baikal, the world's largest and most threatened freshwater body at the time. The Academy trained lawyers and biologists
side by side, as engineers of the new society. Fatal to the system, as it turned out,
Academy members were also allowed to travel abroad. In retrospect, it was inevitable that the Academy would serve as an entry point for emerging concepts
of environmental policy from other parts of the world, none more radical than
the idea of public interest advocacy. And that it would eventually produce someone with the courage to go out and practice it.

Environmental activism was not exactly new to Russia, but it had been on a
very short leash. State-recognized nature protection societies were found at all
levels of government, and they carried out such nonthreatening, love-of-the-
land missions as antipoaching campaigns and erosion control. These societies
evolved as well to serve a communist style, informing function within farm col-
lectives and industrial plants, reporting on pollution compliance, sometimes
stimulating improvements, but if there were no improvements the case was
closed. The idea that a complaint could go farther was laughable, as I was to
discover.

In the 1970s, when environmental activism in the United States was in its
first bloom, I visited several Russian cities as part of a governmental exchange.
There were many speeches and endless rounds of toasts. When it came my turn,
I told the story of a recent lawsuit in which environmentalists had blocked the
construction of a large dam in order to protect a tiny and hitherto unknown
species of fish. The story was received in silence, followed by nervous laughter.
Was I joking? Then came the questions. How could a fish stop a dam? And yet
more unbelievable, how could a citizen stop the government? Whatever was
happening in America was clearly off the leash.

Then, in 1985, came Mikhail Gorbachev, glasnost, and the Russian world
turned upside down. The Chernobyl nuclear catastrophe produced steady revelations of government malfeasance leading to news of more pollution disasters.
Antinuclear protests began. Word came of a scheme to run the rivers of Siberia
backward. Government credibility plummeted. Two years later, the Communist
Party and the Council of Ministers, playing catch-up, passed a resolution, "On

Albert Butzel, center, attorney for the Scenic Hudson Preservation Conference, at the "Hudson River Peace Treaty," settling the litigation. He is accompanied by Frances Reese, left, chair of the conference, and Ross Sandler, right, representing the Natural Resources Defense Council, which emerged from this litigation. Overseeing the signing is Russell M. Train, standing, first chair of the Council on Environmental Quality under President Richard Nixon, who was enlisted to mediate the agreement. Photo courtesy of Albert Butzel.

Robert Boyle, a freelance writer who investigated fishing on the lower Hudson and fell into the Storm King litigation. He went on to found the Hudson River Fisherman's Association, a potent force in the case and a continuing presence in river cleanup. Photo courtesy of Robert Boyle. Photo by Elgin Ciampi.

Antonio Oposa, center, with the codirector of the Visayan Sea Squadron, Elipido "Jojo" de la Victoria, right, and a member of the Philippine National Bureau of Investigation. A short time following this photo Jojo de la Victoria was assassinated on the doorstep of his home. Photo courtesy of Antonio Oposa.

Antonio Oposa, right, with Philippine Supreme Court justice Hilario Davide and wife. Davide's *Minors Oposa* opinion gave legal rights to generations yet unborn and an aspiration that the world is still trying to achieve. Photo courtesy of Antonio Oposa.

Vera Mischenko, who founded the environmental organization Ecojuris in Moscow and went on to challenge major Russian projects, among them the transfer of protected forests to private uses. Photo courtesy of Vera Mischenko and the Environmental Law Alliance Worldwide.

Maitre James O'Reilly, right, who represented the Cree Indian Nation in several cases relating to the Great Whale project, at the Agreement La Paix des Braves between the Cree Grand Council and the Government of Quebec. On his far left is the then–prime minister of Quebec, Bernard Landry, and in the middle, Ted Moses, the Grand Chief of the Cree at the time. Photo by Gaston Cooper.

Mathew Coon-Come, right, Grand Chief of the Cree Nation, during the Native American flotilla that descended the Hudson River to New York City, catalyzing the State of New York to cancel purchase agreements from Hydro Quebec and sparing the Great Whale River. On the left is Lawrence Joseph, Grand Chief of the Federation of Saskatchewan Indian Nations. Photo courtesy of The StarPhoenix, Saskatoon, Canada.

Tokugawa Ieyasu, Shogun of Japan, whose shrine and surrounding cedar trees prompted the first injunction against the Japanese government on environmental grounds, and a legal opinion that anticipated modern environmental law.

Sha Jahan of India and his second wife, Mumtaz Mahal, for whom he built one of the most famous edifices in the world.

Mahesh Chander Mehta, center left, with the author and guests, in 2003. Mehta took his first environmental case before the Supreme Court of India in 1984 to save the Taj Mahal. He went on to become one of the most prolific and successful environmental lawyers in the world. Photo by Eric Dannenmaier.

Dr. Michael Decleris, former justice of the Greek Conseil d'Etat and president of the Fifth Chamber established, at his instance, for environmental law. The Acheloos project was one of the court's first cases, and remains one of its most difficult to resolve. Photo courtesy of Dr. Michael Decleris.

Dr. Glykeria Sioutis, University of Athens professor of public law, vice president of the Greek Environmental Law Association, and lead counsel for the Acheloos project before the Conseil d'Etat. Photo courtesy of Dr. Glykeria Sioutis.

David Syre, Seattle real estate developer and entrepreneur, whose Trillium project in Tierra Del Fuego was intended to demonstrate sustainable forestry but encountered increasingly difficult environmental questions and ultimately financial meltdown. Photo by Kathleen Culver.

Adrianna Hoffman, former director of the Chilean Environmental Commission, whose opposition to the Trillium project led to her dismissal but, ultimately, to the defeat of the proposal. With her is Senator Antonio Horvath, former president of the Committee on the Environment of the Chilean Senate and a lead plaintiff in the lawsuit that blocked the project at a critical juncture on environmental grounds. Photo by Malu Sierra.

the Radical Reconstruction [Perestroika] of Environmental Protection Activities in the Country," and convened a first-ever public hearing on the idea of environmental impact review. It was too little, too late. In 1991, the whole house of cards collapsed, and the stage was set for a revolution in environmental law. Out popped a remarkable series of women lawyers, the first of whom was a PhD graduate of the Academy of Sciences Institute named Vera Mischenko.

Mischenko was no accident. She had studied natural resources and environmental law at Moscow University and written her graduate thesis on "The Effectiveness of Civil Remedies in Environmental Law." In the late 1980s, while still a member of the Institute, she began investigating the construction of a power station in Moscow that was proceeding without environmental permits. There seemed to be no remedy. Wherever she looked she saw the same pattern. Nice-looking law, but that is where it ended. In response, she formed the first, postglasnost environmental organization in Russia, Ecojuris. In 1992, as the new Russian world was taking shape, Mischenko was given a three-month fellowship to study in the United States with two environmental advocacy organizations. She came back home with an agenda for public interest practice, foundation funding, and strategies for litigation.

Back in Moscow, Mischenko was on terra incognita. Russian courts had little experience in gainsaying the actions of the Russian government, and no knowledge of environmental law. On the plus side, Mischenko had at her disposal a set of recently enacted statutes that looked powerful enough to compel compliance even by sovereign agencies unaccustomed to questions and long accustomed to bulldozing their way forward. In 1992, a framework law declared the right of each citizen to a "favorable" environment and its protection against "negative effects" caused by economic activities. The following year, a new Constitution guaranteed the right to a healthy environment and added the rights to assemble, protest, and appeal to the courts for violations of individual liberties. A new Civil Code provided direct access to the Supreme Court. As if made for the Ecojuris cases to come, a new Forest Code reiterated Group One protections and provided that these reserves would not be transferred from public protection without approval of national authorities and, even then, only on a showing of need. A 1995 statute required environmental review. Suddenly there was lots of law. The problem was that it was being broken by the busload.

Mischenko's first lawsuit targeted a railway project between Saint Petersburg and Moscow that, as a route of least resistance, ran through the Valdai and other Group One reserves. As with other projects she had earlier examined, there was no environmental review. She appealed directly to the Supreme Court but, to her disappointment, the judges had no appetite for the issue and came up with a series of procedural reasons to avoid hearing the merits. At the same time, however, Ecojuris launched a media blitz soliciting letters from the public to state agencies, legislators, and the attorney general. More than three thousand people supported the campaign, which was reported on every television channel. Over time, the project monies ran out, some said into the pockets of government officials, and the route was cancelled. Mischenko had fired her first shot across the bow of Russian government decrees and had learned another valuable lesson in the bargain. There was more than one way to win a lawsuit.

The outright transfer of Group One reserves was a tougher nut. They were extremely popular with local officials and developers. Strong odors of payoff and corruption ran up the chain of command. Forest ministry officials saw it as a local affair. "If in the forests of the first group people make a cemetery, should I require exhumation?" one explained. "Because of that, we allow transfers." To be fair, the practice of giving away Group One reserves dated back to the Soviet era and had acquired the mindless legitimacy that comes with custom and habit. Only now in the new, postglasnost Russia there was another factor in the equation: the rest of the Russian people who did not particularly favor losing their parks, mushroom picking grounds, picnic areas, green belts, the sweet spots of their countrysides and the lungs of their cities.

The first rumblings of opposition were local. In 1994, a small town mayor on the outskirts of Moscow approved the construction of a condominium in a protected forest. Faced with an Ecojuris lawsuit and a vigorous local letter campaign, the mayor wound up reversing course and cancelling the project. A few months later, the city of Leningrad sliced a biological reserve in half to make way for new development, only to be challenged by a group called Green Party and stopped by a local court for lack of environmental review. The Supreme Court affirmed. The difficulty with these isolated resistance movements is that the approvals were coming in waves, and swatting at them one by one would hardly check their momentum.

This was a case for Vera Mischenko. Digging in, she discovered that, in the two years previous, the Russian government had transferred away some seventy-five thousand acres of Group One reserves in twenty-two states, across the top of the world. In the Urals, fifteen hundred hectares were ceded for the construction of a waste plant, industrial buildings, and a commercial market. In the Khanty-Mansiyisk region they went to gas stations, roads, and oil development. Other reserves were converted to public housing, private recreational homes, parking garages, and whatever else would generate revenue and political favor. It was pandemic, disposal by a thousand blows. None of the transfers made the case for need. None were accompanied by the required environmental assessment.

All of which brought Mischenko, Zlotnikova, Ecojuris, and several other environmental organizations, accompanied by the newspapers, the television cameras, and a smattering of citizens from across the country, to the small window of the Supreme Court building on Povarskaya Street on a cold day in April 1997, to file suit and launch their rocket that, this time, would reach the sky.

THERE WERE two forest cases. Both were filed in the name of Tamara Zlotnikova, who was also a member of the Russian Academy of Sciences. An active environmentalist in the State Duma, she had introduced the Law on Environmental Expertise and had nearly ten years of legislative debate under her belt. Zlotnikova became the public face of the forest campaign. Passionate and articulate, she would speak first for the plaintiffs in each proceeding. Mischenko was more the strategist, content to take second chair. As Mischenko later said, people thought, this was not just an environmental group against the government, this was a deputy of the Duma against the government. Something had to be wrong.

Zlotnikova I, filed in April 1997, challenged twelve bundled decrees issued by Prime Minister Chernomydrin that effectively opened eighteen thousand acres of Group One forest lands to residential cottages, cemeteries, landfills, service stations, and the familiar range of intrusions. The original plaintiffs also included the All Russian Nature Protection Society—which had traveled quite a distance from its old tree-planting days—ecology groups from faraway Tomsk and Bashkortostan, and even the heads of several local forestry departments, forest professionals finding their voices. As the proceedings went on, they would be joined by an even wider array of public and private organizations, including the Moscow Water Department, which feared pollution and erosion along its aqueducts and reservoirs. Like a civil rights march, the case started with a small band and ended with an army.

The grounds of the complaint were simple. Although the Forest Code allowed the transfer of Group One forests for other uses, these approvals required not only environmental review but "exclusivity," a showing of need. The law seemed clear, but the Supreme Court was at first no more ready for it than it had been for the Group One challenge to the Moscow railway. It refused to hear the case on the grounds that the decrees were too generalized to enforce. Zlotnikova argued that, to the contrary, the decrees had "particular, one-time, real-world consequences—stripping protections from distinct forest habitats." Further, to deny plaintiffs this challenge would deny them access to justice guaranteed by the Constitution.

None of these arguments would have mattered but for the intervention of Supreme Court Deputy Chairwoman Nina Segeeva, a highly respected member of the bench, who agreed with the Zlotnikova team and appealed to the Presidium, a gatekeeper body within the Court, to take the case. The Court reversed itself. There was law here after all. We would go to the merits.

By late fall, the case was becoming notorious. The first hearing, scheduled for the end of November, had to be postponed with the appearance of twenty-two new plaintiffs. A month later, the first session began, relatively quietly. The government, unaccustomed to serious challenge, took the case lightly, with only two attorneys in the courtroom. They would end up with fifteen, plus retained private attorneys and a bevy of other experts, but the die by that time was cast.

At one point a government attorney turned to Mischenko, Zlotnikova, and their female assistants and said, "You women would be better off singing the 'Song of the Bryansk Forest' than trying to present such stupid statements to the court." This did not go over very well. The Court informed him that if he repeated such comments he would be removed from the proceedings. Here was a surprise. Neither disregard nor bullying, time-honored government responses, seemed to work. The government would have to staff up. This was a new day.

Meanwhile, Ecojuris was mounting a political campaign with weekly press releases and widely publicized letters to state agencies and representatives, putting them on the spot, urging them to uphold the law. A second hearing in early February was postponed, ostensibly for the absence of a plaintiff but in reality because the Ecojuris documents had overwhelmed the Court. Somewhat belatedly, the Forest Ministry went on a counteroffensive, its newspaper urging the Court not to be swayed by the "green hysteria" surrounding the proceedings. To the end, its officials could not believe that their decisions were under question. A contemporary observer reported their "smoldering discontent." "What environmental rights are you talking about?" they asked. "You say it is illegal? This obstacle can be overcome."

Finally, in late February, the second hearing began. Zlotnikova and her colleagues produced experts from as far away as the European border and the far side of Siberia to testify about the high value of the Group One forests in their areas and the harm that was being caused by their reclassification. The Forest Ministry, trying to wash its hands of the matter, argued that all it was doing was issuing permits, which were only pieces of paper; it was up to local officials to decide what to do with them. At the same time, a forestry official admitted that "over 80 percent of the reclassified lands in the Cheyablinsk region of the Urals had already been developed." The transfer permits were in fact death warrants, and everyone knew it.

It was hard, however, to read the mind of the Court. By the end of the second day of trial, plaintiffs had seen several motions rejected, including the addition of yet more distant plaintiffs from Karelia in the far north and Sakhalin Island near the Bering Strait, and the rejection of several expert witnesses as well. On the third day, Zlotnikova and company adopted a radical strategy. Under

Russian civil procedure rules, key witnesses, along with attorneys, may make closing statements to the court. They decided to take full advantage of the opportunity. A chain of recognized experts arose to condemn the conduct of the proceedings and to insist on their statutory and constitutional rights. The moment was made all the more dramatic by the declaration of a young woman prosecutor from the Office of the Attorney General, the government itself, who began her remarks by saying, "I have just spoken as a prosecutor, but I would now like to say as a citizen . . . ," and proceeded to ravage the government's case. The decrees were illegal, she said. And there was major harm.

The Court retired to consider its verdict. Outside the building, a picket line of environmentalists had been demonstrating for three days. Inside, they packed the courtroom to the point that there was no room to stand. Two hours later, the Court returned and announced its decision. It found for the plaintiffs on all counts: environmental harm, no environmental review, and no showing of need. All twelve decrees were voided. The room burst into cheers. The people stayed on long afterward, applauding.

Their joy would be short-lived. Vera Mischenko had done her homework in researching the decrees, but her challenge came after the three-month window for challenging government decisions had closed. And so, again on appeal to the full court, the case was reversed and remanded to determine which, if any, of the appeals had been filed in time. Only two challenges were found timely. The other ten had lapsed, and those transfers escaped the net. Zlotnikova and her colleagues filed their own appeal this time and persuaded the high Court that two more of their challenges had been timely. At the end of the day, four decrees were annulled while another eight wriggled free.

Ecojuris kept the pressure on. While the first appeal was pending, Ecojuris filed a new petition, Zlotnikova II, challenging thirteen additional decrees, some of them several years old but at least one other issued, rather audaciously, following the Court's first opinion. The suit also sought a prospective ruling, a declaration that the whole transfer process, without environmental review, was unlawful. Testing new provisions of the Constitution and the Civil Code, the complaint was filed on behalf of "all current and future generation[s] of Russian citizens." Many thousands of Russians sent letters and faxes to Ecojuris after the case's coverage in the media, asking Ecojuris to represent them, their children, and their grandchildren. Shades of *Minors Oposa*.

When the dust settled, the Court found twelve of the thirteen challenges untimely, but in an opinion addressed directly to then prime minister Eugene Primakov, it declared the Group One transfer process invalid. Plaintiffs' constitutional rights to a favorable environment had been abrogated, and the government had neglected its duty to consult with the public before acting. Here was a strong nudge toward a wider notion of democracy. In a sense, it was the last and missing piece of glasnost, the rule of law. Then, once again, the story changes.

IS IT POSSIBLE to have environmental protection without the free-for-all of Western democracy? Russia may tell us. China may tell us. But to date, the answer seems otherwise. Western notions of environmental protection depend on citizen participation, opposition, demonstrations, referendums, and lawsuits to defend against government complicity and to advance the ball. To be sure, environmental participation advances civil society, but it also presumes the opportunity of civil society. It is no accident that the notions of environmental organizations and public interest law came to flower in Russia in the 1990s following perestroika, glasnost, and the disintegration of the Soviet Union. In a few heady years under Mikhail Gorbachev and Boris Yeltsin, with a fecundity rivaling that in the United States in the early 1970s, Russia enacted a wide range of protective environmental statutes, established an independent Ministry of Environment, and sponsored a first-ever Federal Civic Forum to promote the growth of citizen voices and organizations.

The Gorbachev years were seismically disturbing to the Russian people, however. Seventy years worth of icons broke and fell. The Yeltsin period that followed turned into chaos, and the government all but dissolved. Not before, however, in a free-market frenzy, hundreds of former functionaries and freelancers made killings by appropriating everything of value the government owned, including its natural resources, including the trees. Private "oligarchs," overnight millionaires, controlled petroleum, timber, and other concessions. Then came Vladimir Putin.

Ten years after the forest cases, Russia made another of those tectonic shifts familiar to students of its history and displaying the same extremes, back to central authority and strongman rule. The most visible new phenomena were central authority and Vladimir Putin. The federal government had taken over again. The new buzzwords were *vertical executive power* and *managed democracy*, which presented a challenge to Western-style environmental protection because this style of protection is in turn such a challenge to government, wherever it is found. To have to run for election every few years is one thing. It is another to have someone persistently questioning your actions and then taking you to court. In 2001 a New York reporter commented: "Putin is not likely to engage in open political repression, except perhaps, against the environmental movement, which is capable of arousing public opinion—over pollution and health hazards, for example." Environmentalists, he went on, "were capable of interfering with large-scale financial deals in which the administration or its allies have an interest." His comments were prescient.

The subsequent crackdown on all criticism in Russia included a barely concealed mugging of its environmental critics, but the offensive was far more sweeping. Within a few brief years, Putin had taken over television, eliminated the independent media, intimidated journalists (several were "mysteriously" killed, including an American reporter), replaced elected members of parliament with appointed officials, marginalized opposing political parties, nationalized the oil industry, and gone after independent businessmen with a ferocity that shocked even sympathetic foreign observers. It did not particularly shock the Russians, however, and they are the votes that count. In 2004, Putin was reelected with 70 percent of the vote and then saw his approval ratings soar to 80 percent. This is before we come to the environment.

Putin's views here were more complex. On the one hand, he professed allegiance to the environment and the civil rights necessary to protect it. On select occasions, backed into a public relations corner, he made green decisions. On the other hand, he also saw environmental concerns as a danger to the nation. "As soon as we start to do something," he complained, "one line of attack against us is always environmental problems." These problems were not genuine, he continued, but were instead stalking horses for political opposition. Worse, in Putin's view, environmental groups provided a lever for foreign interests to manipulate Russian society and Russian decisions, often for simple pecuniary gain. "We began building a port near Finland," he explained, "and [some companies]—I know this for a fact—invested money into the activity of environmental organizations with the only aim of hindering the development of this project, because it creates competition for them." He saw the motives of foreign infiltrators as even more nefarious. "Sadly," Putin declared in 1999, "foreign secret services use not only diplomatic cover, but also all sorts of ecological organizations."

Motivated by these concerns, as well as by officialdom's age-old resentment of its critics, Putin moved aggressively to curb environmental law and environmental civil society. In 2000 he abolished the environment ministry, the State Committee for Environmental Protection. The Law on Environmental Expertise itself then weakened, the new version called by one observer, "terrible, but better than nothing" and abolished, yet again, the professional Ministry of Forestry, transferring its duties to the Ministry of Natural Resources, which is committed by statute, to production. To Vera Mischenko, it was like "letting the cat guard the cream."

It went downhill from there. Environmental monitoring disappeared, and pollution fees imposed on industry were allowed to expire. Following a referendum signed by two and a half million Russians protesting the elimination of the environmental and forestry agencies, Putin changed the law to prohibit nongovernmental organizations from launching such referenda in the future. The subsequent fate of the Forest Code has been a *Perils of Pauline* saga with monthly twists and reversals of fortune, and no end in sight. A senior forestry expert from the Russian Academy of Sciences, long the unofficial arbiter of such issues, complained; "At first we tried to be active," he said, "then after about the fifteenth version, we threw up our hands." At last reading, the Code facilitated the transfer of Group One forests. This was a new political day and, of course, a very old one.

Government actions against environmentalists themselves have also been extreme. Coincident with their voiced opposition to government proposals, small groups in the hinterlands have been raided, audited, and intimidated and have seen their operating licenses revoked. The Moscow office of Greenpeace was ransacked on the pretense that a cubicle had been built without a permit. When a former Russian navy captain expressed reservations about contamination leaking from discarded nuclear submarines, he was jailed and criminally charged. The same happened to a journalist reporting bad environmental news from Siberia. Not content with case-by-case warfare, in January 2007, Putin signed a bill requiring disclosure of citizen group member lists, finances, and sources of funding. The chairman of the Bellona Environmental Rights Center in Saint Petersburg said, "The Kremlin is building up a mechanism to make them die."

It is against this backdrop of hostility that the fallout of the forest cases must be judged. For a while, the environmental movement boomed. Ecojuris went on to challenge unrestrained oil development in northern Siberia and Sakhalin Island, home to about eight thousand Inuit, large numbers of endangered sea mammals, and much of the nation's seafood. The scenario troubled even some of the businessmen involved. As one western oil executive described, "You go there, and you are surprised, if not horrified, by what you see. It's wells leaking all over the place, and big oil spills in the marshes. So you say, 'What am I going to do?'" What Russia was going to do was fast-track the action. It signed a deal with Exxon-Mobil that waived pollution regulations for drilling wastes and bypassed impact review altogether. In 1999, Ecojuris appealed to the Supreme Court, which invalidated the approvals and remanded the decision. Five years later, Ecojuris was back in court again challenging the same deal.

Ecojuris also took on the nuclear industry, a particularly sensitive issue following the meltdown at Chernobyl. In the late 1990s, the Putin Duma repealed its ban on the import of radioactive waste from other countries, including the United States, opening the way for a multibillion-dollar business. To Russians in the street it looked like selling out their safety for cash they would never see. Ecojuris and other groups launched a referendum to, among other things, reinstate the ban. They garnered some 2.5 million signatures, 500,000 more than required, only to have the government invalidate some 600,000 signatures and, therefore, the petition itself. Ecojuris then went to court, challenging the rejection of the referendum. A more tamed Supreme Court, stepping back from the fray, denied the appeal. Putin won, but one could feel his blood pressure rising.

While all this was going on, the government approved a $15 billion oil pipeline that ran less than one hundred meters from Lake Baikal. Ecojuris and residents of the neighboring city of Irkutsk launched a series of "flash mob" actions, tying blue and black balloons to the trees to represent Baikal before and after the next spill. Five thousand people gathered in protest on the streets of Irkutsk, the city's largest demonstration in decades, too many to arrest. When a state panel voted against the Baikal route, the government hand-picked new members and removed the opponents. Even for Russia, this was getting heavy-handed. In early 2006, Mischenko filed suit, but it was the publicity that counted. Under considerable public pressure, the pipeline company announced a new route some four hundred kilometers from Baikal. Putin took credit for the decision. But he would later characterize the environmental opposition as an example of the very extremism that he was seeking to rein in.

Despite these successes, the odds of winning an environmental issue within Russia have become increasingly long. President Putin has stepped down, as the Constitution required, but he hand-picked his successor and there is little doubt who is in charge. The Supreme Court temporarily found its voice in the forest cases but has since blown hot and cold on judicial review. Asked recently about the forest cases, Mischenko said, somewhat wistfully, that she could never win them today. For the moment, she too is in time out, having left Ecojuris to act as a private consultant, without the aggravation of maintaining an environmental organization in a state that considers them, if not the enemy, then the enemy's unwitting front. What she and her colleagues accomplished, however, is no more erasable than history.

We can say this much with certainty. About twenty years ago, Russia departed from a long tradition of tsarist regimes and Soviet rule to impose a rule of law, environmental law, on government. Most governments—whatever they may preach—do not like rules of law applied to them, and the push-back in Russia has been particularly strong. But the forest cases are there, and the precedent they set continues to challenge government decisions. They may be latent, even dormant for the moment, but everyone up to and including the president is aware that they are there. They are the seeds of live trees.

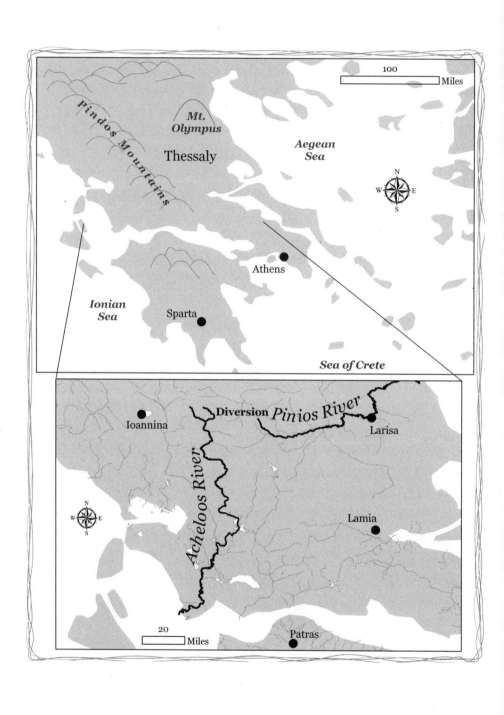

CHAPTER SEVEN

Acheloos

The wild Acheloos may finally be put to good use!
  Engineering News-Record, August 1988

A CHELOOS WAS the god of rivers, and his waters fed the Kingdom of Calydon. The ruler of Calydon had a beautiful daughter named Deianira, whom Acheloos courted for his wife. Unfortunately for the river god, Deianira had also captured the attention of Hercules, the celebrated hero and sociopath, who was also on the market for a wife, having "accidentally" killed his first one. Alternatively, depending on the version, he had killed his children in a fit of rage, blamed his wife, and then given her to a stranger. Faced, then, with a stiff challenge for Deianira's hand, Acheloos tried to reason with Hercules, pointing out that, as a native of Calydon, he would meet favor with Deianira's father. He also insisted on some deference, being a god, but his arguments were unavailing. Hercules replied, "My hand is better than my tongue. You may conquer me in words, but not in a fair fight." Acheloos, preparing himself for a battle that he sensed was hopeless from the start, transformed himself into a bull, but Hercules tore one of the horns from his head and beat him back to his river bed, where he has since remained, wounded for eternity. Now Greece is back to finish the job.

The Acheloos today is the longest river in Greece and easily its most beautiful, rising in a beech grove high in the Pindos Mountains and running nearly two hundred miles to the sea. For the last twenty-five years, the Greek government has been trying to drain the Acheloos and send it to Thessaly. It would have succeeded long ago but for the intervention of environmental law. More particularly, the intervention of a Greek court that turned itself into the most proactive environmental judiciary in all of Europe, if not the world.

The Acheloos litigation has questioned the reach of judicial authority, political authority, and yet a third authority new to this book, that of the European Union, itself a work in progress. We have a triangle here, and no one yet knows which corner will have the ultimate say.

𝄞

THESSALY, a perennial power in the Greek world, spreads north of Athens and east of the Pindos range. Athens might rule the country, but the plains of Thessaly would feed it from wide plains watered by a river of their own, the Pinios, and lakes of every size. Agriculture on this scale led to wealth and independence, enabling the region to take its own lead throughout history, siding with Persia on some occasions and with Athens on others, and later to rule itself as a separate barony until the Ottomans moved south and made Greece their own. The economic and political power of this region is perhaps the only rational explanation for the government's love affair with the Acheloos project today. At bottom, the project consists of a massive transfer of water from a poor region on the other side of the Pindos Mountains to the east and Thesally, where the money lies.

The notion is not new. It was first conceived in the 1920s by an ambitious engineer from, coincidentally, Thessaly, who, after advanced training in the Soviet Union, went on to become dean of the National Technical University in

Athens. Intended to waken the "sleeping giant" of the Thessaly plain, the dream lay dormant until the close of World War II brought the possibility of massive, Soviet-style public works. Instead, a numbing series of revolutions, civil wars, and coups got in the way, retarding the megaproject fever. Then, in the early 1980s, as stability returned, the Acheloos proposal was dusted off and became a centerpiece of the government's development program. At anywhere from $1.4 to $6.5 billion, depending on who is counting, it would be the most expensive project in the country's history.

The engineering was simple, if ambitious. It called for four separate dams and reservoirs on the Acheloos River, two tunnels taking it through the Pindos Mountains, and a long canal delivering it to the Thessaly plains. The target was also straightforward. It would help grow cotton, a crop that drinks water like desert camels. More than 90 percent of the project water was for agriculture, and more than 90 percent of that for cotton. At last, an engineering journal enthused in 1988, the wild Acheloos would be put to good use. To the engineering mind everywhere, water in rivers is waste.

The enthusiasm of the construction community was exceeded only by that of the cotton farmers of Thessaly, who were riding a tide of government programs that made cotton growing profitable, by law. Europe's agricultural policy guaranteed cotton prices and paid heavy premiums for increased production, while its regional development program was funding irrigation works throughout the region. Cotton growers couldn't lose. Subsidies of this scale create a feeling of entitlement in the agricultural mind, in the words of one Greek commentator, "a Testament." In this view the Acheloos project simply executed a promise that had been created by practice and, now, by the need for new water.

The old water was running out. Thessaly farmers had taken their own sources down to the bone. They had so polluted the Pinios River that it was in some stretches unusable; in other reaches, for months of the year, it no longer existed. They had drained lakes that stored millions of gallons of rainwater in order to put a few more hectares into production. They had drilled so many water wells that their aquifers came up dry. Cotton is a thirsty crop, but by the late 1980s an arid country whose soils had been abused for more than two thousand years had become the fifth largest exporter of cotton in the world. The cotton growers of Greece had also become the most heavily subsidized farmers in the world, a prize for which there is no small competition. And the cotton growers of Greece came from Thessaly.

Of course, there were people and other living things on the other side of the Pindos Mountains who were already using the Acheloos. In fact, they depended on it. But they were not Thessaly, and in the late 1980s, as the first Acheloos construction bids were sent out, they seemed as immaterial as a distant breeze.

𝔇

THE BYZANTINE monastery of Saint George at Myrophyllo rests in a high mountain pass west of the Pindos Mountains, opposite Thessaly. Dating back to the eleventh century, it holds a special place in Greek hearts. Its secret passages sheltered the Friends of Greece, the premier resistance movement against the advancing Ottoman Empire and an inspiration for the 1820 revolution when the Greeks took back their own. The walls of the monastery were covered in colorful, free-flowing frescoes, which in 1993, were about to be buried in murky water behind the Messochora dam, phase one of the Acheloos project. The village of Myrophyllo would be inundated as well. Georgios Rapti, the mayor of the town, had not been consulted on the project. "No one has come here to explain," he said. "It is our farmland, our walnut trees, our history and heritage, and eventually our homes on the hillside that will go."

They were not alone. Entire mountain towns would be eliminated from the west slope of the Pindos, their houses made of flat stones piled up on each other like tidy stacks of books, their alleys roofed by vines whose stems were the width of a man's leg and had shaded generations in their time. In a country better known for island beaches and the great sprawl of Athens, these mountain ecosystems are jewels in the sky, the source of clear running water, silver trout, and snow. The streams are crossed by old stone bridges that go back to the time of Rome. With curved arches and elegantly simple patterns, they are about as close to fine cabinetry as one can get with stone. This is where the Acheloos rises. They too would be drowned.

Granted, as the saying goes, you can't make an omelet without breaking eggs. Even Myrophillo's mayor, facing the loss of his town and his people, conceded as much. "We would not stand in the way of progress if it was for the good of Greece," he said, "but all we know is that it is to grow more tobacco and cotton to be ploughed back into the ground and make farmers rich." This was the other problem with the Acheloos project. It was unmistakably a dog.

To begin with, it was a dog with two heads, depending on where it was being shown. By the late 1980s the European Community was beginning to have second thoughts about supporting crops like cotton, which were grown in such abundance that it was also paying farmers not to grow them. Seeing the handwriting on the wall, Greece presented Acheloos as an electric power project in order to qualify for Community funding. Meanwhile, project sponsors back home were presenting it as an agricultural venture to rescue the Thessaly plain. They knew what was real and what was window dressing.

Compounding the project's identity crisis was the fact that the claimed power and irrigation benefits drank from the same glass. The more water one stored for power the less was available for agriculture, and the reverse was likewise true. At which point, in the words of the *London Guardian*, the scheme "descend[ed] into farce." The Greek Power Corporation complained the project would actually reduce the water supply to its existing plants. It was demanding to be paid sixteen million pounds in compensation. Not a good beginning.

The numbers got worse from there. Cotton production would not increase sevenfold as predicted; best case, it would be lucky to increase by 50 percent. Low inflation would not keep costs down; inflation, in fact, was soaring. The costs of operating the facilities, some highly complex, and fixing them when over decades of use they began to break down, were omitted from the debit column, as were the costs of actually getting the water to the fields. One report likened these machinations to "the thief of mythology, Procrustes, who cut or stretched the bodies of those he robbed so that they would fit his bed."

Not that the Greek government didn't try for a good report card. It contracted three times for independent analyses of the Acheloos project, but each one had found it a loser. On the last try, the government turned to a British firm,

Morgan Grenfell, giving it a very short deadline and even more limited information, which was not to be questioned. The ensuing report, which reads like an excuse for bad homework ("taking in mind the time restrictions," which "allowed neither the extensive collection . . . of hydrological data, nor the use of the most developed methods of hydrology technology") ended with a cold embrace: if cotton prices remained at an all-time high and inflation at an all-time low, the Acheloos might break even. Not long afterward the director of Morgan Grenfell was retreating from even this prediction, saying that "anyone who suggests we endorsed it [the Acheloos] is being economical with the truth." No one was owning up to this one.

None of this, of course, mattered to the agricultural industry in Thessaly nor to the government in Athens. The point of projects like these is not to justify the money but to deliver it, particularly where the moneys are offered, as in Monopoly, at the beginning of the game. Also irrelevant was the fact that Thessaly farmers were wasting water as if it were their last day on Earth. The prevailing custom was to irrigate crops throughout the heat of the day with "water cannons" that shot streams of liquid high into the air, from whence they descended "like a sprinkling rain." About half of it descended. The other half was lost to evaporation before it hit the ground. The irrigation canals in the region were both unlined and uncovered, so much of the water in transit either leaked down into the soils or evaporated as well. At the same time, growing monoculture crops on exhausted soil required ever greater loads of pesticides and fertilizers, all of which filtered into the groundwater and what surface water remained.

By the 1980s then, Thessaly cotton was growing on chemicals and borrowed time. The Pinios was shot, and water wells were starting to pump up brines. The response to these problems was not to water at night instead of by day, nor to water along the ground rather than by cannons in the air, nor to line the feeder canals, nor to cover them on top, nor to begin to charge farmers increasing rates for the use of water, which would induce them to conserve. Way off the table was any notion of rotating crops to allow the land to recover, or substituting other crops more sustainable in a future all could see was going to bring higher energy prices and more intense cycles of drought. Thessaly's solution was far more simple. It would bring over the Acheloos River no matter how much times had changed, and it was not going to budge. It had waited long enough and it had Athens on its side.

THERE WAS another government in Europe, however. Its formation had been a lot slower than that of the United States, which had managed to package itself in less than twenty years, but then again the wars of Europe had been going on for two millennia among people who spoke different languages and had learned to hate each other from childhood. Americans call the construction of their government the Miracle at Philadelphia, and it was indeed remarkable, but the case could be made that a comparable event was launched in Europe fifty years ago and is still in motion. The question on both sides of the Atlantic was the same: as between the central government and the member states, push comes to shove, who held the power?

It took the United States two tries to agree on a national authority that could get things done. The member states of Europe moved with equal caution, and what emerged in the Treaty of Rome was something like the American Articles of Confederation, but even more diffuse. It was originally named the European Community, not Union, and for good reason. There would be no fixed presidency, but a leader who rotated frequently among the member states. Laws could be passed only by state government ministers, and only unanimously, which meant that a single unwilling government had the veto. Even when enacted, these laws, in the main by "directives," only set goals and let the states adopt programs to accomplish them. A commission in Brussels would supervise state performance from afar. So would a European Court of Justice, but only after a lengthy process aimed at reconciliation. In sum, a more indirect and deferential superauthority would be hard to imagine. If it had been imaginable, they would probably have adopted it instead.

When it came to environmental policy, the Community's power was not simply indirect. It was nonexistent. The whole arrangement was directed by the Treaty, and the Treaty was based on free trade. Commerce was the magnet that brought these countries together, and the initial pact committed them to the removal of trade barriers and little else. There was nothing in the Treaty about environmental protection, not a word. One would think, then, that Greece and its sister countries had little to fear from Brussels over their environmental policies. If indeed they had any policies. In fact, however, the opposite happened.

In the 1970s, the Community began to pass environmental laws. Lacking explicit authority in the Treaty to do so, Brussels teased it out of a duty to "harmonize" national laws to prevent economic disparities. The theory worked for environmental programs like pollution control where some states might try to lure industry with weak regulations. Over time, though, the idea of protecting the environment in order to equalize commerce seemed increasingly fictitious, and so Europe did a straightforward thing. It dropped the fiction and changed the Treaty. It would protect the environment in order to protect the environment, and it would go on to say how. These amendments would jolt Greece and its designs on the Acheloos River.

The new provisions were dramatic. They dropped the requirement for unanimity, which enabled the passage of tough laws over the objections of a few recalcitrant states. In the same vein they beefed up the role of the popularly elected Parliament, giving it an equal vote at the table. The vox populi was now in play, and the European vox populi was decidedly green. A spate of green directives would follow.

At the same time, the amendments declared that environmental protection would be guided by several overriding principles: pollution should be abated at the source, the polluter should pay, and development should be "sustainable" over time. Read literally, these principles offended industry and developers of every stripe. No rational enterprise wants to pay for pollution controls if the costs can be passed on to the general public, nor is the rational enterprise eager to control discharges at the source if it can get the government to bring over the Acheloos River and flush them away instead. The principle of sustainability was even more threatening, because no one could predict what it entailed. Which left it for courts to decide.

As the Acheloos project came on, then, in the late 1980s, it would face a rising focus on environmental problems in Brussels and a new set of laws to address them. One of the first of these laws adopted a mechanism which at that time, as we have seen, was traveling the world: environmental impact assessment. Europe followed with an assessment directive, and Greece was obliged to follow suit. This said, the basic leave-it-to-the-states philosophy of the European Union remained in place, which left the process to the Greek government and its judiciary.

Two thirds of the Greek government was no problem to Thessaly. It had carried the day with the legislature and the presidency. The judiciary was another matter, a cipher really, because it too was emerging from the long darkness of the Second World War, followed by a civil war, and then a military coup. No one knew what the judiciary would do.

THE FIRST time the Acheloos project went to court it emerged with a black eye and a bloody nose. The year was 1994, and a group of environmental organizations led by the Hellenic Ornithological Society and the World Wildlife Fund filed a lawsuit against the venture, its first impoundments already well under construction. The defending agencies formed a mighty phalanx, including Agriculture; Industry, Energy and Technology; National Economy, and Tourism; and the lead agency for the project, Environment, Planning and Public Works. Their very names bespoke the difficulties of getting an environmental word in edgewise. Three of the four had nothing to do with environmental protection, and indeed pursued missions that would be complicated by the requirements of environmental law. The name of the fourth, Environment, Planning and Public Works, misspoke where the power lay.

Public works, in any country, holds the political constituency. It builds things from which people make money. Planning on the other hand is popular nowhere and is usually reduced to half-hearted exercises in zoning. Environment, the third part, is allowed at the dance but is usually found standing by the wall. It might seem strange then, to read a news report that a Mr. George Souflias, the "Minister of Environment," waxed enthusiastic in the news about the completion of the Acheloos project. His reported title was misleading. He was first and foremost the minister of public works, and this project was his adopted child.

The Acheloos opinion came as a rude shock to power. The Council of State, the supreme tribunal for administrative issues, began by according environmental groups the right to sue not because they had members that were harmed in a certain way but, rather, because their purpose was to protect the environment. It next announced environmental protection to be a "fundamental principle," for the benefit "not only of the present generation, but also of those who will follow." *Minors Oposa*, again. At which point the court took off the gloves.

What followed was a blistering critique of the Acheloos project, a litany of its adverse effects on the "exceptionally rich flora and fauna of the region"; the disruption of lives, communities, and transportation systems; the loss of the Acheloos delta, the continuing contamination of both the Acheloos and Pinios basins, and the high risks of moving aquatic organisms from one self-contained ecosystem to another. Clearly, in the words of the trade, this was an "educated" court. The Ministry of Environment, Planning and Public Works had tried to mask the project's impacts by cutting it into pieces, treating a single dam or diversion canal, where it was obvious that the total effect was larger than its parts. The court saw the impacts as "dynamic," not "linear," and called for a "composite" review that put the whole together. The ball went back to the agencies.

All of which is worth a pause. We are in Greece circa 1990, one of the least developed countries in western Europe and just emerging from nearly fifty years of chaos. The Acheloos was the biggest development bonanza in the country's history, supported with religious zeal by the dominant political party and the power of Thessaly. It was on a roll. Environmental lawsuits were a new phenomenon, just beginning to trickle in to a court system trained to protect the government from outside litigants like an elite regiment of the Royal Guards. Greek law schools barely mentioned the word *environment*, and then only as a small appendix of administrative law. The number of lawyers in environmental practice could be counted on one hand without using the thumb. Where then, did a Council of State opinion like this one come from? The answer, like so many in history, is that it came from a remarkable person at the right place and time.

DR. MICHAEL DECLERIS is an intellectual in the Greek tradition, educated at the Universities of Athens and London, ending with a doctorate of laws from Yale. His first interests were in public policy and the workings of government, but he soon immersed himself in the sciences, particularly the workings of large-scale ecological systems. His work shows a steady trend from the question of governance to the even more elusive question of sustainable development. The ranks of environmental lawyers around the world include a strain of those who became fascinated with the challenges of science, and Decleris seems to have been one of them. At the time the Acheloos project came along he had been a member of the Council of State for over two decades and was now its vice president. More germane to the Acheloos, he was in his tenth year heading a new branch of the Council, Section V, exclusively dedicated to environmental cases. It was no accident. He had created Section V. Michael Decleris was an intellectual who also got things done.

The very existence of Section V affected the Acheloos opinion. An environmental court, a concept still foreign to the United States, offers the advantage that it learns the law and the agencies it is dealing with. A plaintiff does not have to struggle to educate a new judge, often impatient and a little timid toward the unknown, on how an environmental program is supposed to work. Nor does the environmental side have to convince the judge that the government—which is presumed to do no wrong—can actually do wrong, at times repetitively, even deliberately. It does not take many cases against a ministry like Environment, Planning and Public Works for the judges to conclude that there is a bad attitude here and to stop granting it the benefit of the doubt. That kind of understanding about an environmental program —in this case, the impact review process—and how agencies tend to thwart it—in this case, by dividing the process into pieces—jumps from the Council's opinion. Section V saw what was going on.

Decleris's problem was, having arranged a new branch for environmental cases, he did not have much law to apply. Greece did not join the European Community until 1980, and did not pass even a framework environmental statute until 1986. In the absence of legislation, all the Court had to work with was the Greek Constitution, which stated opaquely that environmental protection was an "obligation of the state," and that the government should take "special measures" to conserve it. There was nothing about citizen lawsuits, impact assessment, or sustainability. So Section V invented them. It took the Constitution and within a few years created a roadmap for environmental impact review, and strong protections for coastal areas, urban ecology, and other sensitive pieces of the landscape. And the right of Greek citizens to enforce them.

Not without controversy. The most heated complaint of the Council's critics is that it legislated, and the loudest acclaim of its supporters is that it legislated. Decleris was open about it. Like other scholars, he saw the Greek government not only failing its environmental responsibilities but inherently incapable of meeting them. The legislature was paralyzed, he would write, even where required to act by treaty, as in the case of wetlands protection where a convention had been signed and then ignored for twenty years. The executive remained paralyzed as well, "in thrall" he wrote, "to an all-powerful, party-political and everlasting patronage system which abhors order because it feeds on and is strengthened by disorder." These are not the words of an anarchist. They are those of an expert on government systems who had published half a dozen books on the subject. Decleris continued, with perhaps the Acheloos in mind: "The governments of the day, reserving most of their time and energy for economic development and projects of all kinds, act only opportunistically and in a fragmented way on behalf of the environment." He concluded, perhaps with the farmers of Thessaly in mind, "The regulatory vacuum is exploited by various private interests to create faits accomplis to their own advantage, which are then as a rule accepted by the State."

To Decleris, the environmental crises could not wait for the utopia of government reform. Natural resources were being destroyed right now, and what was being lost could not be replaced. The Byzantine monastery high in the high Pindos valley was going under eight feet of water and would be gone forever. The same fate awaited endangered deltas, coastlines, and species. The judicial role was to fill the gap. It is one of the most controversial, and controverted, judicial roles in the world. But it just might save the Acheloos.

The Ministry of Environment, Planning and Public Works offered a classic response. It proceeded with construction. Within record time it pumped out a new project decision and redeclared itself good to go.

VASSILIS ANAGNOSTOPOULOS takes another view. He is an elected official in Thessaly and has supported the Acheloos diversion from the start. The way he sees it, the farmers in Thessaly were caught in a trap. The government encouraged them to switch from cereal crops to cotton in order to boost foreign exchange, reinforced by European programs that were throwing money at them to put ever more acreage into production. At the peak, draining their water to the last drop and adding heroic loads of chemicals, Thessaly farmers were pulling in three and four crops of cotton a year. Thessaly had no hand in promoting these policies, of course. It was all the government's fault. Bridling at project delays, he says that if the government was "now going to spend over half a billion euros" from "what little money the Greek people can afford" for more studies, then "they might well be the worst administrators ever." On which possibility, the environmentalists might agree.

Anagnostopoulos finds an ally in Dr. Glykeria Sioutis, an attorney who has been defending the Acheloos project before the Council of State for the past thirteen years. A few early missteps in the paperwork aside, she thinks the project is sound. Thessaly needs the water, she explains, and there is too much of it, a "surplus" in her words, on the other side of the Pindos. Of course, she is paid to represent the project, and the agriculture industry in Thessaly is not exactly an indigent client. On the other hand, Sioutis is also a professor of administrative and environmental law at the University of Athens, with a respectable number of publications on environmental policy to her name. Her complaint is that the Council of State "overstepped its bounds," to the point of "scandal."

Were we invisible in a room with Michael Decleris and Glykeria Sioutis, we might at this point eavesdrop on the following conversation:

Decleris: Are there no decisions of the Council on Acheloos with which you agree?

Sioutis: Well, I represented the project in the first case, in 1994, and your ruling requiring a broader impact statement was correct. It was required by law.

Decleris: But there was no law. We had a skeletal directive from the EU and no guidance from the government. We had to interpret the Constitution to find that "composite" requirement. Was that improper?

Sioutis: It was at least limited, because the experts in the ministry could go back and fix the statement. You did not dispute their scientific findings. But in the next decisions you went too far. You found the impacts to be serious and unacceptable, when they found the opposite. There you stepped out of bounds.

Decleris: Would you have us take the ministry's statements at face value, without a serious look? This is after all the same ministry that is promoting the project.

Sioutis: These are statements of science, and lawyers are not scientists. We have to stay within our roles.

Decleris: But are they of science? The weight of scientific opinion says that the impacts on the Acheloos system will be devastating, and violate several European policies as well. Including some rather important ones on endangered habitats and water quality.

Sioutis: Where scientists disagree, we defer to the agencies. Otherwise it is judicial chaos.

So it would go among the lawyers. Meanwhile, the project would—and did—roll forward. The village of Mesochora attempted to save itself from the flooding by showing that reducing the height of one dam under construction would have spared it and the monastery, with no loss in power production. No reduction was made. Instead, the government incurred yet more costs paying damages to the displaced residents of the town, including families who had lived there for centuries. The people in the way of the Acheloos venture were not just dealing with a project. They were dealing with the attitude of a project that had considered itself invincible and was now beginning to feel under siege.

Shortly after the new impact statement emerged, Hellenic Ornithological and its allies went back to court to challenge it as little changed from before. In 1999, Section V ordered the project to be scaled back in order to spare historic and cultural landmarks. The court had issued such decisions before, imposing development limits to protect unique resources, but this was its first application to so large a venture and it offended attorney Sioutis. One of the affected sites was an old stone bridge, associated with an ancient church. In poor condition, she contended, the bridge was "doomed anyway." No steps had been proposed to preserve it. Yet here came an opinion saying that the bridge must be saved. Another example of a court out of control.

This time, the court was explicit in ordering the construction to stop, and so it did, for the next two years. Meanwhile, however, the Greek government had appropriated over two hundred million dollars toward completing the project, and that was a great deal of money just sitting around. And so, in 2003, the ministry issued yet a third environmental statement and let the bids once more. Two years later, the Council of State issued yet a third opinion rejecting the project, this time because the project did not conform to European water law. A new directive required that water quality not be impaired by dams or diversions, and that private beneficiaries pay full project costs. The Acheloos project violated both principles, but for the fact that Greece, rather handily, had done nothing to implement them. It was the Council's reliance on this directive that most upset Sioutis, and to understand her complaint, we need to bring Europe back on stage.

The European Community never intended to implement its directives from afar. Instead, the member states would implement them, which soon presented a problem. Some members were not about to, leaving the Commission with the chore of trying to cajole countries like Greece into action or, after protracted jawboning, taking them to the European Court. Which might then, after more years, impose a fine. These were not rare cases. One quarter of all the Commission's docket against member states—for violations of everything from labor laws to social services to commodity prices—concerned the environmental directives. Environmental law is that hard to make happen. In recent years Greece had been found in violation of the Wild Birds Directive, Natural Habitats Directive, Water Directive, and Nitrates Directives, to name only those directly connected to the Acheloos case. Other European policies to protect the economy and culture of mountain communities were being ignored as well. In the meantime, while these disputes between the Commission and Greece ran their course, projects like the Acheloos ran free.

Enter a remedy to plug the gap. Certain European directives, if their requirements were specific and left no room for escape, were found to have "direct effect" and constitute national law by themselves, without waiting for state action. This doctrine was the invention of the European judiciary, and the idea was that member states should have nothing to gain by dragging their feet. The doctrine was all the handle Decleris needed. Once a European directive like the new one on water had the effect of Greek law, anyone, including the Hellenic Ornithological Society, could take the government to court to enforce it. Which, potentially, was very bad news for the Acheloos project. Unless the Greek government could find an escape valve.

𝒟

IN EARLY 2006, following the Supreme Court's third Acheloos opinion and yet another rebuke from the European Court of Justice on its overall compliance, the minister of Environment, Planning and Public Works pulled a double coup. The European directives on water and habitats were in his way, but both had a loophole that allowed states to opt out for projects of "overriding public interest." Exploiting the opening, the minister went to the Greek parliament and requested that it pass laws to implement both directives, long overdue, while at the same time exempting the Acheloos as a project of overriding significance. Which the parliament did, scoring two goals for the Thessaly–Athens team. It met the minimal demands of the European Commission. And, by making the declaration legislative, it finessed review by the Greek Council of State. The Council could declare a ministry action to be against the law, but the parliament *was* the law. For Thessaly–Athens, it looked like victory at last.

The Commission stood down. Having ended its funding for Acheloos some years back, it declared that it had nothing more to do with the project. The monster that the Commission had fed and nurtured was no longer its concern.

Environmental groups, undeterred, bounced back to the European Commission with a new claim. Greece was violating their treaty rights to environmental protection. They also asked the Greek Council of State to refer the question to the European Court of Justice, which, after some back-and-forth, it agreed to do. As the dust continued to swirl, Acheloos remained contested in three separate venues, the Commission in Brussels, the European Court in Geneva, and the Greek Council of State in Athens. Anyone who complains that environmental laws tie up development projects in red tape would have a field day here. Yet sometimes, and often in public interest law, red tape is the only thing that human rights have. On the one side is money. On the other side is process.

Meanwhile the Acheloos project, which flaunted nearly every environmental principle of the European Union and every legal principle of the Greek

Council of State, stood impatient in the wings, pawing the floor, ready to go forward.

✆

PLATO saw it. Two thousand years ago he wrote of the abuse of Roman-occupied lands along the Mediterranean coast "like the skeleton of a sick man, all the fat and soft earth having wasted away," only the "bare framework" remaining. Two hundred years ago George Marshall, as ambassador to Turkey, traveled the area and wrote his master work, *Man and Nature*, which pointed out that the sandy wastes of North Africa had once been the breadbasket of Rome. Civilizations as old as the Aztec and as young as the homesteaders of Oklahoma have also stripped their soils, outrun their water, come on dry times, and expired in the dust. They have done so even more rapidly with cotton, which after several decades left the soils of the American South too sour to plant, and then did the same in Uzbekistan, turning Asia's fruit bowl into Dustbowl Two. On a short time frame, very short, what Thessaly is doing to the Acheloos River may be argued as tenable, taking another region's water to postpone the day of reckoning. Over even a medium term, however, everything it is doing—from the crops it is planting to the manner in which it grows them—is doomed to crash. This is before the oncoming crunch of energy costs and climate change.

But are these legal questions? We can perhaps steal secretly back to the room with the lawyers Sioutis and Decleris for a final snippet of their conversation:

> *Sioutis:* Sustainability depends on political, not legal, choices. Any departure from the judicial role is wrong.
> *Decleris:* But sustainability is also a legal norm.
> *Sioutis:* In trying to define it, however, you are legislating.
> *Decleris:* Not at all, I am interpreting the law.

Which would end it, except for the second act of the story of Hercules and Acheloos, the river god. On his way home with Deianira, now his bride, brave Hercules faced another river, the Evenus, made impassible by recent storms. As he pondered his dilemma, the centaur Nessos arrived on scene and offered to carry Deianira across in his ferry. Hercules agreed with the plan, and went across first with the couple's belongings to prevent any thievery on Nessos's part. But as he reached the far shore, looking back, he saw Nessos attempting to carry Deianira away. Enraged by yet another challenge so soon after his defeat of Acheloos, he shot a poisoned arrow at the centaur, wounding him fatally. As Nessos lay dying, he told Deianira to take a sample of his blood as a charm to win back Hercules' love, should he ever tend to stray. Which she did.

Not long following, Hercules was again off to war and had set his sights on yet another attractive princess, Iole. Learning of the relationship, and remembering Nessos's dying words, Deianira sent her husband a gift, a robe of gold treated with Nessos's blood. When Hercules donned the robe, however, the blood, still tainted by the poisoned arrow, began to burn his skin. The harder Hercules struggled, the more tightly the robe clung. Certain that his wife had betrayed him and suffering the agony of the burning robe, he ordered his men to immolate him on a pyre at Mount Oeta. Which they did.

You can defeat Mother Nature for a while. Then it becomes very difficult.

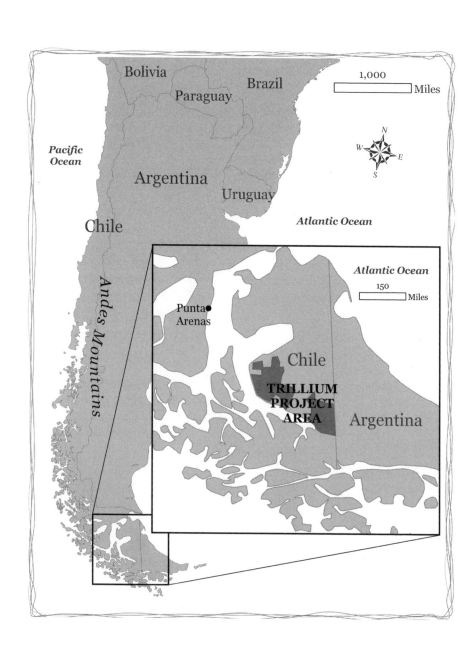

CHAPTER EIGHT

Trillium

I told David Syre the first time I came back from seeing the property in Tierra del Fuego, I said, "David, you have bought a national park which has some timber."

Dr. Jerry Franklin, Forest Ecologist, University of Washington, 2004

IN THE WINTER of 1520, Fernando Magellan was nosing his way down the flank of South America in search of passage to the treasure of the day, the spices of the far Pacific. Henry Hudson and others were about to probe the northern route, and Christopher Columbus had just attacked the middle, certain that he had found China. Magellan took a southern course, and it was brutal.

Dogged by sea ice, sabotage, mutiny, unspeakable weather, useless charts, an unyielding landmass, and superstitions about the sea world so paralyzing that he had to command his crew by guile and torture, the captain general nosed into yet another lead. The strait widened, storms howled in his face, and to his left and right rose steep forests of small trees, rocks, and ice. It looked promising. Whatever was ahead seemed open to the ocean beyond. In the evening, they spotted distant fires on the port side, which they took for signs of life. They saw no one, but the fires made an impression, and Magellan called the land mass he was passing Tierra del Fuego. Within a year he would be hacked to pieces on a small island, half a world away.

Three hundred years later, Charles Darwin and the *Beagle* rounded the same strait and did a little more exploring. Within only a few feet of shoreline they found "a dense forest with dozens of types of ferns; windblown and stunted trees; silky moss; and a layer of spongy tundra." The place was strangely fertile. The same diet of frozen mist and squall that daunted the human heart produced woods so thick that "it was necessary to have constant recourse to the compass." The few native people Darwin encountered were stunted in their growth and "hideous" in appearance to the point he could hardly see them as fellow creatures, "inhabitants of the same world." There were few souls worth converting and no gold. Nothing here to claim the European heart.

So Tierra del Fuego remained, an isolated dab at the foot of the continent and a dragon at the gate to the Pacific Ocean. One sailed by Tierra del Fuego, God willing, as quickly as one could. The thick and stunted forests also remained untouched, off the radar of a globalizing world. Until the 1990s, when an enterprising businessman from Seattle, Washington, decided to buy them and cut the timber. Suddenly Tierra del Fuego mattered, halfway up the chain of the Andes Mountains to Santiago, Chile, and back to the boardrooms of corporate North America. The furor was certainly a surprise. Who could possibly care about some dwarf trees at the bottom of the world?

IN 1993, DAVID SYRE purchased over half a million acres of real estate that he had never seen. He was looking for forests, and this was one was available. The fact that it was ten thousand miles away from his headquarters in Seattle was no obstacle. He had sent two foresters to Tierra del Fuego, and they reported that the purchase was a "terrific value," with 650,000 acres of virgin timber, most of it hardwood, a local community hungry for jobs, and a country with no hint of environmental compunctions and falling all over itself to attract foreign investment. Better yet, the headquarters of the company trying to sell the land was located only an hour's drive away, in Vancouver. Syre drove north to make the deal.

Syre was used to taking chances, and winning them. Tall, soft-spoken, and personally charming, even his adherents used the word "aggressive" when speaking of his ventures. Syre had fought his way back from polio at an early age to a series of investments that put him, then in his early fifties, at the top of a $450 million enterprise that stretched from Alaska to the tip of South America. He started out in real estate by building a 176-unit condominium complex near Glacier Park, then a shopping mall in his hometown of Bellingham, Washington. He purchased "at fire sale prices" large chunks of downtown Denver, Vancouver, Ketchikan, and Anchorage. He opened a business park named Cordata and a nearby resort called Semiahmoo. He did nothing by halves here, not even the names.

At the same time, Syre was diversifying. He bought out a manufacturer of sunglasses, and then another of bicycle helmets. He had a model farm and agricultural theme park in mind as well—Hollyhock Farms. Then he started buying forests, a cluster from Boise Cascade and another on Whidbey Island in Puget Sound, which is when he made his first mistake. He began clear-cutting them. Worse, he committed the cardinal sin of a timber operator; he clear-cut where people could see it, and clear-cut timber is as ugly as a fire-bombing. It was such bad form that the state lands commissioner sent him a "blistering" letter of reprimand, not about the cutting, but about its visibility. Syre was making the timber industry look bad.

Projects like these create their own controversy. His shopping mall provoked a storm of protests from people who preferred their old stores and less traffic, and his Hollyhock Farms was blocked by neighbors. Some got nasty. They dumped sawdust in his lobby and held a "group vomit." One spat at him in the street. His timber cuts, memorialized in photographs, were called "savage" and "destructive." It was a stigma that would last, to the detriment of his next big play, the Río Cóndor project in Tierra del Fuego.

Syre did not choose the southern tip of Chile by accident. He wanted to do more in timber, and the prospects around him were grim. Apart from the buzz his own projects had caused, by the 1990s the Pacific Northwest was embroiled in controversy over its remaining forest stands. Denuded slopes were choking off salmon streams all the way inland to Idaho, and the coastal forests were so depleted that deep woods species like the spotted owl and the marbled murrelet were being pushed to extinction. More to the point of a farsighted businessman, the good timber was gone, logged out for decades in a spree led by the below-cost sales of the U.S. Forest Service.

Syre considered Canada, but with most forests north of the border in government hands it seemed a risky investment. He looked into New Zealand, but discovered that other companies had beaten him to the punch. His plans to enter Russia's vast storehouse of timber crashed when his business contact there was assassinated and found stuffed in the trunk of a car. By comparison, Chile was a piece of cake. There was nobody else of consequence there, a stable military regime only beginning to cede real power, and an unusual forest product. The primary tree of Tierra del Fuego was the lenga, which, with a hard red core turning white toward the bark, had high-end potential for furniture and interior carpentry.

It was to be done the right way. To Syre himself, and to many whom he recruited, he was green at heart and had an ambitiously green project in mind for Tierra del Fuego. They would showcase the world's largest venture in sustainable forestry. Syre would only cut the amount of lenga that could regenerate on the island, a perpetual source of trees and revenue. He would even help the regrowth along by tree thinning, and by growing seedlings in nurseries. He would reduce the knots in the trunks by trimming off their limbs, making the lumber more marketable. In the words of his operations manager in Chile, which could be the words of a forest manager anywhere in the world, the uncut trees of Tierra del Fuego were "over mature." They were too old; they had stopped growing; they might as well be dead. Syre saw his team as coming to the rescue:

We thought over time, we would improve the environment for all the different species of people and birds and animals that depend on it. Now it's just sort of decadent and about as much lives as dies each year—is [*sic*] pretty much in balance and you'd have a much wider variety of habitat because you would have different kinds of growth taking place.

Syre and company were not just improving Tierra del Fuego with a new port, a sawmill, a wood drying plant, an energy plant, an airport, and twelve hundred miles of forest roads. They were improving Mother Nature.

There were two problems with Syre's approach. The first was that nobody in the vast array of technicians at Syre's disposal, including those in the Chilean government, knew anything about the lenga forests of Tierra del Fuego, much less how to regenerate them. The second was political. Syre's team was stepping into a country that was in much greater flux than they, even with the Chilean experts on his payroll and in the government itself, had reason to believe.

AT FIRST blush, Chile in the early 1990s looked like the ideal place for a US investor, and that was no accident. For the past seventeen years it had been under the thumb of General Augusto Pinochet, a dictator with a strong penchant for free market economics. The best of both worlds, some might say. Granted, Pinochet had ousted a democratically elected president, Salvador Allende, but his coup was backed strongly by the US government, which indeed had a hand in it, and by the time David Syre came along it seemed a distant memory, if a memory at all. Chilean authors since have described a sort of collective amnesia that settled on Santiago that ignored the dictatorship and took the profits in return. One could not blame Syre for treating it the same way.

Chile's profits came largely from selling its natural resources. Some three thousand miles long and less than three hundred miles across at its widest point, Chile formed a "dagger pointed straight at the heart of Antarctica" (as Henry Kissinger had derisively called it). Its primary resources were minerals in the north and trees to the south. Chile had taken a brief run at nitrates, mining islands of guano until the dung ran out, and had been exploiting copper, its number one export, for some time. The trees were a new opportunity. Most of the world's timber came from northern climes with large, uniform stands of trees, few in species and seemingly endless in number. With the world construction boom that followed the Second World War, suppliers began to look below the equator, but the view was disappointing. They saw large stands, to be sure, but with a bewildering diversity of trees that made them difficult to market. The answer was to take them all down and replace them with fast-growing, northern species—soft pine, for example. Thus came a surge of pine plantations to South America and to Chile in particular. Before long, almost half of its original forest inventory had been replaced by two foreign tree types, eucalyptus and radiata pine.

The Pinochet government saw nothing but dollar signs. It sold forestlands to foreign corporations at pennies on the acre. It eliminated the cap on foreign investments, waived their taxes for fifty years, paid three-quarters of the costs of developing pine plantations, and lifted a ban on exporting raw forest products. Most of the trees were cut into chips for the pulp industry, which boomed, and mountains of chips were soon lining the Chilean coast awaiting shipment abroad. Raw wood became the country's number two export—in the words of the government forest agency, the "new copper." It might seem anomalous that a government so ostensibly committed to markets without government intervention that its financial managers were dubbed "the Chicago Boys," would also commit itself to lucrative subsidies aimed at sacking its natural resources to be sold abroad. One difficulty with subsidies on this scale, of course, is that they do not allow the market to weed out marginal ventures, as was about to be seen in Tierra del Fuego.

In 1993, David Syre was once again at the right place at the right time for a deal. He bought forests for his Río Cóndor project at prices ranging from $5 to $50 an acre, when surrounding lands were selling for ten times that amount. He got his price largely because prior owners had gotten an even better one from the government, said to be in the order of $1.50 an acre. In 1991, a company called Magallánica Industrial had aimed to grind some 250,000 acres of lenga forest into wood chips and sell them to Japan. It might have succeeded had the company lent the slightest attention to environmental impacts and paid its workers on time. Instead, within a period of less than two years, the Chilean forest ministry, overstretched and underfunded as it was, managed to fine Magallánica fourteen times for violations of its none-too-stringent management plan. Magallánica stopped paying its employees altogether. When it ended production and pulled out of Punta Arenas, it left behind a mountain of wood chips that ignited into a "massive, slow-burning fire." Magallánica sold to a Canadian company, Cetec-Sel, which also had a mind to clear-cut the forests and market the chips. When Cetec-Sel ran into money problems and permit delays, it was ready for Syre to drive up from Seattle and take the project off its hands.

Syre was coming with something different. He thought cutting up such fine wood for chips and pulp was barbaric, "like using old-growth fir to make tissue paper." He put down $30 million for the initial purchase and went out to raise funds for the rest. He could afford the payment. A Chilean economist later calculated that his government would be paying Syre two dollars in subsidies for every dollar he invested. Syre called the project Río Cóndor, but it would be forever known by the name of his Seattle corporation, the majority owner in the venture, Trillium Ltd. By the time Syre was done, his expenses would triple—before a single tree was sold.

WHILE ALL appeared calm on the surface, Chile was a nation in transition. Indeed, like many Latin American countries, transition seemed to be the normal order of things. In less than two hundred years it had seen four civil wars and ten military coups. These upheavals revealed the struggle, common to the entire continent, between a ruling oligarchy and almost everyone else. There were not all that many large landowners, bishops, and generals in Chile, but they presided over the banks, the Sunday masses, and the heavy weapons to the extent that even the occasionally elected governments were safely under their control. When a civilian president showed signs of leaving that box, as one did in 1924, and as Allende did again in 1970, the Chilean military, backed by the church and the nation's wealth, stepped in and took over. In Allende's case the air force strafed and then bombed his office; they later said he committed suicide. Meanwhile, the root problems of social services, and distribution of resources remained unsolved. Even today, following three decades of prosperity that Chileans call their economic miracle, the country has one of the most disproportionate stratifications of wealth in the world. It also spends the second-highest amount of money on military defense in South America after Brazil, a country five times its size. The national coat of arms bears the legend, "por la razón o la fuerza."

For the seventeen years following the Pinochet coup it had been pretty much la fuerza. The economy improved. Civic democracy went on ice. The mass killings and disappearances abated early on, but citizens continued to disappear without explanation and never appeared again. Union activity was on a very short leash. Social organizations were explicitly apolitical. When, finally, under strong international pressure, Pinochet agreed to national elections, he lost and in 1989 was replaced by a new president. So began a slow transition, during which Pinochet remained a member for life of the Chilean Senate and his former subordinates in firm control of the military, from whence he came. His presence, and the threat of his return, remained.

Nevertheless, at the time Trillium came to Chile, civil society was in an uncertain thaw. The first new shoots of opposition and free speech were beginning to appear, along with a brand new phenomenon that relied principally on both opposition and free speech: environmentalism. These indications were not front page and were easy to overlook, but through long-suppressed civic organizations, a few legislators, and even courts of law, environmentalists were ready to test the air. Even had he seen all this, David Syre would probably not have been concerned about its impact on the Río Cóndor project. The Chilean government seemed to have environmental issues under its thumb.

Indeed, Chile's response to environmental concerns was extremely cautious. It believed in the free market, it believed in its economic miracle, it was finally struggling back to a government approximating democracy, and it was not about to let anything rock the boat. While the Pinochet government paid lip service to the rising phenomenon of environmentalism and tasked a committee to develop a system for impact review, years went by and no such system appeared. Finally, in 1993, transitional President Aylwin issued an executive order directing impact assessments for all public works. Review of private projects such as Trillium's Río Cóndor, however, remained optional.

The following year the legislature placed environmental review in the hands of a new czar, the National Commission on the Environment (CONAMA). On one level, the Commission looked like a powerhouse, with a veto over any project on environmental grounds. Looking more closely, however, it had the power only to make recommendations to a council of government ministers, that is to say to the very agencies proposing the projects under review. It was not, further, an independent body, but instead reported to the secretary of state, in effect the White House, which imposed yet more political pressure on the decision. This kind of pressure induces paralysis, which is what happened. CONAMA's first statutory duty was to develop the regulations for impact review. Years went by. They didn't happen. Into the vacuum stepped Trillium's Río Cóndor project. The only requirements around were President Aylwin's order, and because the project was private they did not apply to Trillium at all.

This is where David Syre, depending on who is telling the story, made his grandest gesture or his fatal mistake. He voluntarily submitted his project for environmental review. Enter the problems of the lenga forest.

SYRE'S DECISION to submit an environmental impact statement seemed risk free at the time, and would demonstrate his bona fides to the Chilean authorities. Sustained yield had become the catchphrase for forestry in America and, after all, trees are trees—you cut them, they grow back. Here in Tierra del Fuego it would be no different. Indeed, according to Syre's project managers it would be easier, because there was basically just one kind of tree. In order to sustain the ecosystem, all that was needed was to grow that one tree back. A "naturally occurring monoculture," in the words of a Trillium land steward, was "much simpler" to maintain than other forests, "like a farm where you are growing wheat." How hard could that be?

With this understanding, the Syre team set out to create a model for the sustained harvest of the lenga of Tierra del Fuego. He would not clear-cut them, as his predecessors had intended, and as he had done back home. Instead he would cut some of them, weed them out, leaving other adults standing to "shelter" new trees growing up. He called the process "shelterwood" cutting, a name implying comfort and protection, and his accompanying diagrams showed, first, an original stand of trees, then a few trees on a cut-over landscape, and then, happily, these same adult trees surrounded by smaller ones, pushing up around them like children on a playground. Syre had confidence in his experts and his models. He hired a prestigious consulting firm, Dames and Moore, to prepare the impact statement. He had nothing to hide. To the contrary, he wanted to show the world.

Tierra del Fuego, however, was a different place, vastly different from anywhere that Syre and his experts had ever worked before. No one had ever tried sustainable forestry in an environment this hostile and this precarious for all life, including trees. It wasn't just the climate, which was cold almost all the time, frozen much of the time, and subject to ferocious winds and storms that could break apart a passing ship in minutes, to say nothing of lone trees on the landscape. It was also basically rock. The top soil was wafer thin, an inch or two in places, anchored only by the roots of the very plants Trillium was intending to remove. It was, in the words of a Chilean scientist, "young soil"; indeed he said it was a "miracle" to have stands of trees on this type of soil at all. Further, most of the nutrients of the forest were in the bodies of the trees themselves, not on the ground, so when you thinned the stands—and Trillium was proposing to take out 60 percent of the trees in its first cut—you also removed the food source for what would regrow. The nutrient cycle was "very, very slow." Worse still, once these stands were cut open to the winds and rains, they would be open to erosion as well, and there wasn't that much soil to erode before you were back to bare rock. The very thickness of the natural stands, which grew so closely together they literally linked branches at the top, was also their only defense to the gales that blew across Tierra del Fuego like the wrath of God. To some scientists, even shelterwood cutting was a highly problematic operation.

They were not alone. Though the local reaction to Río Cóndor was initially positive, if guarded, it would soon turn sour. To begin, the locals had been badly burned before by the Magallánica project and others like it. Foreign companies had come in with big promises, stripped the land, short-changed the locals, and left them with burning piles of waste. A community leader in the town of Porvenir spoke for many: "In the beginning, I was really hopeful . . . because . . . the project they were bringing in was marvelous [*sic*]," with developments such as new schools, drying sheds, even a deep new port. The logging would be "moderate," and they would even "bring in plants" to regrow, so hopes were high.

Then came the bad news. The deep port fell out of the plan; it would not be necessary. The local mills dropped out next; it would be easier to buy an existing mill to the north. It all began to smell like bait-and-switch. Rumors also started circulating that this might not be so moderate a cut after all. A forest with trees dating back to the time of Joan of Arc would be reduced to trees half their size and perhaps a decade old, laced with forty miles of new forest roads each year, more than a thousand miles in all. The same previously enthusiastic community leader later reflected, "so hopes were high of proposals that came crashing down, and we started seeing that it wasn't like it had been promised." Once the plan was "analyzed better," she said, was when "the tough battle started."

They, too, were not alone. To a fledgling environmental community stretching its wings after the long period of Pinochet, this was the latest in a two-decade string of insults ranging from uncontrolled mining, toxic copper smelters, and the nationwide fire-sale on native forests. Here was a priceless and irreplaceable ecosystem, a "cold jungle" at the bottom of the world, about to go on the block to yet another foreign corporation for short-term profits that would largely go abroad, leaving Chile holding the bag. They connected with the skepticism of the few scientists and locals willing to express their reservations. Slowly they began a campaign.

ɔ

THE SYRE team submitted its environmental report in 1995, and all still appeared well. Based on its own reviews, COREMA, the regional branch of CONAMA, approved the project on the understanding that Trillium would later prepare a "sustainable management plan" and commit to only a "selective harvest" of the lenga forest. Further, the company offered to set aside a quarter of its purchase—largely the quarter without the trees—as a biological preserve and reference point for future management decisions. The conditions were all very rational and acceptable to Trillium. It had never intended clear-cutting, it maintained.

The problem surfaced with the report of COREMA's technical committee, which had some very different things to say. Composed of scientists from several Chilean agencies, the committee dedicated the first six pages of its report to "positive environmental aspects" of the project. The next eighteen pages were pure criticism. There was no inventory of the forest, which would form the basis for any intelligent evaluation or plan. There were no data on tree growth, rates, or cycles in the area; the data provided came from very different environments. Nor were there data on "extraction impacts," and the inevitable pull toward more harvesting created by a machine whose profitability depended on harvesting, once the machine was in place. On this basis, the technical committee recommended against the project. Instead, COREMA overrode its experts and approved the plan.

Two things followed. The first was that CONAMA, in turn, approved the project, subject to several monitoring conditions that were to be made more specific in the future. Everything was going according to form. The second was that environmentalists went to court to enjoin the approvals. They filed suit against the COREMA approval when it first came down, and then they filed against the CONAMA approval. This was not according to form. It was new.

The heart of both lawsuits was that the Chilean agencies were giving away a national treasure based on conditions that seemed unenforceable and, further, unlikely to work. The difficulty with these claims is that agencies make unwise and politically twisted decisions every day of their lives. Nothing in law required COREMA or CONAMA to be intelligent or, in the end, environmental. Indeed, these agencies had been established the way they were precisely in order to keep politics at the helm. Accordingly, as might be expected, both lawsuits were rejected by the lower courts. The environmentalists, led by two members of the "green bench" in the Chilean legislature, took their appeal to the Constitutional Chamber of the Supreme Court, where the two cases were consolidated for hearing. It was their last roll of the dice.

They were rolling at a propitious time in history, and one of the few unlucky times for David Syre. Environmentalism was moving from soft to hard, from the field of science to law. In the United States, *Storm King* and other cases were based on statutory commands. The jump-start in many other countries of the world was their constitutions, and thereby hangs a tale.

Back in 1972, after Rachael Carson and Jacques Cousteau had shocked the world with their disclosures of a threatened planet, national governments convened in Stockholm for a summit on this new phenomenon, environmental protection. As with many summits of this nature, the participants did not really foresee making commitments, but it seemed necessary to offer the gesture. A group of activists, however, were led by Cousteau, who had quit the French delegation to play a more aggressive role. They held a countersummit with their own agenda, paralleling the official one, but treating each issue the day before it would be taken up by the official event. Quickly seized on by the press, their resolutions became, in effect, the agenda to which the government delegations had to respond. One of their more dramatic resolutions was a declaration of a right to a healthy environment. Who could oppose that? Who even knew what it meant? And so, emerging from Stockholm was an official declaration that nations should establish a constitutional right to a clean environment. Most delegations in attendance went home, did just that, and no more. Of all the resolutions adopted, this one seemed the most innocuous.

The notion of a constitutional environmental right, once stated, lay dormant for years. It might have remained so in Latin America but for a second constitutional right, a procedure really, that would propel it forward. The process is variously called an action of amparo or tutela, and it works like a habeas corpus. One story goes that a Spanish judge was dining on the veranda one day when a group of soldiers came down the street, kicking and propelling a prisoner ahead of them. The prisoner called out, "protect me!" ("amparo!"), at which point the judge ordered the soldiers to stop and held a hearing on the matter, and the prisoner was freed. Whatever the true origins, Spanish and Latin American jurisprudence has long afforded special adjudication for constitutional rights. In these cases a plaintiff may go directly to a judge, bypassing the labyrinth and delays of civil practice. All of which would be academic, but for the fact that enterprising lawyers dug up the forgotten environmental rights in their constitutions and began seeking direct review for violations of their "right to a clean environment," whatever that might mean. Trillium would be the first case in Chile to say.

✍

THE CHILEAN SUPREME Court found that it meant a great deal. The decision was close—three votes to two—but it reached a remarkable conclusion by equally remarkable reasoning. Chilean law provided amparo relief for government actions that were illegal and arbitrary. CONAMA's approval did not seem illegal—after all, CONAMA was authorized by statute to make exactly the kind of decision it made—but to the finely trained judicial eye the approval was caught in a sort of catch-22. Chilean law required impact reviews on the basis of CONAMA regulations, but, of course, CONAMA had never issued these regulations, ergo no review based on them took place, so the review that did take place was unlawful. The fact that Trillium submitted its own review voluntarily and in accordance with President Aylwin's directive did not save the day. The Syre team could be forgiven if they thought themselves adrift in something of a wonderland at this point. If the Supreme Court was correct here, no action affecting the environment in Chile was lawful because there were no CONAMA regulations. Meanwhile, Trillium, who had tried to cooperate, was the one in the trap.

The Court's more difficult question was whether the CONAMA approval was "arbitrary." Here the opinion split, but the majority sided with the COREMA technical committee jot for jot. Identifying the expert agencies on the committee by name—Forestry, Fisheries, Livestock and Agriculture, Water, Public Health—they found the criticisms to be significant and the government's assurance that their problems would be fixed later to be unsatisfactory. Particularly so when the committee had gone on to recommend that the project be denied. Furthermore, the majority said, the Chilean constitution guaranteed a right to environmental protection, which required "the maintenance of the original condition of natural resources," reduced only by "a minimum of human intrusion." The Court here was requiring more than a process for impact review. It was requiring an environmental result that, in the Court's view, CONAMA must be "vigilant" to secure. In the face of so much contrary expertise, CONAMA's approval failed the test.

The center ring of the Trillium opinion, however, was the question of whether the plaintiffs had the right to be in court at all. Those who were residents of Tierra del Fuego had shown no special injury to themselves. As for the environmental plaintiffs, they lived more than a thousand miles away in Santiago. Few of them had ever even been to Tierra del Fuego. Who in the world were they to complain? Basically, said the dissent, theirs were only "diffuse" interests, common to all, part of living in modern society and no excuse for opening the courthouse door. The majority, on the other hand, found that everyone had constitutional rights to a clean environment, so everyone could vindicate them, including those in Tierra del Fuego and those in Santiago, half a world away. Trillium was not the only interest in trouble here. Whatever CONAMA approved anywhere in the country from now on could be challenged by members of the general public on environmental grounds. The opinion had detonated a bomb.

THE EXPLOSION made waves. The first was to spring loose CONAMA's impact regulations, which had been stalled for seven years. The decision had flipped the default position. Up to here government and industry could go forward with their projects without bothering about regulations that, among other things, would bring nosey environmentalists into their business. Following the ruling, the same government and industry had to get the regulations out in order to move their projects forward. The effect was magic.

The opinion also galvanized Syre into a new round of defense. He assembled a dream team of US forestry experts, including critics of timber practices in the Pacific Northwest. It hired the opposing lawyer from its Bellingham shopping center imbroglio to be a project watchdog. It hired a turnaround expert from the Plum Creek Timber Company, which had its own checkered history in forest management, to handle public relations. It arranged endorsements from the field of biodiversity and ecosystem management, scientists whose names and publications drew crowds. It lined up the approval of several well-known international conservation organizations, including The Nature Conservancy, who supported sustainable forestry as a way to offset a pandemic of clear-cutting around the globe. Even Greenpeace, known for its hard-nosed brand of environmentalism, was cautious toward the Río Cóndor project at first, favoring an approach more conditional than oppositional. Still confident of success, Syre's troops would redo the impact assessment posthaste and resubmit it. Syre remained committed to making Río Cóndor a world model of sustainable forestry.

The Trillium decision, however, had one more impact. It gave Chilean environmentalists a jolt of adrenaline that would carry them forward for years. They would need it, because the court victory proved only temporary, and the fight ahead was going to be long, expensive, and straight uphill. They did an unprecedented thing in a country so fractious and new to the game as Chile. They agreed to set aside their competition for press and funding to form a national network of over 150 organizations, scientists, local activists, ecotour guides, and companion groups in the United States, Canada, Argentina, Australia, even Russia. At this point the environmentalists didn't just want a better project, they wanted no project. In fact, they were shooting yet higher. They wanted to create a reserve for cold-climate forests starting in Tierra del Fuego and extending around the world. They even had a name for it, worthy of some of the names conjured up by David Syre. They called it the Gondwanaland Project, a Lord of the Rings–sounding amalgam of the regions involved.

Within months, Trillium was back with a new plan and a new assessment. Burned the year before by the Supreme Court and the attendant press, CONAMA did its homework this time. It assembled its own blue-ribbon team to scrub the project. That the Commission would ultimately approve Río Cóndor was foreordained. It remained after all a political body. But its staff imposed, and the Commission approved, no fewer than one hundred conditions on the project that were to prove onerous indeed. Trillium's annual cut of timber was severely trimmed. Restoration benchmarks had to be met at each step before additional logging continued. Most innovatively, Trillium would post an "ecological insurance" bond to assure the performance of all of its obligations. The performance bond requirement in particular stuck in Trillium's craw, so much so that the company filed suit against CONAMA for exceeding its authority. A challenge such as this, however, went against the grain of David Syre's public persona. He was guaranteeing a sustainable project. So why wouldn't he be willing to back that up?

The environmentalists appealed CONAMA's approval again to the Supreme Court, but they lost this time, five votes to zero. The agency had crossed its t's and dotted its i's. The Court would not gainsay it again. But the time between these two decisions was a precious win for the environmental opponents of Río Cóndor, and increasingly costly to David Syre. There were information problems ahead, a drumbeat of bad press, and looming money problems. At some point, the project might not be worth the candle.

$\mathcal{D}$

DAVID SYRE now had the green light and an economic challenge. The more environmental he made the project appear, the less profitable it became. The lands he agreed to set aside would now included some important lenga forest, and every reserved hectare of trees was board feet that would never reach the mill. To Chilean environmentalists, the numbers just didn't add up. "We saw that they had a very huge industrial [project] to use the wood . . . the kinds of saws, the saw mill, the plants," one commented, "but when you look at the forest . . . it is impossible to get all this kind of material to feed the industry." A professor of forestry at the University of Chile concluded that Trillium could harvest one thousand hectares a year, maximum. Trillium was counting on nearly three thousand hectares. One fear was that Trillium would get the permit and then sell it to another timber company. "They could disappear; declare bankruptcy or things like that." It had happened before with Magallánica and Cetec-Sel.

Trillium countered that its nurseries and management practices would increase rates of growth but, internally, it knew it had a problem. The method might not work. Trillium's chief forester later commented that they "could probably have a very viable sustainable forest operation with probably 25% of the property"—a considerable reduction in ambition—but even that would require "group selection" rather than the shelterwood model. By group selection he meant cutting in wide patches, all of the trees, clear-cuts. One could imagine the reception such a proposal might receive. It never became the new model, even while the old one bogged down.

Months following the second Supreme Court decision, Trillium announced a first cut of lenga trees. It started bulldozing roads and powered up the saws. Then it stopped. The Chilean Forestry Commission was giving it fits over the permit conditions, and when the company submitted its revised plan and $70,000 in fees they were rejected as inadequate. Suddenly, in the fall of 1998, Trillium announced that it was putting Río Cóndor on hold, laying off all but three of its Chilean employees, and moving across the border to Argentina to focus on a project there, called Lenga Patagonia. Its head of forestry operations stated that there would be nothing Chile could do to get the company back for the moment "except maybe give us a clean [assessment] and say forget all these conditions . . . all this crap." The Trillium locker room was not a happy place.

Meanwhile, the environmental opposition was flourishing. Local and national critics of Río Cóndor had grown so strong that they drowned out the efforts of other groups to find a compromise. Adriana Hoffman, a former director of CONAMA then heading the Defenders of the Chilean Forest, made common ground with Pat Rasmussen of the America Lands Alliance, and together they began to take the message to Trillium's home turf, Seattle and Bellingham. They returned to Chile with photographs of Trillium's operation on Whidbey Island. Trillium's modus operandi, they said, was "clear-cut, build roads and spray herbicides." They also turned up the choice bit of information that Trillium's public relations man had been ousted from another timber empire, Louisiana-Pacific, which had been indicted on fifty-six counts of misconduct by the US Department of Justice for pollution violations. It was also under investigation for the sale of house sidings that, despite its representations, "began crumbling and sprouting mushrooms."

Back in Chile, grassroots activists took to the streets, with imagination. In June 1998, on the International Day of the Environment, they staged a play in pantomime in which an actor representing President Frei took a chainsaw, rented from a local hardware store, from another player representing Trillium. The rain was pouring down at the time, and there was no one watching, save a few members of the press, when two hundred Chilean police officers, four to a demonstrator, suddenly appeared and carted them off to jail. That was not good press for the company. On another occasion, following CONAMA's second approval of the project, a small group of protesters showed up at its headquarters and took off their pants, telling all who would listen that the agency lacked the "cojones" to turn the project down. Reportedly, CONAMA employees in sympathy with the protestors were "laughing their heads off." The beat went on. A US campaigner on forest issues who went to Chile to join the action later commented, "I came down here and there is a handful, and I know them, a handful of people with no experience who stood up against a 500,000 acre logging plan that would have sailed through in any other country and they stop it, postpone it, postpone it, postpone it, stab it, jam it, jam it, tilt it, knocking it off balance, but never really hitting a good frontal blow. . . . I couldn't believe it, it's unbelievable."

At the same time, Hoffman, Rasmussen et al. were shaping an offer for David Syre. He could sell his holdings for an international park of the "most unique forests in the Southern Hemisphere." They started an Adopt-a-Tree-in-Tierra-del-Fuego campaign in Bellingham and eastern Washington. For his part, Syre's public comments remained bullish on Río Cóndor. In 1999, he was talking about using the Cóndor forests as a carbon sink and selling the credits to carbon-emitting industries. In a 2002 speaking event hosted by Yale University, entitled Sustainable Development, Can It Work? An Entrepreneur's Experience in Tierra del Fuego, he advised, "Always have a great sense of hope because you will finally prevail."

Then the money ran out. Projects the size of Río Cóndor are not financed out of the pockets of their proponents but are leveraged on loans, and when they run into delays and difficulties, more loans. In 2000, Trillium, already in hock over this and other ventures, borrowed $56 million at a "hefty" interest rate of prime plus 5 percent. When the lender, in turn, crashed from assorted financial and criminal difficulties, it was bought out by one of the largest investment banks in America, Goldman Sachs. At that point, Trillium owed $30 million on its Río Cóndor project alone. It handed over the property to quit the debt. A silk-stocking Wall Street investment firm now owned the lenga forests at the bottom of the world. What on Earth could they do with it? "We work with money, not trees and animals," said a company officer. Hoffman and Rasmussen had an idea for them.

The idea took hold. Goldman handed the Trillium portfolio over to the company's charitable trust, and the trust, in turn, to the Wildlife Conservation Society, an international organization with a track record for managing wildlands in South America. Goldman also put $6.6 million onto the table to cover the costs of running the reserve for the first three years and offered to match another $6 million raised by the Society. Not just Goldman the bank, either. A considerable piece of these monies was contributed by its employees who were said to have "taken the project to heart." Some monies were in all likelihood contributed by Henry Paulson, CEO of Goldman at the time and an ardent conservationist. The decisions were made "at the highest levels in the company," it was said.

What followed was a love-in. A Goldman spokesman called it "a gift to the people of Chile." The office of the Chilean president said it was "a very interesting project, very good, because it creates a protected area in a zone that is very fragile ecologically." Adriana Hoffman called it "unbelievable." Pat Rasmussen added that it was "exactly what she and her allies were looking for." Even Trillium came on board. According to their managing director, this was what the company had wanted all along. The new reserve was "not all that different" from the Río Cóndor project; "it was always our intention to put about 70 percent of the land into conservation zones," he said.

THE AFTERSHOCKS of the Trillium case continued to rumble for years. Its momentum carried the newly fledged environmental community to places it had only dreamed of on paper, and had no realistic hope of achieving. One was the Gondwana Forest Sanctuary, first conceived of as an alternative to the Río Cóndor project, more aspiration than plan. Then, in 1998, as Trillium was showing the first cracks in its armor, an environmental foundation bought up lenga forests between the Río Cóndor project and the Argentinean border, next to an Argentine park, blocking any timber expansion in that direction. This purchase set the stage for a joint dedication, by Chile and Argentina, of a 4.6 million hectare cross-border nature reserve to be jointly managed, with core zones of absolute protection, surrounded by rings of limited agriculture and tourist development. Joint management by Chile and Argentina, mortal antagonists, who would have imagined such a thing? Meanwhile, Chilean environmentalists were advancing the Gondwanaland network of "frozen forests" to Tasmania and New Zealand. Riding the tide, anything seemed achievable.

Then, yet another gift fell from the sky, only Chile nearly rejected it. In the early 1990s, an American billionaire named Douglas Tompkins was quietly buying a twelve hundred square mile stretch of forest for a conservation park to the north of Río Cóndor. Tomkins had made his money in outdoor gear, the Esprit and North Face clothing lines, and was deeply green. His park would be supported by ecotourism and other light-impact uses. Other North Americans had made small conservation purchases in Chile but this property ran in a narrow swath from the Pacific Ocean clear to the Argentinean border. A coalition of the Chilean military, church leaders, and private landowners—the Big Three of Chilean history—came out against the purchase on familiar-looking grounds: Tomkins was in reality trying to establish a Jewish state and was presenting a threat to national security. That Tompkins was a foreign owner only helped the case against him. The press picked up the cry, painting the proposal in dark colors. Of course, the fact that David Syre and Trillium were also foreign owners did not appear to bother them. Trillium was going to make money the old-fashioned way. Tompkins was going to do something new, and green, and they were simply not ready to go there.

The Trillium outcome changed the Chilean mind. It was legitimate to be green and to make money, less money to be sure, but more sustainable money over time. Tompkins won approval and his lands are now the Pumalín Park. They inspired a Chilean businessman, Sebastián Piñera, to buy nearly one thousand square miles of forest for a nature preserve on Chiloé Island, also just north of Tierra del Fuego. Better yet, he would invest another $20 million to cover its operations, boosted by anticipated revenues from tourism. Chilean suspicions, however, remained. Private parks were beginning to drive the conservation agenda of the country. On the other hand, the Chilean forest ministry had to manage areas fifty times the size of Chiloé Island on an annual budget of $5 million, total. The numbers did not match the job. It was no accident that Goldman Sachs, looking to put its Río Cóndor property into long-term care, chose an international conservation organization. No accident, but insulting all the same.

The impact of the Trillium case on Chilean environmental policy is more ambiguous. CONAMA, the official protector of the environment, remains a heavily conflicted organization. The first Supreme Court decision was such a shock that CONAMA's director was sacked. Her replacement was compliant. He spoke of "balance," which is the standard code of agencies that do not make environmental protection a priority, and added, as if reassuring his superiors that the agency would remain their servant, "[w]e are, in fact, part of the government." He continued by explaining, "I think it would be strange if we were not close to the government on development issues." Strange or not—after all, legislatures routinely task government agencies with duties such as the protection of public health that are not supposed to be carried out on the basis of politics— Chile's lead environmental agency remains on a short leash, more advisory than decisional, and under the watchful eye of a government dedicated to commerce first and to the rest where it doesn't get in the way.

The Chilean legal system has also retreated from the opportunities offered by the Trillium opinion. The right to sue by citizens remains, as does the Court's ratification of the importance of environmental protection. On the other hand, few injunctions against government decisions, however misguided, have followed. According to a CONAMA attorney now in private practice, the courts have taken an increasingly narrow view of the Trillium principles, reducing judicial review to the question of whether permitting agencies filled out the proper forms. The constitutional right to protect the environment—the basis of the first Supreme Court opinion—has been lost in the interminable hallways of administrative law. One has the impression that it will be a hot day in Tierra del Fuego before the Chilean judiciary goes this way again. This said, the decision produced one ineludible effect. An intact, virgin, and very unusual forest park at the southern tip of the world.

THE QUESTION remains: What, in the context of the Río Cóndor project, does sustainable development mean? To the Trillium team, the option was to develop wisely or to watch the area succumb to a series of fly-by-night operations. They saw their task as a technological one, to offer an alternative to people who would otherwise take the trees to the ground. In Syre's view, the environmentalists were frustrated precisely because, whatever their objections, "[Trillium] had answers." As his chief forestry consultant put it, their opponents didn't give a damn for sustainable forestry. "[T]he reality was," he said, "they did not want any trees cut. They wanted it all preserved." To the ecological forester, to the sustainable natural resource developer, the absurdity of this position speaks for itself.

Of course, Trillium did not have all the answers. There is serious doubt whether the project really was sustainable over time. The conditions necessary to protect the environment made any logging questionable, and logging on a scale sufficient to pay off US investors was going to run out of trees. Then what? One look at the track record of the sustained yield practices of the US Forest Service shows the relentless pressure of politicians, the timber industry, and local communities to cut a little more. And then a lot more. Or one could look to the sea, where sustained yield has been the golden rule of fisheries management for the past fifty years, during which most fisheries collapsed. In the real world, the concept of sustainability has a very hard time holding the line.

Beyond these practical difficulties, however, there was another force at work here, and the Syre team put its finger on it. They were facing a new kind of environmentalism on the move here, and it was not driven by reason but by a passion for living spaces that defies logical plans for their development. Pat Rasmussen spoke for thousands of people who will never see Tierra del Fuego and could not spell the name of the lenga tree without a dictionary when she said, after it was all over, "[s]ome places are wild and should stay that way." The same impulses won a wilderness system in the United States, after thirteen years of to-the-last-ditch opposition from commodity groups to whom the very idea of leaving nature alone was insane. The same impulses have risen up repeatedly to defeat proposals for opening the Arctic National Wildlife Refuge to oil and gas drilling. There would be only a small amount of drilling on a huge landscape that no more than one protesting environmentalist in ten thousand would ever visit in a lifetime, but for these people, and they are not insane, it is the idea of a wild place that matters. And that is enough.

Reflections

I am the only prosecutor in the state assigned to enforce environmental laws. I try to prevent unlawful clearing of the forest. But nobody wants me to succeed. The people are against me, the politicians are against me, and the courts are against me. I keep trying. I initiate proceedings against violators. My worry, though, is that if I win one of these cases, they will kill me. What should I do?

Statement from a Prosecutor in Amazonia, Brazil, 1987

THERE IS A TIME toward dark when I take my dog down to the edge of the Mississippi River where she hunts for something forbidden and I can walk through the trees. One evening we happened on a group of kids around a fire and, as we were passing, one of them asked, "Aren't you on television"? I said that no I wasn't, but from time to time they might ask me a question. Suddenly the boy said, "I know, you're the Communist!" I stood there at the edge of the light, wondering where that came from, and then it struck me. I asked whether by any chance his father worked in a law firm downtown. The boy looked amazed, as if I'd guessed his birthday. I left the fire ring imagining the outburst that must have taken place in his household when my face appeared on the television screen, saying something about environmental protection. Perhaps *communist* was not even the strongest word used.

And this is in America, before we go abroad.

Yet, environmental law is happening abroad, and it is being driven, as it was in the United States, by an idea so simple and compelling that it can be squelched for a while but not forever. Ordinary citizens can, through legal process, make their governments protect the environment when that may be the last thing their governments want to do. America invented this option and indeed has since built citizen lawsuits into many of its environmental programs, but that does not make them popular. Nor are they welcome in other countries with slender traditions of democracy and judiciaries long joined at the hip to political power. Against this backdrop, environmental cases are prompting a kind of institutional renaissance where courts have seen the natural world collapsing and responded to the bell. They have not decided what should be done, but they are beginning to say what may *not* be done under principles as latently powerful as the "right to a healthy environment."

But is this really the judicial role? No question more dogs environmental law in the United States than this one. Although most judges have answered it affirmatively all the way to the Supreme Court, an unpersuaded rear guard sees citizens' suits as the *Invasion of the Body Snatchers*, a threat to good order. If environmentalists have a problem with lopping the top off of Storm King Mountain, they argue, or sending the Acheloos River to the plains of Thessaly, let them take it to the legislature. That's democracy. Judicial decision making, they contend, is tyranny.

Their argument has two problems. The first is that these same critics of environmental litigation are the first to praise it where private interests are the ones filing suit, say an industry with an unwelcome limit on its discharge permit. In their world, industry can sue to oppose a tough permit but the public cannot sue to oppose a weak one. Their scales of justice tip only in one direction. The second problem is that, in each of the cases we have seen, the democratic process had worked. Every one of the countries in this book had adopted laws and constitutions by popular and representational vote. The only question left was whether the government could ignore them. In saying no, the courts were not short-cutting democracy. They were making sure that it was not a charade.

This said, if we were to conclude from this book that environmental law-suits are easy wins and that courts are moving aggressively to protect the natural world we would be deluding ourselves. Environmental protection remains a very hard road, against odds as steep as the human impulse to make as much money as quickly as possible, deny unpleasant news, and leave others holding the bag. By running against these instincts environmental law makes powerful enemies every day of its life, and few powerful friends. Not many people amass fortunes by treating nature kindly, nor do they get named for a dam or highway they didn't build. All the momentum runs the other way.

What environmental lawsuits do is help balance the scales. Courts of law, to the extent they are impartial, are the one venue beyond routine capture by the money and politics that drive the other two branches of government. Standing in a courtroom, for this brief moment Vera Mishenko and Al Butzel are the equals of the Russian state and the Consolidated Edison company. The decisions they ultimately receive may not be made entirely on the merits; after all, judges are human beings too, but they are more likely to be made on the merits than in other forums. Of course, in many countries the judges are not impartial, including some places in the United States. Several current Supreme Court justices have never voted in favor of an environmental position before them, of any kind, in their recorded lives. You have better odds of winning in Las Vegas. Several of them are particularly affronted by citizen enforcement of environmental laws. In a recent opinion concerning climate change, four of the nine Supreme Court justices denied the right of plaintiffs to be in court at all. The terrible irony here is that America, the birthplace of the environmental rule-of-law, is now within an ace of retreating from it as the rule lights up the rest of the globe.

To this challenge we now add the practical difficulties of bringing environmental lawsuits, in any country. They make no money for the environmental side. They do not seek damages, and there are no contingency fees for winning representation. Nor do plaintiffs like the Northern Cree or residents of the

Acheloos valley have the resources to carry lawsuits like these on their own, which, in several of the cases described in this book, went into their second decade. The defendants, meanwhile, enjoy the services of free government lawyers and private attorneys whose bills are written off like martinis as normal business expenses. From an economic perspective, environmental litigation is suicide. Then comes the difficulty in finding experts who will dare to testify against the government—which may be their employer, or may fund their employer—or against companies that bankroll the research of their field. Entire university departments depend on the chemical, electric power, and pharmaceutical industries; indeed it is an unusual one without corporate sponsors, and so the pool of experts available to environmentalists challenging these interests becomes as unbalanced as the money. When Kermit the Frog observed that it was not easy being green, he surely had environmental litigation in mind.

All the more remarkable, then, what happened. No one orchestrated it. Rather, it has been a convergent evolution, the same kind of approaches evolving from similar, although quite unconnected, precursors. Storm King and Nikko Taro came down within a few years of each other. In retrospect, one of the striking impressions of this book is that virtually any of the judges involved would have decided any of these cases in the same fashion. They saw the world and their duty toward it in a new way. It is not possible to convene them, but it is possible to recognize them: the Honorable John Oaks of Storm King, Kenzo Shiraizi of Nikko Taro, Albert Malhouf and Paul Rouleau of the Great Whale, Hilario Davide of *Minors Oposa*, Kuldip Singh of the Taj Majal, Neena Segeeva of Lenin's Trees, Michael Decleris of Acheloos, and the majority panel in Trillium. And to thank them for the time they have bought us to reclaim the Earth.

Acknowledgments

Where to begin? I think with the people who have educated me the most about their countries, my international students at Tulane University and in schools abroad. I will identify below a handful who worked with me directly on this project, but all of them, whether in the classroom or in casual conversation, contributed an idea, an experience, a piece of the reef. I am certain that, in the aggregate, I have learned more from these students than I have been able to teach them.

I also want to thank several people directly involved in these histories for their information and critiques. I have met only a few of the principal actors in this book but I have corresponded with many, and to a person they were generous with their suggestions and time. To this cadre I want to add academics in other countries, where in some cases I was starting from zero in both the culture and the law.

The stories themselves were written over a period of years, often with research students who graduated and were replaced by others. We worked in teams. For this reason, rather than present them in a single lump, it seems more fitting to identify them by story, and so with enormous gratitude for their assistance, they are:

STORM KING: Courtney Harrington (Tulane Law School Juris Doctor [TLS, JD] '03); Jennifer Marshall (TLS, JD '01); Albert Kahn Butzel, Attorney at Law, New York City; and Robert H. Boyle, Hudson River Fisherman's Association.

NIKKO TARO: Osamu Nagatomo (TLS, Masters of Laws [LLM] '04), Hiroshi Kobayashi (TLS, LLM '05), Professor of Law, University of Nagasaki, whose assistance continued after his return to Japan; Lucas Lavoy (TLS, JD '07), and Professors Tadashi Oksuka, Waseda University School of Law; Toshirio Ochi, Sophia University; and Mineo Kato, Yokahama National University.

MINORS OPOSA: Jennifer Hoekstra (TLS, JD '07), Patricia Syquia (TLS, JD '05), Minging You (TLS, LLM '07), and Antonio A. Oposa Jr., Attorney at Law, Manila.

GREAT WHALE: Christa Fanelli, Cashauna Hill, and Tinnetta Rockquemore; all of the Tulane Law School graduating class of '05; Lena Giangrosso (TLS, JD '07); Ken Brynaert, Canadian Wildlife Federation; Martha Kosuch, Friends of the Oldman River; and Edwin Small Legs, Peikan tribe of the Blackfoot Nation.

TAJ MAHAL: Galia Aharoni (TLS, JD '09); Sara Porsia (TLS, JD '05); Elizabeth Ristroph (TLS, JD '04); Arjyia Majumdar, Attorney at Law, Delhi; and M. C. Mehta, Attorney at Law, Delhi.

LENIN'S TREES: Ilya Fedyaev (TLS, LLM '05); Lois Kim (TLS, JD '07); and Svitlana Kravchenko, University of Oregon School of Law.

ACHELOOS: Sara Cline (TLS, JD '07); Diana Czank (TLS, JD '09); Alexander Markopoulos (TLS, JD '08); Dr. Michael Decleris, former member, Council of State, Athens; and Dr. Glykeria Sioutis, Professor of Law, University of Athens.

TRILLIUM: Dana Steinberg (TLS, JD '07); Matthew Finklestein (TLS, JD '09); Felipe Leiva (TLS, LLM '05), whose assistance continued after his return to practice in Santiago; Dr. Jorge Varela, Environmental Consultant, Santiago; and Javier Vergara, Attorney at Law, Santiago.

Lastly, I would like to recognize the art of Richard Campanella of Tulane University, an historian and geographer in his own right, whose careful maps guide us through these stories. Likewise, I am also grateful to the Colorado Law

Review, Georgetown International Environmental Journal, Boston College International and Comparative Law Review, Tulsa Law Review, and University of Hawaii Law Review for their editing on previous versions of this work and their permission to rewrite, edit, and publish this book.

In the end, and recognizing that I could not have written this book without the generous contributions of so many individuals, writing remains a solitary endeavor, and whatever faults are found here, and whatever offense I may have given by omission, description, or point of view, are my responsibility entirely.

Oliver A. Houck
March 2009
New Orleans, Louisiana

Notes

Introduction

1   *In no other.* Tom Turner, *The Legal Eagles*, THE AMICUS J., Winter 1988, at 25, 27 (quoting David Sive). Mr. Sive, professor of law emeritus at Pace University, was a founding father of American environmental law.

Chapter 1 Storm King

8   *grander and more.* John Cronin and Robert F. Kennedy Jr., THE RIVERKEEPERS, at 21.

8   *the shadow of.* Francis F. Dunwell, THE HUDSON RIVER HIGHLANDS, at 52.

9   *exhale . . . sweetest odors*. Robert H. Boyle, The Hudson River: A Natural and Unnatural History, at 34.

9   *such a sweet.* Boyle.

9   *Frederick Law Olmsted.* Central Park, Dunwell, at 142, Olmsted's later design of the 1890 Chicago Exposition is well told in Erik Larson's THE DEVIL AND THE WHITE CITY.

9   *THE CORNWALL HYDROELECTRIC.* "Con Edison's Proposed Hydroelectric Project, Cornwall, New York," brochure, reprinted in Dunwell, at 203.

9   *THE CON ED.* Natural Resources Defense Council, E-law: What Started it All?, at http://www.nrdc.org/legislation/helaw.asp (last modified May 5, 2000).

9   *Proud to provide.* Allan R. Talbot, POWER ALONG THE HUDSON.

10 *To Con Ed's.* Talbot, at 73. "From the perspective of an engineer, the Hudson Highlands are custom made for pumped storage."

10 *We're dealing with . . . that.* Boyle, at 99, describing a conversation with officials of the US Army Corps of Engineers.

10 *Dig We Must.* Boyle, at 157.

10 *Dig They Must.* Id.

10 *the company everyone.* Boyle, at 156.

10 *misinformed bird watchers.* Id.

10 *buzzards and vultures.* Id.

11 *His problem was.* Talbot, at 96–97.

11 *It is a.* Dunwell at 215; Boyle at 22, 38–40; Talbot, at 112.

11 *What was different.* Dunwell, at xi.

12 *famine they do.* Id.

12 *The Indians caught.* Id., at 42.

12 *their women lascivious.* Id., at 38–39.

12 *who look for.* Id.

12 *The striped bass.* Cronin and Kennedy Jr., at 24–25.

12 *New York Harbor.* Writing in 1944, one author observed: "The bulk of the water in New York Harbor is oily, dirty, and germy. Men on the mud suckers, the big harbor dredges, like to say that you could bottle it and sell it for poison. The bottom of the harbor is dirtier than the water. In most places, it is covered with a blanket of sludge that is composed of silt, sewage, industrial wastes, and clotted oil . . . The sludge rots in warm weather and from it gas-filled bubbles as big as basketballs continually surge to the surface. Dredgemen call them 'sludge bubbles.' Occasionally, a bubble upsurges so furiously that it brings a mass of sludge with it. In midsummer, here and there in the harbor, the rising and breaking of sludge bubbles makes the water seethe and spit. People sometimes stand on the coal and lumber quays lining the Gowanus Canal and stare at the black, bubbly water." Joseph Mitchell, The Bottom of the Harbor, 37–38 (1944), cited in William Least Heat-Moon, BLUE HIGHWAYS, at 12.

13 *They're going to.* Cronin and Kennedy Jr., at 29.

13 *Churchill hearing that.* Cronin and Churchill, at 29.

13 *like a Brown.* Boyle, at 172, quoting Yale Professor Vincent J. Scully Jr.

13 *Why waste time.* Talbot, at 100.

13 *any large lake.* Boyle, at 171.

14 *The winter months.* Boyle, at 159–160; Cronin and Kennedy Jr., at 30.

14 *He was given.* Boyle, at 160.

14 *He was a.* Talbot, at 115–116.

14 *He was also.* Talbot, at 124; Albert Butzel, draft memoir of Storm King Case, on file with author.

14 *It was my . . . court.* Butzel memoir, at 2.

15 *Garrison was pleased.* Talbot, at 126.

15 *public interest.* Id. at 126–127.

15 *Asked at one.* Butzel memoir, at 12.

16 *Don't get your.* Id.

16 *The appellate decision.* Scenic Hudson Preservation Commission v. Federal Power Commission, 354 F.2d. 608 (2d Cir. 1965) (hereinafter "opinion").

16 *an area of.* Opinion, at 613.

16 *seriously undermined.* Talbot, at 128, quoting from the Federal Power Commission brief on appeal.

16 *by their activities . . . interest.* Opinion, at 614.

16 *public interest.* Opinion, at 617.

16 *an umpire, calling.* Opinion, at 619.

16 *A few short.* Calvert Cliff's Coordinating Comm. v. United States Atomic Energy Comm'n, 449 F.2d 1109 (D.C. Cir. 1971).

17 *On remand for.* Scenic Hudson, at 468–481.

17 *It would accommodate.* Id. at 465–466.

17 *The Commission seemed.* Butzel memoir, at 24.

17 *A split panel.* Scenic Hudson, at 481.

17 *The "preservation of . . . impose.* Id. at 475.

17 *swallow . . . its craw.* Id . at 491 (dissenting opinion of Judge Oakes).

18 *These fish would.* Cronin and Kennedy Jr., at 34.

18 *The Atomic Energy. AEC Averts Fish Kills,* note 36.

18 *Closed cycle cooling.* Editorial, *A Peace Treaty for the Hudson,* N.Y. TIMES, December 20, 1980, at 24.

18 *In May 1974.* Hudson River Fisherman's Association v. the FPC, 498 F.2d 827 (2d Cir. 1974).

19 *one of the.* Editorial, note 41, at 24. The description of the settlement terms that follows is taken from this account.

19 *We lost the.* Suzanne DeChillo, *Battler for a Clean Hudson,* N.Y. TIMES, February 15, 1981, 2 § 22, at 6.

19 *We raked in.* Id. at 1.

20 *The founders of.* For a full description of Scenic Hudson's achievements, Scenic Hudson, at http://www.scenichudson.org/about/history.htm (last visited March 5, 2002).

20 *Butzel went to.* Sierra Club v. United States Army Corps of Eng'r, 772 F.2d 1043 (2d Cir. 1985); Sierra Club v. United States Army Corps of Eng'r, 701 F.2d 1011 (2d Cir. 1983).

20 *cleaner and more.* Rimer, note 6, at B1.

Chapter 2 Nikko Taro

23 *Build a small.* Nikko Tourist Information, *Ieyasu's Last Instruction and Toshogu Shrine*, 2004, at http://www.nikko-jp.org/english/nature/tousyouguu.html (last visited June 15, 2009).

23 *The Nikko Toshogu.* Built at the order of Shogun Tokugawa Ieyasu to Kugawa, the shrine also honors two of his illustrious predecessors, Minamoto Yorimato (deceased 1199) and Toyotomi Hideyoshi (deceased 1598). Japanguide.com, *Toshogu Shrine*, in NIKKO, at http://www.japan-guide.com/e/e3801.html (last visited October 23, 2004).

24 *Ieyasu won the.* "Tokugawa Ieyasu," Sadler, A.L. (1937). The Maker of Modern Japan, p. 164. Ieyasu 2, at 4–5.

25 *Within these confines.* The first Portuguese arrived, by accident (sailors blown off course) in 1543. Traders and Jesuit missionaries soon followed. "Japan," THE WORLD BOOK OF KNOWLEDGE, Vol. J–K (1987) at 44; Japanguide.com, *Muromachi Period :1333–1573),* in HISTORY, at http://www.japan-guide.com/e/e2134 .html (last visited June 9, 2002).

25 *These affairs ended.* Japan-guide.com, *Edo Period (1603–1867)* e.g. in HISTORY, at http://www.japan-guide.com/e/e2128.html (last visited November 18, 2002). There is evidence that, had Ieyasu lived longer, he would have taken a more open path with Europe and the West. Louise Jury, *Portrait of a Warlord,* THE INDEPENDENT (LONDON), May 6, 2005, at 18, 19. Turning inward, instead, the country experienced an explosion of cultural life that was uniquely eastern. Id.

25 *sensing the approach.* WebJapan.org, Nikko Toshogu Shrine, http://web-japan.org/ atlas/architecture/arc05.html (last visited March 25, 2009).

25 *Nothing important stays.* Nikko Toshogu Shrine, Id.; Construction of the elaborate shrine is said to have involved "4.5 million craftsmen and laborers working for 17 months at a cost of 200m [$370 million US] in today's money. The receipts and wages bills are still kept within the shrine complex." Jury at 18.

25 *The road from.* Toshogu Shrine Religious Org. v. Minister of Construction, 710 HANREI JIHO 23 (Tokyo High Court) 1973, HANREI JIHO 23 (Utsonomiya Dist. Ct. 1969); JULIAN GRESSER, KOICHIRO FUJIKURA & AKIO MORISHIMA, ENVIRONMENTAL LAW IN JAPAN pp. 212–215 (translation), p. 213. Legend has it that a liege of the Tokugawa, unable to contribute money to the construction of the Shrine, was permitted to plant a double wall of cedar trees, now "100 feet high, snaking across the plan for 25 miles." Hugh Johnson, "On seeing the Forest for the Trees," NEW YORK TIMES, May 19, 2001, at 3.

26 *a venerable giant.* Gresser, p. 213.

26 *The most impressive.* The Shinto Online Network Association, Civilization of the Divine Forest, http://jinja.jp/english/ci-1.html (last visited March 15, 2009).

26 *first temples of.* Pliney, NATURAL HISTORY. XII.2. "Trees were the very temples of the gods," Philemon Holland, translator (1601): Gaius Plinius Secundus The Historie of the World. Book XII.1, located at http://penelope.uchicago.edu/holland/pliny12.html.

26 *The Romans marked.* Homeric Humn 5, 257–272. Homer, Homeric Hymn 5 (To Aprhodite), p. 22 of Hesiod, Homeric Hymns, and Homerica by Hesiod and Homer, trans. Hugh G. Evelyn-White, Digireads.com Publishing, 2008 (describing sacred forests as "the holy places of the immortals and never mated them with the axe").

26 *The Greeks carried.* J. D. Hughes, *Sacred Groves of the Ancient Mediterarean Area: Early Conservation of Biological Diversity*, in Ramakrisham note 20, at 103. The Christian Bible's Book of Genesis has Abraham building an altar in the holy oaks of *Genesis 21:33* (King James) ("And Abraham planted a grove in Beersheba, and called there on the name of the Lord, the everlasting God.").

26 *So it was in the Baltics.* Jay H. C. Vest, Will-of-the-land: Wilderness among Primal Indo-Europeans, 9 ENVTL. REV. 323–329 (1985).

26 *So it was in Africa.* M. Anana 1997 Religion and conservation in Ghana in: Leyla Alvanak and Adrienne Cruz (eds.), Implementing Agenda 21: NGO Experiences from around the world. United Nations Non-Governmental Liaison Service Geneva 99–107.

27 *how do you.* C. W. Nicol, "The Sacred Forest," cited in "Civilization of the Divine Forest."

27 *Our country, as.* "Ours is a splendid and blessed country, the Land of the Gods beyond any doubt." Hirata Atsutane (1776–1843), cited in ALEX KERR, DOGS AND DEMONS: TALES FROM THE DARK SIDE OF JAPAN (2001), at 13.

27 *The Nihonshoki, Chronicles.* The Shinto Online Network Association, at 4. The earthstory that follows is taken from this source.

27 *In the isolation.* Paul Watt in *Civilization* (describing Shinto as "religion of the forest"); Paul Watt, "*Shinto & Buddhism: Wellsprings of Japanese Spirituality*," in ASIA SOCIETY'S FOCUS ON ASIAN STUDIES, VOL. II, NO. 1, ASIAN RELIGIONS (Fall 1982), at http://www.askasia.org/frclasrm/readings/r000009.htm (last visited August 9, 2005) (describing early Shinto as "an amorphous mix of nature worship, fertility cults, divination techniques, hero worship and shamanism"); "Shinto", WIKIPEDIA (July 27, 2005), at http://en.wikipedia.org/wiki/Shinto (last visited August 10, 2005) ("the most immediately striking theme in the Shinto religion is a great love and reverence for nature"). Wellsprings of Japanese Spirituality.

27 *To be in.* Johnson, at 22: "Today their shrine's sweeping tile roofs are gray rollers tapped and tossing in fjords of immense cliff like sugi [cedar trees]. They stand in great docs of granite among Piranesi an staircases, among roaring runnels, with moss and ferns infiltrating wood and stone, steps and lanterns and the stony boles of the titanic trees, the main pillars of this incomparable temple."

28 *shin tao, . . . Gods.* ReligiousTolerance.org, Shinto, at http://www.religioustoler-ance.org/shinto.htm (last visited June 15, 2009).

28 *Asphalt blanketing the.* Kerr, at 50.

29 *According to its.* Toshogu Shrine Religious Org at par. 1.

29 *Even the National.* Id. at 6. Apparently the Park Council's urging, the treed slope of the road would be leveled and replanted with cedars. Kobayakawa, summary of facts.

30 *At eighty trillion.* KERR, at 13–50.

30 *It won't be.* Id. (citing J. Ryall, Next Big Tourist Destination—The Moon, JAPAN TIMES, June 22, 1996 [quoting Matsumoto Shinji]).

30 *The buy-in.* Kerr, at 20. (A good percentage [traditionally about 1 to 3 percent of the budget of each public project] goes to the politicians who arrange it.)

31 *Bureaucrats educated in.* Kerr, at 23.

31 *Almost all of.* Roderick H. Seeman, "New Highway Company Reform," Japan Law info, 2005. http://www.japanlaw.info/law2004/JAPAN_LAW_2004_NEW_HIGHWAY_COMPANY_REFORM.html (last visited March 21, 2009).

31 *bulging coffers.* Kerr, at 48.

31 *so that people.* Id. at 29, quoting Nakaoti Yutaka, Governor of Toyama Prefecture.

32 *When the Japanese.* Id. at 290.

32 *the blade of.* Interview with Osamu Nagatomo, L.L.M. Candidate, Tulane Law School, May 10, 2004, describing Japanese education and attitudes. Mr. Nagatomo is now a practitioner in Tokyo.

32 *Their officials were.* "From the peaks of lofty superiority, the bureaucracy surveyed the rest of society with vast disdain—the maxim, officials honored, the people de-spised [Kanson minpi], epitomized the prevailing attitude.'" GRESSER, p. 230.

33 *descended from heaven.* Id., p. 107.

33 *increase of industrial.* Shiro Kawashima, *A Survey of Environmental Law and Policy in Japan,* 20 N.C. J. INT'L L. AND COM. REG. 231, 232 (Winter, 1995).

33 *Copernican changing time.* Shiro Kawashima, A Survey of Environmental Law and Policy in Japan, 20 N.C. J. INT'L L. & COM. REG. 231, 232–233(1995).

33 *The first case.* GRESSER, at 4. The description of this Furukawa mine case that fol-lows is taken from this source, Id. at 4–8.

34 *little compensation, or.* Dr. Kenneth Strong, *Tanaka ShEozEo: Meiji Hero and Pioneer Against Pollution,* 67 JAPAN SOC'Y OF LONDON 6, 10 (1972).

34 *A series of.* GRESSER, at 12, 13; Kawashima at 234–236. The description of the Akali case is taken from these two sources.

34 *Toyama itai-itai . . . hurts!".* GRESSER, at 30.

34 *Big Four.* GRESSER, at 29–64, Kawashima at 239–240. The description of the Big Four cases that follows is taken from these cases.

35 *The only environmental.* GRESSER, at 215 [Park Council's approval], attaching sev-eral hopeful but unenforceable conditions, such as to "minimize the cutting of inter-fering trees"; the Ministry of Health and Welfare also approved.

36 *appropriate and reasonable.* "The minister of Construction or the prefectural governor may authorize the project only when the project fulfills all of the below enumerated conditions: . . . (3) the project plan is one which will contribute to the appropriate and rational use of the land." Mark A. Levin, Essential Commodities and Racial Justice: Using Constitutional Protection of Japan's Indigenous Ainu People to Inform Understandings of the United States and Japan, 33 N.Y.U. J. INT'L L. & POL. 419, 457 n.137 (2001) (quoting [Land Expropriation Law], Law No. 219 of 1951, art. 20[3]).

36 *The land in.* The quotes that follow are taken from this opinion. Toshogu Shrine Religious Organization.

37 *no feasible and.* 23 U.S.C. § 138, note 61; Citizens to Preserve Overton Park, Inc. v. Volpe (rejecting decision to route highway through park for failure to show no feasible and prudent alternative 401 U.S. 402 [1971]).

38 *derelict on the.* Ala. Pub. Serv. Comm'n v. S. Ry. Co., 341 U.S. 341 (1951).

38 *Lawsuits would be.* KAWASHIMA, at 263 (describing the Osaka airport case, "After a twelve-year dispute, the Supreme Court in 1981 permitted the recovery of a portion of the damages sought, but dismissed the injunction because the plaintiff petitioners had mistakenly chosen civil rather than administrative procedure."

38 *And so, even.* GRESSER, at 149–165 and Kawashima 216–270 describing these and other cases.

39 *Although the plaintiff.* Toshogu Shrine Religious Organization at 3.

39 *He is known.* Otsuka, note 179 (citing Gunma Chuo Bus, 14 Gyosaishu 2255 [December 25, 1963] and *Kojin Taxi*, 14 Gyosaishu 166 [September 18, 1963]). The Professor concludes that these decisions are considered "to have made a large contribution towards Japanese administrative litigation and jurisprudence." Id. The importance of the Nikko Taro decision is noted by, among other Japanese scholars, Professor Mitsvo Kobayakawa of Tokyo University in the legal publication Bessatsu Jurist. ("The court decision is an important decision that has been often referred to not only in the interpretation and application of Land Expropriation Law but also in discussing administrative discretion in general.")

39 "The way of". Tadashi Otsuka, Memorandum (October 25, 2005), on file with author. (citing Gunma Chuo Bus, 14 Gyosaishu 2255 [December 25, 1963] and Kojin Taxi, 14 Gyosaishu 166 [September 18, 1963]). The professor concludes that these decisions are considered "to have made a large contribution towards Japanese administrative litigation and jurisprudence."

40 *Rather, they developed.* Stefanie Beyer, "*Environmental Law and Policy in the People's Republic of China,*" 5 CHINESE J. OF INT. L. 185, 190 (2006).

40 *Traditional philosophy.* Tsuyoshi Kimoshita, "Towards Comparative Law in the 21st Century—East and West in Legal Cultures and Mondern and Post Modern Law" (undated, on file with author).

40 *Highway Approved Near.* Shawn Pogatchnik, Road Past Holy Hill Divides the Irish: Disputed Highway Will Ease Bottleneck, TIMES-PICAYUNE, May 15, 2005, at A-23.

40 *Japan's immediate problem.* Roderick H. Seeman, "New Highway Company Reform," Japan Law info, 2005.

41 *And yet, the.* After long negotiations (reportedly, seven years), objects from the shrine have been lent for display to the Royal Armouries Museum in London, accompanied by two Shinto priests. Jury.

Chapter 3 Minors Oposa

44 *Pieces of a.* ANTONIO A. OPOSA, A LEGAL ARSENAL FOR THE PHILIPPINE ENVIRONMENT (2003).

44 *The Laws of.* ANTONIO A. OPOSA, JR., THE LAWS OF NATURE AND OTHER STORIES 177 (2003) [hereinafter LAWS OF NATURE] ("To repeat: If enforcement is to be effective, it must be swift, painful and public.").

44 *He would bring.* Selected by his classmates at Harvard's graduate school of law to give the commencement address, Oposa spoke not on the law, but "On Friendship and Laughter." Ma. Ceres P. Doyo, Mother Nature Lays Down the Law, INQUIRER (Manila), April 30, 2006, available at http://archive.inquirer.net/view.php? db=0 &story_id=74179. Within the Philippines, Oposa has become a breeder reaction for environmental protection, across the board. For the range of his activities, Antonio A. Oposa, Jr. Curriculum Vitae, available at http://www.oposa.com/oposa_ family/cvaao198.htm. By way of example, in 2004, Oposa spearheaded an effort to create an environmental ombudsman to prosecute public complaints; in 2005 he filed on behalf of the Philippine bar's environmental section the first complaint before the ombudsman against illegal solid waste dumping by the City of Manila. Rox Pena, *Enforcing the Solid Waste Law,* SUN STAR, May 13, 2005, available at http://www.sunstar.com.ph/static/pam/2005/05/13/oped/rox.pe.a.html.

44 *He is not.* DOYO; ("Here is one lawyer who says he is not in love with the law, not in the way others wax poetic over legal philosophies and the sheer beauty they find therein. 'For me, law is a tool, a thinking tool to guide human conduct . . . I was not in love with law when I started off.'"). Visayan Sea Squadron Begins Patrols in Philippines, 9 INECE NEWSL. (Int'l Network for Envtl. Compliance & Enforcement), February 2004, available at http:// inece.org/newsletter/9/regional_asia.html.

44 *in their time.* Antonio Oposa, Dedication of "The Laws of Nature" to the Tulane University Law Library, April 2005. Laws of Nature; ANTONIO A. OPOSA, JR., THE LAWS OF NATURE AND OTHER STORIES 177 (2003). ("To repeat: If enforcement is to be effective, it must be swift, painful and public.")

45 *Legend has it.* Jill Cynthia, The Monkey Eating Eagle Pithecophaga Jefferyi, http:// boojum.as.arizona.edu/~jill/Cynthia/report.html (last visited January 16, 2007), at 11.

45 *frailocracy . . . and to.* History, Wikipedia.org, History of the Philippines, http:// en. wikipedia.org/wiki/Philippine_history (last visited January 11, 2007); see also Alan

Grainger and Ben S. Malayang II, "A model of policy changes to secure sustainable forest management and control of deforestation in the Philippines," Forest Policy and Economics, Vol 8, Issue 1, January 2006 at 5.5. For a revealing discussion of China's great Treasure Fleet that, with ships up to 480 feet long, dominated trade in this region in the early 1400s, GAVIN MENZIES, 1421: THE YEAR CHINA DIS-COVERED AMERICA (2003).

45 *The wood of.* MARITES DANGILAN VITUG, THE POLITICS OF LOGGING: POWER FROM THE FOREST 11 (1993) (quoting Beveridge addressing the US Senate in January 1900).

45 *In 1898, the.* "Philippine History," The Columbia Encyclopedia, Sixth Ed. By the time of American intervention, the Philippine independence movement had wrested control from the Spanish over all of Luzan but a section of the city of Manila. Id.

46 *The trees began.* Cf. VITUG, MARITES DANGILAN VITUG, THE POLITICS OF LOGGING: POWER FROM THE FOREST 11 (1993) (quoting Beveridge addressing the U.S. Senate in January 1900), (statement of U.S. Senator Beveridge), at 12.

46 *Get out the.* Id., at 12–13. "It was American colonial forestry in the Philippines, however, which continued the systematic denudation of the forests. George Ahern, first American director of the Bureau of Forestry, presided over the passage of a forest law in 1904 that gave the bureau power to issue timber concessions on whatever scale and duration they deemed a lumberman's resources could match. Nearly 20 million hectares of forest lands were under his control." VITUG, at 12.

46 *By 1934, only.* Id., at 11.

46 *The United States.* Id., at 25.

46 *Timber concessions went.* MICHAEL L. ROSS, TIMBER BOOMS AND INSTITUTIONAL BREAKDOWN IN SOUTHEAST ASIA 55–56, 61–70 (2001).

46 *By the mid-1950s.* VITUG, at 13.

46 *In 1969, President.* ANTONIO P. CONTRERAS, THE KINGDOM AND THE REPUBLIC: FOREST GOVERNANCE AND POLITICAL TRANSFORMATION IN THAILAND AND THE PHILIPPINES 50 (2003); SOUTHEAST ASIA SUSTAINABLE FOREST MANAGEMENT NETWORK, UPLAND PHILIPPINE COMMUNITIES: GUARDIANS OF THE FINAL FOREST FRONTIERS 6-12 (Mark Poffenberger and Betsy McGean, eds.) (1993).

46 *After his reelection.* VITUG, at 25.

46 *If Necessary,* I. VITUG, at 25. For the ambiguous, on-again, off-again environmental policies of President Marcos, Id.; ROSS.

47 *At the same.* VITUG, at 20, n. 14.

47 *The President's mother.* Id. at 22.

47 *In 1971, a.* VITUG, at 25; CONTRERAS, at 56.

47 *balanced and healthful.* CONST. (1987), Art. II, § 16, Art. XII, § 4 (Phil.). Section 16, Article II of the 1987 Constitution reads in full: "The State shall protect and advance the right of the people to a balanced and healthful ecology in accord with the rhythm

and harmony of nature." Minors Oposa v. Factoran, 224 S.C.R.A. 792 (S.C., July 30, 1993), reprinted in 33 I.L.M. 173 (1994), at 177–178. Art. II, § 16.

47 *environment . . . exploit . . . environment.* Providing for the Reorganization of the Department of Environment, Energy and Natural Resources; Renaming it the Department of Environment and Natural Resources, Exec. Ord. No. 192 (1987) (Phil.).

47 *Somehow when we.* LAWS OF NATURE, at 163.

48 *Nobody knows how.* DOYO. The account of the fire and Oposa's upbringing and education that follow are taken from this source; and from Interview with Antonio A. Oposa, Jr., Lawyer, in New Orleans, La. (April 1, 2005). Description of the arrest of the logging ship is taken from these sources.

49 *The liquidation of.* Cf. LAWS OF NATURE, at 166 (quoting Robin Broad, The Political Economy of Natural Resources: Case Studies of Indonesian and Philippine Forest Sectors, J. OF DEVELOPING AREAS, April 1995, at 29 [cited in ABRAMOVITZ, STATE OF THE WORLD 29 (1998)]).

50 *The Department had.* Minors Oposa v. Factoran, 224 S.C.R.A. 792 (S.C., July 30, 1993), reprinted in 33 I.L.M. 173, 179 (1994).

50 *That was already.* Approximately 850,000 hectares of virgin forest remained. Id.

51 *one can imagine.* The account of finding plaintiffs and the quotes that follow are taken from Oposa email. Email from Antonio A. Oposa Jr. to Oliver A. Houck, Professor of Law, Tulane University Law School (August 6, 2006) (on file with author) [hereinafter Oposa email]. Oposa states that his most difficult feat of persuasion was his convincing his wife, a "practical minded person" who did not see why he had to "tackle the entire Philippine Government." Id., at 178.

51 *The suit was.* Juan Antonio Oposa, Anna Rosario Oposa, Jose Alfonso Oposa, Roberta Nicole Sadiua, Carlo Flores, Amanda Salud Flores, Patrisha Flores, Gianina Dita R. Fortun, George II Misa, Ma. Concepcion Misa, Benjamin Alan V. Pesigan, Jovie Marie Alfaro, Maria Concepcion T. Castro, Johanna Desamparado, Carlo Joaquin T. Narvasa, Ma. Margarita Saenz, Jesus Ignacio Saenz, Ma. Angela Saenz, Marie Gabrielle Saenz, Kristine King, Mary Ellen King, May King, Golda Marthe King, David Ian King, David Endriga, Francisco Endriga, Therese Victoria Endriga, Jose Ma. Avaya, Regina Ma. Abaya, Marilin Cardama, Mario Jr. Cardama, Mariette Cardama, Clarissa Oposa, Ann Marie Oposa, Nagel Oposa, Imee Lynn Oposa, Philip Joseph Quipit, Stephen John Quipit, Isaiah James Quipit, Bughaw Cielo Bibal, Crisanto Bibal, Anna Bibal, Daniel Bibal, Fransisco Bibal. *Minors Oposa*, 33 I.L.M. at 174–175.

51 *taxpayers' action.* Challenges to government actions by those claiming to represent all taxpayers have not found favor in US courts. Frothingham v. Mellon, 262 U.S. 447, 479 (1923). In this case, the Philippine Court sidestepped the taxpayer aspect and found class representation more directly: "The subject matter of the complaint is of common and general interest not just to several but to all the citizens of the

Philippines. Since the parties are so numerous it is impossible to bring them all before the court." *Minors Oposa*, 33 I.L.M. at 184.

51 *the unabated hemorrhage. Minors Oposa*, 33 I.L.M. at 176.

51 *The government filed.* Oposa email.

51 *sufficient definiteness.* Daniel V. Gatmaytan, *The Illusion of Intergenerational Equity:* Oposa v. Factoran as *Pyrrhic Victory*, 15 GEO. INT'L ENVTL. L. REV. 457, 463 (2003), at 461.

51 *Nothing in the.* Id.

51 *political color . . . public policy.* Id.

52 *He questioned Oposa's.* Oposa, Environmental Activism.

52 *intergenerational equity* . For a discussion of intergenerational equity, EDITH BROWN WEISS, IN FAIRNESS TO FUTURE GENERATIONS: INTERNATIONAL LAW, COMMON PATRIMONY, AND INTERGENERATIONAL EQUITY (1989); Edith Brown Weiss, Our Rights and Future Obligations to Future Generations for the Environment, 84 Am. J. Int'l L. 198 (1998); Edith Brown Weiss, Intergenerational Equity in International Law, 81 AM. SOC'Y INT'L L. PROC. 126 (1987); Edith Brown Weiss, *The Planetary Trust: Conservation and Intergenerational Equity*, 11 Ecology L.Q. 495 (1984).

52 *the rhythm and.* Minors Oposa v. Factoran, 224 S.C.R.A. 792 (S.C., July 30, 1993), reprinted in 33 I.L.M. 173, 181(1994).

54 *Justice Davide, who.* Hon. Chief Justice Hilario G. Davide, "The Role of the Judiciary in Scaling Up Poverty Reduction" speech, World Bank Global Conference on Scaling Up Poverty Reduction, Shanghai, China, May 25-27, 2004. Justice Davide went on to write an inspired dedication for Oposa's book on Philippine environmental law; ANTONIO A. OPOSA, A LEGAL ARSENAL FOR THE PHILIPPINE ENVIRONMENT (2003).

54 *The great trees.* From the world's leading producer of timber, only a few decades ago, the Philippines now is one of the largest importers in all of Asia, suffering, in the year 2000, a US$517.2 million forest trade deficit. VITUG, at 25; Contreras, at 47.

54 *In 1991 a.* VITUG, at 1.

54 *in 1999, another.* The Wrath of Nature. ASIA WEEK, August 20–27, 1999, available at http://www.asiaweek.com/asiaweek/99/aw.0702.to.0820/0820/nat5.html.

54 *In 2006, it.* Carlos H. Conde, *Danger of Philippine Landslides Often Ignored, Critics Say*, N.Y. TIMES, February 21, 2006, at A3.

54 *You could look.* GATMAYTAN, at 467–468, whose phrases describing the case ("since the practice [timber cutting] continues, it is difficult to see how Oposa can be construed as a victory for the environment," the Court's rulings on intergenerational equity were mere "obiter dictum," the concept of intergenerational equity "has no practical effect," and, in the end, the case remains "largely ignored") seem rather extreme. Oposa would be, and is, the first to say that his case did not stop logging in the

Philippines; Oposa, Environmental Activism. But that it provided the momentum to curb commercial harvests and, then, a number of other unsustainable practices, seems beyond cavil. See the discussion following.

55 *The case gave. Environmentalists were pressing. Coordinated Enforcement*, Antonio A. Oposa Jr., *Using Coordinated Enforcement to Protect Forests from Illegal Logging in the Philippines*, in 2 FIFTH INTERNATIONAL CONFERENCE ON ENVIRONMEN- TAL COMPLIANCE AND ENFORCEMENT, PROCEEDINGS (Jo Gerardu & Cheryl Wasserman, eds., 1998) [hereinafter Coordinated Enforcement], at 235, 239; ANTONIO A. OPOSA JR., 4TH INT'L CONF. ON ENVTL. COMPLIANCE AND ENFORCEMENT, INTERGENERATIONAL RESPONSIBILITY IN THE PHILIP- PINE CONTEXT AS A JUDICIAL ARGUMENT FOR PUBLIC ACTION ON DE- FORESTATION 2 (1996) [hereinafter "International Responsibility"], at 5 ("Given a sympathetic bureaucracy, the government administrators may just be looking for ad- ditional ammunition with which they can enact a policy that they wanted to do in the first place but could not on account of political considerations and sensitivities.").

55 *By 2006 there.* REX VICTOR O. CRUZ & JUAN M. PULHIN, VERIFOR, COUNTRY CASE STUDY 7, REVIEW OF MULTISECTORAL FOREST PROTECTION COM- MITTEES IN THE PHILIPPINES tbl.1 (2006), at 3.

55 *The annual rate.* Mongabay.com, Philippines: Environmental Profile, http:// rainforests.mongabay.com/20philippines.htm (last visited January 19, 2007).

55 *DENR cancels 8,000 . . . logging. DENR cancels 8,000 timber permits due to illegal log- ging,* MANILA TIMES, January 10, 2006, available at www.manilatimes.net/ national/2006/jan/10/yehey/top_stories/20060110top9.html; Illegal-logging.info, Filipino Region Imposes Logging Ban: NGO Caution WTO Implications, April 14, 2006, www.illegal-logging.info/newws.php?newsId=1378 (last visited January 19, 2007); Tonette Orejas, *14 Draw prison terms for illegal logging,* PHILIPPINES DAILY INQUIRER, April 27, 2006, at 17, available at http://archive.inquirer.net/view .php?db=0&story_id=73830; *Ban on illegal activities in Shilan forest sought,* SUN STAR BAGUIO (Phil.), May 13, 2006, http:// www.sunstar.com.ph/static/bag/2006/ 05/13/news/ban.on.illegal.activities.in.shilan.fore (last visited January 14, 2007).

55 *The last native.* Great Ape Trust: Orangutan Research Project Destined for Great Ape Trust, available at http://www.greatapetrust.org/media/releases/2003/nr_11a03.php (last visited January 19, 2007).

55 *The Brazilian ecologist.* Jorge Cappato, *Who Was Chico Mendes?,* UNITED NATIONS ENVIRONMENTAL PROGRAMME GLOBAL 500 FORUM, available at http:// www.global500.org/feature_6.html (last visited January 14, 2007).

56 *our struggle for.* Nora Boustany, *Risking His Life for Grass-Roots Environmentalism,* WASH. POST, April 29, 2006, at A12, available at http://www.washingtonpost .com/wp-dyn/content/article/2006/04/28/AR2006042801970.html, at A12.

56 *It challenges a.* Daniel A. Farber, *From Here to Eternity: Environmental Law and Future Generations,* 2003 U. ILL. L. REV. 289 (2003) (assessing the discounting of

future impacts); FRANK ACKERMAN & LISA HEINZERLING, PRICELESS: ON KNOWING THE PRICE OF EVERYTHING AND THE VALUE OF NOTH-ING (2004) (challenging cost-benefit decisionmaking); Douglas A. Kysar, *Law, Environment, and Vision*, 97 NW. U. L. REV. 675 (2003) (promoting "ecological economics").

56 *Perhaps the most.* Concerned Residents of Manila Bay v. DENR, RTC (Imus, Cavite, September 13, 2002), discussed in Rosemary Lyster, *Philippines Regional Court Reiterates Constitutional Right to Environment: The Manila Bay Case*, ASIA PAC. J. ENVTL. L., vol. 7, issues 3 & 4, 2002, at 1, 1.

56 *The complaint was.* Id.; LAWS OF NATURE, at 137 ("In the case of Manila Bay, fisherman attest that 90 percent of what their fishing nets catch is pure and simple garbage—plastics, cans, foam, and the other discarded flotsam and jetsam of the modern human being. While the standard for fecal coliform bacteria for marine waters fit for swimming is only 200 units, in the mid-1990s some parts of Manila Bay's waters were found to contain almost one million units.").

56 *The modern trend.* LYSTER, at 3.

56 *The plaintiff's attorney.* The Manila Bay case, with its attendant publicity and its manifold difficulties in fashioning judicial solutions for environmental problems at political stalemate, reflects the reluctant-warrior philosophy of a seasoned environmental lawyer. Oposa would write, for all its jurisprudential value and implications in constitutional and political law, remedial law, and environmental law, the important lesson learned is that "environmental controversies and issues are not resolved by legal action and in the legal forum"; Oposa, Environmental Activism, at 5. However, he continued, environmental lawsuits secure a vital role in stimulating "the molecules of thought" in the minds of government and the general public, in subjecting the conflict to "dispassionate scrutiny" and orderly consideration, and by providing ammunition to a "sympathetic bureaucracy," which they can "enact a policy that they wanted to in the first place" but did not have the clout; Id., at 3–4. One senses him recalling his dealings with Secretary Factoran in *Minors Oposa*.

57 *Jurists and scholars.* Gatmaytan; Ma. Socorro Z. Manguiat and Vicente Paolo B. Yu III, *Maximizing the Value of Oposa v. Facotoran*, 15 GEO. INT'L ENVTL. L. REV. 487 (2003); Paul A. Barresi, *Beyond Fairness to Future Generations: An Intragenerational Alternative to Intergenerational Equity in the International Environmental Arena*, 11 TUL. ENVTL. L. J. 59 (1997); Pail A. Barresi, *Advocacy, Frame, and the Intergenerational Imperative: A Reply to Professor Weiss on "Beyond Fairness to Future Generations,"* 11 TUL. ENVTL. L. J. 425 (1998); G. F. Maggio, *Inter/Intra-Generational Equity: Current Applications Under Constitutional Law for Promoting the Sustainable Development of Natural Resources*, 4 BUFF. ENVTL. L.J. 161 (1997).

57 *Quotations from it.* Convention on Access to Information, Public Participation in Decision-Making and Access to Justice in Environmental Matters, art. 7, June 25, 1998, 2161 U.N.T.S. 447. Section 7: "[7] *Recognizing also* that every person has the

right to live in an environment adequate to his or her health and wellbeing, and the duty, both individually and in association with others, to protect and improve the environment for the benefit of present and future generations." To be sure *Minors Oposa* did not invent these concepts, but it gave them legitimacy and momentum for their incorporation in law.

57　*One of the.* INECE Newsletter.

57　*the Amazon of.* Id.

57　*He persuaded the.* Visayan Sea Squadron Begins Patrols in Philippines, NEWSLET-TER 9 (INECE Secretariat, Wash., D.C.), February 2004, available at http://inece .org/newsletter/9/regional_asia.html.

57　*One of Oposa's. Bantay Dagat Chief Attacked at Gate of His House,* SUNSTAR, April 13, 2006, available at http://sunstar.com.ph/static/net/2006/04/13/bantay.dagat .chief.attacked.at.gate.of.h.

57　*On April 12, 2006.* Id.

57　*The triggerman turned. Cop Nabbed on Slay of Bantay Dagat Chief,* SUNSTAR, April 19, 2006, available at http://www.sunstar.com.ph/static/net/2006/04/18/cop.nabbed .on.slay.of.bantay.dagat.chief.

58　*crisis . . . danger" and "opportunity.* LAWS OF NATURE, at 45.

58　*Immediately following the.* Oposa email.

58　*We can turn.* Id.

Chapter 4 Great Whale

62　*fiasco," "embarrassment," . . . ups.* GEORGE N. HOOD, AGAINST THE FLOW: RAFFERTY-ALAMDEDA AND THE POLITICS OF THE ENVIRONMENT 128 (1994) (stating that there were a litany of screwups); Carol Goar, *The Politics behind Ottowa's Concern for James Bay,* TORONTO STAR, July 18, 1991, at A17 (stating that it was a fiasco and an embarrassment).

62　*Rainfall follows the.* STEWART L. UDALL, THE QUIET CRISIS 121–122 (1963), at 94. For a detailed critique of water resources development in the western United States, MARC RESINER, CADILLAC DESERT (1986).

62　*storms of snow.* IAN FRAZIER, GREAT PLAINS 196–197 (1989).

62　*A Canadian who.* HOOD, at 6.

63　*He arrived to see.* Id. at 8.

63　*Rafferty-Alameda Dams.* TORONTO STAR, July 5, 1991, at D10.

63　*environment . . . was born.* For background on sportsmen's organizations, WILLIAM T. HORNADAY, OUR VANISHING WILD LIFE: ITS EXTERMINATION AND PRESERVATION 53–61 (1913); George Reiger, *Hunting and Trapping in the New World,* in WILDLIFE AND AMERICA: CONTRIBUTIONS TO AN UNDERSTAN-ING OF AMERICAN WILDLIFE AND ITS CONSERVATION 42, 44, 46–47, 52

(Howard P. Brokaw ed., 1978); Richard H. Stroud, *Recreational Fishing*, in WILD-
LIFE AND AMERICA, at 53–84; THOMAS B. ALLEN, GUARDIAN OF THE WILD:
THE STORY OF THE NATIONAL WILDLIFE FEDERATION, 1936–1986, at 147
(1987).

63 *Meanwhile, north of.* Telephone interview with Ken Brynaert, former executive director, Canadian Wildlife Federation (May 20, 2005). The description that follows of
the Canadian Wildlife Federation is taken from the interview.

63 *our foundling fathers . . . growth.* The author was General Counsel to the National
Wildlife Federation during this time, and worked closely with Kimball. Among other
things, he saw Kimball oppose his own hunting and fishing constituency on several
occasions in the larger interest of environmental protection.

64 *The United States broke.* Marbury v. Madison, 5 U.S. 137 (1803).

65 *US courts, over.* For a description of Commerce Clause challenges to environmental
law, Robert V. Percival, *"Greening" the Constitution-Harmonizing Environmental and
Constitutional Values*, 32 ENVTL. L. 809, 830–33 (2002); Christine A. Klein, The Environmental Commerce Clause, 27 HARV. ENVTL. L. REV. 1 (2003).

65 *FEARO.* Environmental Assessment and Review Process Guidelines Order, SOR/84-
467 (1984) (Can.), available at http://www.ceaa-acee.gc.ca/013/0002/earp_go_e.htm
[hereinafter EARP Guidelines Order]; Roger Cotton & John S. Zimmer, *Canadian
Environmental Law: An Overview*, 18 CAN.-U.S. L.JJJ. 63, 75 (1992).

65 *[H]istory will show.* 22 September Proceedings; Saskatchewan, Legislative Assembly,
Debates and Proceedings (Hansard) (22 September 1987) (Mr. Lyons) 4-7, available
at http:// www.legassembly.sk.ca/hansard/21L1S/87-09-22.pdf [hereinafter 22 September Proceedings]. Wilkinson v. Rafferty-Alameda Bd. of Inquiry, [1987] 64 Sask.
R. 170. at 5–6.

65 *mere description. Can. Wildlife Fed'n Inc.* , 3 F.C. at 313–314, at 322.

66 *A scant two.* Can. Wildlife Fed'n Inc. v. Canada (Minister of the Env't), [1989] 2
W.W.R. 69 (F.C.A. Can).

66 *As Ken Brynaert.* Interview with Ken Brynaert.

66 *News of the.* HOOD, at 70 (describing the proponent's reaction as an "unbelievable
blow").

66 *madder than hell . . . moon."* Id. at 71–72.

66 *Dreams in the.* Id. at 158–159.

66 *Getting the Better.* Id. at 81.

66 *If there be . . . obvious. Can. Wildlife Fed'n Inc.* , 4 C.E.L.R. (N.S.), at 225.

67 *rumbled on into.* HOOD, at 82. (photo caption).

67 *to the high.* JACK GLENN, ONCE UPON AN OLDMAN: SPECIAL INTEREST
POLITICS AND THE OLDMAN RIVER DAM 17 (1999); Ed Struzik, *Supreme
Court Decision Caps 2 Decades of Acrimony over Dam*, EDMONTON JOURNAL,
January 24, 1992, available at http://www.nisto.com/cree/lubicon/1992/19920126

.html, at 13–24; Univ. of Guelph, Guelph Water Management Group, Land Use and Settlement in the Oldman River Watershed, http://www.uoguelph.ca/gwmg/wcp_ home/Pages/O_he_lu.htm (last visited April 18, 2006) [hereinafter Guelph, Land Use and Settlement].

67 *religious ecosystem.* GLENN, at 207 (quoting Milton Born With A Tooth).

68 *By the early 1900s.* Univ. of Guelph, Guelph Water Management Group, Peigan (Pikuni) and Blood (Kainaiwa) Nations, http://www.uoguelph.ca/gwmg/wcp_ home/Pages/O_he_fn.htm (last visited April 18, 2006).

68 *The federal government.* GLENN, at 22.

68 *no environmental concerns.* Struzik.

68 *something with a.* Telephone Interview with Martha Kostuch, Founder, Canadian Environmental Network, May 30, 2005. The description of the early opposition that follows is taken from this interview.

68 *pot smoking social.* GLENN, at 51.

69 *absurd, nonsensical, and.* Struzik.

69 *Then, in the.* Friends of the Oldman River Soc'y v. Canada (Minster of Transp.), [1990] 1 F.C. 248 (Fed. Ct. Can.), rev'd by Oldman River I, 2 F.C. 18.

70 *shams, signed by.* Telephone interview with Edwin Small Legs, tribal council member, Blackfoot Confederacy, June 3, 2005. The descriptions of Milton Born With A Tooth and Edwin Small Legs that follow are taken from this source.

70 *we didn't know.* Id.

70 *ground breaking ceremony.* GLENN, at 77.

70 *somebody had to.* Interview with Edwin Small Legs.

70 *I'll do it . . . jail.* GLENN, at 91.

70 *No more courts . . . country.* William Walker, *Ottowa Refuses to Shut Down Oldman Dam*, TORONTO STAR, May 22, 1992, at A15.

71 *on ice.* GLENN, at 103. The description of the panel's actions that follows is taken from this source.

71 *Of course we.* Id. at 113.

71 *The protection of.* Oldman River II, 1 S.C.R., at 16.

71 *Trojan horse.* Jean Leclair, *The Supreme Court of Canada's Understanding of Federalism: Efficiency at the Expense of Diversity*, 28 QUEEN'S L.J. 441, 424–30 (2003).

72 *decommission it.* GLENN, at 113.

72 *technically adolescent.* Id.

72 *teetered on the.* Id. at 129.

72 *official emblems.* Id. The account of the trial that follows is taken from this source.

72 *I can tell.* Interview with Edwin Small Legs.

72 *I'm going to.* GLENN, at 114.

72 *A Festival of.* Id.

72 *festival of death.* Id. at 115. Telephone interview with Martha Kostuch, Founder.

73 *put up or.* Glenn, at 116.

73 *[A] respectful affirmation . . . Alberta.* Id.

73 *more like a.* Jim Morris, Oldman Dam Draws Controversy: Alberta Project Hotly Debated for 34 Years, THE REC. (Kitchener-Waterloo, Ont.), August 15, 1992, at F10; Martha Kostuch soldiered on citing Canada's failing environmental politics to the Environmental Committee of the North American Free Trade Agreement, with Oldman Dam as Exhibit A. Press Release, Friends of the Oldman River, Further Delay in Release of Commission for Environmental Cooperation's Factual Record on Canada's Non-Compliance with Environmental Laws (June 24, 2003) (explaining Ms. Kostuch's position with respect to the dam issue). At the same time, Friends of the Oldman River was submitting a detailed five-year critique to the Canadian Environmental Assessment Agency of its performance under the new Environmental Assessment Act. Martha Kostuch, CEAA 5 Year Review (2003), available at http:/www .ceaa.gc.ca/013/001/0002/0004/0001/kostuch_f.htm. The organization and reputation of the Society gained during the Oldman Dam fight were being put to new environmental ends.

73 *monument to government.* Morris.

73 *In April 1971.* Jamie Linton, *The Geese Have Lost Their Way,* NATURE CANADA, Spring 1991, at 28–29.

74 *In one corner.* BOYCE RICHARDSON, STRANGERS DEVOUR THE LAND: THE CREE HUNTERS OF THE JAMES BAY AREA VERSUS PREMIER BOURASSA AND THE JAMES BAY DEVELOPMENT CORPORATION 22 (1975), at 20, 22, 27, 327–329; Harvey A. Feit, *Hunting and the Quest for Power: The James Bay Cree and Whiteman Development,* in NATIVE PEOPLES: THE CANADIAN EXPERIENCE 101, 112–113 (R. Bruce Morrison and C. Roderick Wilson, eds., 2004) [hereinafter *Hunting and the Quest for Power I*], at 113–114 (providing background information for the discussion of the La Grande River project that follows).

74 *In the opposite.* CATHOLIC ENCYCLOPEDIA (2005), available at http://www .newadvent.org/cathen/04477a.htm; *Hunting and the Quest for Power I,* at 101.

74 *naturally generous, good-tempered.* CATHOLIC ENCYCLOPEDIA.

74 *high in morality.* Id.

75 *religious occupation.* Harvey A. Feit, *Hunting and the Quest for Power: The James Bay Cree and Whitemen in the 20th Century: Part I: The Contemporary Cree Hunting Culture* (2004), available at http:// arcticcircle.uconn.edu/CulturalViability/Cree/Feit1/ feit1.html.

75 *suspicious . . . over-exploiters. Hunting and the Quest for Power I,* at 101.

75 *dialogue of the . . . necessary.* RICHARDSON, at 23, 27.

75 *It's not ok . . . here.* Id. at 42.

75 *It is quite . . . it.* Id. at 104–105 (photo caption between pages).

76 *When you talk.* Id. at 246.

76 *like losing my.* Id. The testimony of Job Bearskin: It can never be that there will be enough money to help pay for what I get from trapping. I do not think in terms of money. I think more often of the land because the land is something you will have for a long time. That is why we call our traplines, our land, a garden.

76 *not to disturb.* Id. at 26.

76 *What were the.* RICHARDSON, at 42.

76 *When I go.* Id.

76 *He can tell.* Id. at 46.

76 *His 170 page.* Id. at 20, 296–297.

77 *Well, Maitre O'Reilly.* Id. at 300.

77 *If you don't.* RICHARDSON, at 302.

77 *the lack of . . . centres.* Id. at 313; Kanatewat v. James Bay Dev. Corp., [1973] 41 D.L.R. (3d) 1.

77 *a considerable number . . . recreation.* RICHARDSON, at 313.

78 *salutary shock . . . transformation.* Id. at 314.

78 *Follow the Energy . . . complex.* Jamie Linton, *The Geese Have Lost Their Way*, NATURE CANADA, Spring 1991, at 28.

78 *alarming rates of.* Linton, at 30.

79 *Well, my children."* Sam Howe Verhovek, *Power Struggle*, N. Y. TIMES, January 12, 1992, § 6, at SM16 (stating that the electricity generated in the Canadian North races down the transmission lines that stretch like forests of steal across the taiga, into New York state and ultimately that crosses a grid that reaches into every home, apartment, factory and office in the state).

79 *The geese have.* Linton, at 30.

79 *As the Great.* Verhovek.

80 *[C]onquerors are not.* SEAN MCCUTCHEON, ELECTRIC RIVERS: THE STORY OF THE JAMES BAY PROJECT 34 (1991), at 42.

80 *That the James . . . inevitable.* MCCUTCHEON, at 148, quoting Camille Dagenais, former head of SNC, an engineering contractor for Groupe Lavalin, which constructed the La Grande complex, Grand Council of the Crees (of Quebec), *Cree Legal Struggle against Great Whale Project (2000)*, http://www.waseskun.net/cree.htm, at 145.

80 *In my view.* MCCUTCHEON, at 148.

80 *considerable magnitude . . . approach.* Cree Reg'l Auth. v. Canada (Fed. Admin.), [1992] 1 F.C. 440, 447 (T.D. Can.) [hereinafter Cree Reg'l Auth. I]. The description of the Communicators to Quebec and Hydro-Quebec are taken from this source.

81 *[a]n extensive period.* Id.

81 *if the development is.* Cree Reg'l Auth. v. Quebec (Procureur Gen.), [1991] 42 F.T.R. 160, 161-63 (Can.) [hereinafter Cree Reg'l Auth. II], at 164 [The following quotes are from this opinion], at 164.

82 *never submit . . . illegal.* William Walker, *Who Controls the Environment?*, TORONTO STAR, July 14, 1991, at B4, quoting Lisa Bacon, Quebec Minister of Energy.

82 *Hydroelectric development is.* MCCUTCHEON, at 185–186.

82 *agreement in principle.* MCCUTCHEON, at 138; Verhovek.

83 *arrogant and contemptuous,". . . mislead.* MCCUTCHEON, at 159.

83 *carefully airlifting animals.* Verhovek.

83 *an accomplice to.* Id.

83 *Largely at my.* Richard M. Flynn, Letter to the Editor, NEW YORK TIMES, January 26, 1992, § 6, at 6.

84 *the public interest.* Quebec (Attorney Gen.) v. Canada (Nat'l Energy Bd.), [1991] 3 F.C. 443 (Fed. Ct. Can.) [hereinafter Quebec (Attorney Gen.) I], at 453–454.

84 *future construction of.* Quebec (Attorney Gen.) v. Canada (Nat'l Energy Bd.), [1994] 1 S.C.R. 159, 189 (Can.) [hereinafter Quebec (Attorney Gen.) II].

84 *In March 1994.* Quebec (Attorney Gen.) II, 1 S.C.R. 159, at 191.

84 *expressly refrain . . . determinations.* Id. at 192. [The quotations that follow are taken from this opinion.]

85 *As long as.* Mark Clayton, *Canadian Court Ruling Heartens Native Groups*, CHRISTIAN SCI. MONITOR (Boston, Mass.), March 2, 1994, at 4.

86 *the most magnificent.* Boyce Richardson, James Bay Crees Surrender Their Great River Rupert to Industrial Development: Rely on Quebec Promises in Return (October 26, 2001), http://www.ottertooth.com/Reports/Rupert/News/rupert-surrender3.htm; MCCUTCHEON, at 141.

86 *I feel it.* Id.

87 *nothing in this.* Id. The author writes: "the Crees have, in a sense, stripped themselves naked before their long-term adversaries, and are now hoping they will keep their promises as they have not done in the past." Id.

Chapter 5 Taj Mahal

89 *Mahatma Gandhi had.* The description of the political chaos, government reaction, and civil and political rights litigation that follows is taken from BIPAN. CHANDRA, IN THE NAME OF DEMOCRACY: J.P. MOVEMENT AND EMERGENCY, Penguin books (India, 2003). S. P. Sathe, *Judicial Activism: The Indian Experience*, 6 Wash. U.J. L. & Policy 29, 41–59 (2001); Adam M. Smith, *Making Itself at Home Understanding Foreign Law in Domestic Jurisprudence: The Indian Case*, 24 BERKELEY J. INT'L. L. 218, 234–235 (2006).

90 *The story resumes.* M. C. Mehta, Address at the Environmental Law Conference, University of Oregon School of Law (March 2003) [hereinafter Mehta Presentation]. The description of M. C. Mehta and his first encounter with the Taj Mahal that follows is taken from this source. Additional information on M. C. Mehta may be

found at Person of the Year, FIRST CITY MAGAZINE, 1999; Vinod Behl and Onkar Singh, The Green Crusader, SUNDAY OBSERVER, March 13, 1994; Dehli's Green Warrior, ASIA WEEK, August 25, 1995; Vir Sing, Environment: Bringing The Polluters to Justice, EARTH TIMES/ASIA, February 16, 1977; Susan P. Evangelista, "Biography of Mahesh Chandler Mehta: The 1997 Ramon Magsaysay Award for Public Service", at http://www.rmaf.org.ph/Awardees/Biography/BiographyMehta Mah.htm; TLS, TULANE ENVTL. News, Fall 2003, at 7.

90 *too greedy, they.* Mehta Presentation, p. 3; MC Mehta Visits TLS, p. 7.

90 *the Taj Mahal is.* Id.

90 *Neither words nor.* FREDERICK SLEIGH ROBERTS, FORTY-ONE YEARS IN IN-DIA 154 Chapter XX, para. 48 (2005).

91 *But when one.* Mehta v. Union, A.I.R. 1997 S.C. 723 (hereinafter "TAJ MAHAL"); Those recent estimates put the figure at 3 million visitors in 2004 ; See also The Taj Mahal: History and Facts, http://www.buzzle.com/articles/the-taj-mahal-history-and-facts.html.

91 *and adorns the.* A 2007 "global poll" places, once again, the Taj Majal with an updated "seven wonders of the world," in company with the Roman Colosseum, Machu Picchu, and the Great Wall of China. Barry Hatton, "Wonders of world get update," THE TIMES PICAYUNE, July 8, 2007, at A-3.

91 *Leaping back in.* STANLEY WOLPERT, A NEW HISTORY OF INDIA (Oxford, 2000), 24–60; JOHN F. RICHARDS, THE NEW CAMBRIDGE HISTORY OF IN-DIA—THE MUGHAL EMPIRE (Cambridge, 1993), 6–7; Theodore A. Mahr, *An Introduction to Law and Law Libraries in India*, 82 L. LIBR. J. 91 (1990). The description of early Indian history that follows is taken from these sources.

91 *We may take.* WOLPERT, at 165, 166; RICHARDS.

91 *The reigns of.* Muni Lal, SHAH JAHAN (Delhi, 1986), at 190–203.

92 *On one such.* Id.; David Carrol, THE TAJ MAHAL, Newsweek Book Division, New York, 1977, at 15. An early European reference to this epic love affair is that of a French traveler in 1663; Francois Bernier, "Letter to Monsieur de la Mothe le Vayer. Written at Delhi the first of July 1663," in TRAVELS IN THE MOGHUL EMPIRE, A.D. 1657–1668 (Westminster: Archibald Constable & Co.) 1891 at 293, cited in Taj Mahal, at par. 2, 12 ("Chah-Jehan raised [the Taj] to the memory of his wife Tage Mehale, that extraordinary and celebrated beauty, of whom her husband was so enamored it is said that he was constant to her during his life, and at her death was so affected as nearly to follow her to the grave."). The description of the Shah and his wife that follows is taken from LAL and Carrol, Id.

92 *The Taj was.* IBN HASAN, THE CENTRAL STRUCTURE OF THE MUGHAL EM-PIRE AND ITS PRACTICAL WORKING UP TO YEAR 1657, at 81 (photo. reprint 1967) (1936); CARROL, supra note 166, at 15. (1967) 81; Carrol, at 15.

92 *The central dome.* Taj Mahal, par. 10. The legends that follow are taken from this source.

92 *Legend, one of.* Id.

92 *Legend also has.* Id., at par. 14.

92 *Other legend says.* Id., at par. 13.

92 *and yet another.* Id., at par. 15. Marvin H. Mills, *An Architect Looks at the Taj Legend*, http://www.geocities.com/Athens/Ithaca/3440/tajm.html (contending that the structure could not have been built in the time allotted, and that its configuration indicates that it was superimposed on an existing palace).

92 *Others claim that.* Marvin H. Mills, An Architect Looks at the Taj Legend, http://www.geocities.com/Athens/Ithaca/3440/tajm.html (last visited March 6, 2009) (contending that the structure could not have been built in the time allotted, and that its configuration indicates that it was superimposed on an existing palace).

92 *Still others contend.* Mills, at 4 (observing, in addition, that both the Shah and his wife were "cruel, self-centered and vicious" as evidence that the Taj was not a monument to love); Manish Chand, *Love Is Fine But Taj Is a Monument of Power as Well*, India eNews, December 3, 2006, available at http://www.indiaenews.com/art-culture/20061203/30997.htm (citing Austrian historian, Ebba Koch).

92 *The essential truth.* Richards, at 123–124. The physical description that follows is taken from this source, and TAJ MAJAL, at 3–10.

93 *For reasons that.* Carrol, at 133–134.

93 *It is said.* Id. (describing attempt at demolition); Saurabh Sinha, East India Co tried to sell Taj Mahal, Times of India, August 20, 2005; Amy Waldman, The Taj Mahal Is a Glorious Survivor, NEW YORK TIMES, May 16, 2004 (alleged attempts to sell).

93 *All agree, however.* Id., at par. 14–15; Carrol, at 134. TAJ MAHAL paras. 14–15.

93 *BY THE 1960s.* Id.; *Taj Mahal*, at par. 5; T. K. Rajalakshmi, *Toxins and the Taj*, http://www.unesco.org/courrier/2000_07/uk/signe.htm.

93 *From there, it.* Taj Mahal, at par. 5. Thomas C. Meierding, *Marble Tombstone Weathering and Air Pollution*, North America Annals of the Association of American Geographers 83 (4), 568–588 (1993). There is, apparently, no antidote to this form of erosion save that of reducing the pollution, Michael Reddy, *Preserving and Protecting Monuments and Historic Sites*, U.S.Geological Survey, available at http://www.brr.cr.usgs.gov/projects/SW_corrosion/teachers-pupils/index.html.

93 *Air pollution destroys.* Meierding.

93 *Each layer of.* Taj Mahal, at par. 9, (citing report of National Environmental Engineering Research Institute).

93 *The interior walls.* Id. at par 5.

93 *The rot was.* Id.

94 *Some six and.* Id.

94 *The city of.* DAVID L. HABERMAN, RIVER OF LOVE IN AN AGE OF POLLUTION (U. of Cal. Press, 2006) 92; *DJB blamed for poor Yamuna water quality*, The Hindu, New Delhi, August 6, 2004; available at http://www.thehindu.com/2004/09/06/stories/2004080608550300.htm.

94 *In fact the.* HABERMAN.

94 *There were also.* The Taj Mahal: Pollution and Toursim, available at http://www .american.edu/TED/taj.htm, at 14a.

94 *Indeed, there were.* Id.

94 *True, Indian culture.* India is a nation of many religions, but Hinduism, followed by Buddhism, predominates. Both faiths teach a reverence for nature. Hindu sacred texts, beginning with the Vedas (c. 1750–600 BC) speak of the sanctity of Earth, and the epic Mababharata (c. 500–200 BC) warns that when humans despoil nature "the lives of the living will be ruined with the world." Vashudha Narayanan, *Water, Wood and Wisdom: Ecological Perspectives from the Hindu Traditions*, 130 Daedalus, Vol. 4, 179 (2001). Ainslie Thomas Embree et al., 1 SOURCES OF INDIAN TRADITION (1988).

94 *Mahatma Gandhi, reacting.* E. F. SCHUMACHER, SMALL IS BEAUTIFUL: A STUDY OF ECONOMICS AS IF PEOPLE MATTERED (1973), Part 1.

94 *tryst with destiny.* R. Gaiha and V. Kulkarni, *Is growth central to poverty alleviation in India?* , 52 J. Int'l Aff. 145 (1998). Morris D. Morris, *Growth of the Large Scale Industry to 1947*, in Dharma Kumar (ed), THE CAMBRIDGE ECONOMIC HISTORY OF INDIA (1989) 553.

94 *Temples of Modern.* Paul R. Brass, *The Politics of India since Independence*, in THE NEW CAMBRIDGE HISTORY OF INDIA (1990).

94 *He offered subsidies.* A. Vaidyanathan, *The Indian Economy since Independence*, in THE CAMBRIDGE ECONOMIC HISTORY OF INDIA, at 947.

94 *and rich incentives.* Id.

94 *By the mid.* A. Grover, *India Report* APJEL Vol. 1 (1996) at 91; Asha Krishnakumar "Importing Danger," *Frontline*, December 6–19, 2003, http://www.hinduonnet.com/ fline/fl2025/stories/20031219001908600.htm.

94 *Mining and manufacturing.* Reserve Bank of India, *Report on Currency and Finance*, 1973–4 at 63.

94 *Other industrial output.* Id.

95 *On the one . Address of Prime MinisterIndira Gandhi at the United Nations Conference on the Human Environment*, Stockholm, June 14 1972, cited in SHYAM DIVAN AND ARMIN ROSENCRANZ, ENVIRONMENTAL LAW AND POLICY IN INDIA, 2d ed., 31–32) (hereinafter Divan and Rosencranz).

95 *India genuflected towards.* C. M. ABRAHAM, ENVIRONMENTAL JURISPRUDENCE IN INDIA (1999) 65–70. Jasmeet Kaur Madham, *India*, in ENVIRONMENTAL LAW AND ENFORCEMENT IN THE ASIA PACIFIC RIM (2002), 215; Harish Salve, *Justice between Generations: Environment and Social Justice*, in SUPREME BUT NOT INFALLIBLE: Essays in Honour of the Supreme Court of India (2000), 360; Armin Rosencranz and Michael Jackson, The Delhi Pollution Case, The Supreme Court of India and the Limits of Judicial Power, 28 Columbia Environ-

mental LJ 222, 232–234 (2003). The consensus among observers is that the environmental agencies, whatever other handicaps they faced, simply lacked the will to act.

95 *Born into a.* Id.; *Person of the Year*. The description of Mehta's background that follows is taken from this source and others.

96 *He married Radha.* The description of Mehta's marriage, move to Delhi, and immersion into the Taj Majal that follows is taken from these sources.

96 *It had started.* 163 US 537 (1896).

96 *The opinion was.* S. P. Sathe, at 43-48 (discussing case and reaction to it by the public, and, subsequently, the Court).

96 *Smarting from the.* The reversal began with a series of civil rights cases, lead among them Maneka Gandhi v. Union of India, A.I.R. 1978 S.C. 597, invalidating the government's impoundment of a citizen's passport without due process of law. Id., at 54–56. Another seminal challenge was the Judges Transfer Case, A.I.R. 1982, S.C. 149, permitting private lawyers to challenge the transfer of judges for allegedly political reasons.

96 *no person shall.* INDIA CONST. art. 21.

96 *wider meanings that.* Maneka Gandhi, A.I.R. 1978 SC 621, at 709.

96 *flexible enough to.* Francis Coralie Mullin v. Administrator Union Territory of Delhi, A.I.R. 1981 S.C. 746.

96 *fundamental rights.* INDIA CONST. art. 32. Adam M Smith at 237.

96 *Moreover, one could.* Id. Adam Smith, p. 154.

97 *One of the.* Dehradun Quarrying Case cited as Rural Litigation and Entitlement Kendra, Dehra Dun v. State of Uttar Pradesh, A.I.R. 1988 S.C. 2187 (letter to Court), and Mahesh R. Desai v. Union of India Writ Petition, A.I.R. 1988 S.C. 988 (complaint from journalist).

97 *to whom a . . . courts.* People's Union for Democratic Rights v. Union of India, A.I.R. 1982 S.C. 1473.

97 *social justice is.* Judges Transfer Case, A.I.R. 1982 S.C. 189. For the wide range of "representative" standing afforded to groups to protect the interests of the affected public; Sathe, 78–79.

97 *It began to.* Divan and Rosencranz, at 143–147, and cases cited therein, describing these new mechanisms.

97 *It created committees.* Id.

97 *collaborative efforts . . . justice .* P.U.D.R. v. India, A.I.R. 1984, S.C. 1477–1478. In one case involving rickshaw operators, the Court addressed a measure restricting licenses to owners not by striking down the law but by negotiating a scheme whereby those who did not own their own rickshaws could obtain loans from the Punjab National Bank to acquire them. Sathe, at 78–79. The Court was not content with addressing the lawfulness of a problem; it was going to solve it.

97 *lachrymose millionaires . . . indulgence.* Justice Krishna Iyer, *Judical Justice: A New*

Focus towards Social Justice, April 1985 (lecture published by Campus Law Centre, University of Delhi, N. M. Tripathi Private Ltd.), at 145.

97 *It was submitted.* Id.

97 *Friends advised Mehta.* Mehta presentation. The description of the colloquy that follows is taken from this source.

98 *In the middle.* In re Union Carbide Corp., 634 F. Supp. 842, 844 (S.D.N.Y. 1986).

98 *Estimates of deaths.* In re Union Carbide Corp. Gas Plant Disaster at Bhopal, 634 F. Supp. 842, 844 (S.D.N.Y. 1986). The description of the casualties that followed is taken from this source.

98 *With great reluctance.* Id., at 867.

98 *Union Carbide paid.* Union Carbide settled the transferred case in India for $470 million. The payout for over 8,000 lives and 300,000 injuries came to an average of $1,500 per person. Editorial, *Champagne and Toxic Gas*, SAN JOSE MERCURY NEWS, November 28, 1984.

98 *Within a few.* Divan and Rosencranz, at 143–145.The resulting spate of environmental legislation and administrative structures is described herein.

99 *Ganga was sunken.* T. S. Eliot, *The Wasteland*, in COLLECTED POEMS, 1909–1962 at 51, 68 (1963).

100 *Hindu myth presents.* Payal Sampat, THE RIVER GANGES' LONG DECLINE, World Watch, July–August 1996, p. 5; Vasudha Narayanan "Water, Wood and Wisdom: Ecological Perpectives from the Hindu Traditions," *Daedalus* Fall 2001 at 179.

100 *It is said.* M. C. Mehta v. Union of India, A.I.R., S.C. 1998 at 1037, 1038 (Ganges River).

100 *impure objects like.* Manu Smriti 4:56, reported in M. Banarsidass, *The Laws of Manu*, New Delhi, 1964, quoted in Narayanan at 179.

100 *There was a.* Mehta presentation.

100 *huge quantities of.* Id.

100 *In late 1984.* M. C. Mehta, Harnessing the Law to Clean Up India, Multinational Monitor, July–August 1998, at 16. The description of the fire that follows is taken from this source.

100 *One tenth of.* Payal Sampat, *The River Ganges' Long Decline*, World Watch, July–August 1996, at 24.

100 *Into the river.* Id.

100 *Fecal coliform counts.* Jill McGivering, *Clean-up for Filthy Ganges*, BBC News (2003), available at http://news.bbc.co.uk/2/hi/south-asia/2860565.stm (interviewing Manoj Nodkarni, Centre for Science and Environment).

100 *Not surprisingly, one.* RLE Kendra v. Dehradun v. State of Uttar Pradesh, A.I.R. 1985 S.C. 652.

101 *Out of caution.* M. C. Mehta v. Union of India, A.I.R. (1988) S.C.R. 530 (hereinafter GANGES) at 534.

101 *He based his.* Rural Litigation and Entitlement Kendra v. State of Uttar Pradesh (Dehradun Quarrying Case), A.I.R. 1985, S.C. 652.

101 *Rather, it implicated. Ganges River,* 1988 S.C.R. 530, at 555

101 *But how, mused.* Mehta presentation.

101 *He suggested that.* Id. The description of the service of process and appearance of the defendants that follows is taken from this source.

101 *The Court grouped.* Id.

101 *It accepted data.* Divan and Rosencranz, at 144.

101 *It took industry.* Mehta Presentation, at 7; Ganges River, 1988 S.C.R. 530.

101 *It conducted no.* GANGES A.I.R. 1988 S.C.R. at 552–555.

102 *industries was "irrelevant".* Id.

102 *Just as all.* Id.

102 *turning point.* Mehta presentation.

102 *Those that did. Ganges River,* 1988 S.C.R. 530, at 555.

102 *Instead, they too.* Id.

102 *over the next. S.C. Orders Closure of 84 Industries in U.P.,* The Hindu (International Edition), vol. 21, no. 4 (Madras, India), January 2, 1995, at 13, reported in C. M. Abraham, at 112.

102 *We are conscious. Ganges River,* 1988 S.C.R. 530.

102 *It is too. Taj Mahal,* at par. 32.

103 *necessary anti-pollution. Taj Mahal,* Id. at para. 6 (citing study of an expert committee on the state of the Taj that had been "annexed along with the writ petition" and similar studies).

103 *On May 3.* Id. at par. 7.

103 *It stated that.* Id. at par. 8.

103 *Indeed, 212 did.* Id.

103 *With a view.* Id. at par. 10, pars 9, 12.

103 *The deadlines were.* Id. at par. 10 (requiring the Department of Industries to file a list of all air polluting industries within the Taj region "within a week from today); Id., at par. 11, requiring the Department of Environment and Forests to identify an authority to prepare a survey within three weeks, and the Court registrar to send notice of this order within three days).

104 *primary duty . . . safeguard.* Id. at par. 13.

104 *indicate in positive.* Id.

104 *positive assistance.* Id.

104 *nothing positive has.* Id.

104 *We want [a].* Id.

104 *no helpful response.* Id. at par. 14.

104 *Citing several articles.* Id. at par. 46.

104 *three statutes and.* Id., at par. 51 A (g).

104 *and three principles.* Id., at par. 29 (including the Precautionary Principle, the Polluter Pays Principle, and Sustainable Development).

104 *eliminated at any.* Id. at par. 30.

104 *one percent chance . . . involved.* Id.

104 *It ordered the.* Id., at par. 31, 32.

104 *It ordered government.* Id., at par. 32.

104 *It ordered the.* Id.

105 *Turning to the.* Id.

105 *shifting bonus.* Id.

105 *The Court had.* Mehta Presentation at 6, 12–13.

105 *Now it went.* Id.

105 *The Court's running.* TAJ MAHAL par. 32, 35.

105 *It has required.* M.C. Mehta v. Union of India, (1998) 8 S.C.C. 711.

105 *The Archeological Survey.* Atwood, at 125, n. 110.

105 *Having rid itself.* Tata Group, http://www.tata.com/company/profile.aspx?sectid= a4Nd8IHyrqI=.

106 *In another Mehta.* Rosencranz and Jackson, at 232–234. The article recites a similar history of government resistance to its own, and the Court's, public health mandates, Id. M. C. Mehta v. Union of India, A.I.R. 1998, S.C. 206 (Delhi Pollution case).

106 *There are limits.* Divan, *Cleaning up the Ganga*, Economic and Political Weekly, July 1, 1995, at 1557, cited in Divan and Rosencranz, at 147, 149.

106 *judicial activism.* Rosencranz and Jackson, at 244–253; Sathe, at 88–107; Atwood, at 116–117. Correspondence from Professor Shudhir Chopra to the author, February 28, 2005, stating: "The problem with the Indian decision is that it did not stop the activity, only created a much more corrupt system where many lawyers of administration now take a huge cut. Second, it has established a bad precedent in law, what was meant to be solved by proper legislation has been left with judges who cannot legislate the details," email dated February 28, 2005, on file with author. Each commentator expresses reservations about how far the Court can and should go. None suggest an alternative, however, given the chronic reluctance of the executive branch to enforce the law; Id., "Perhaps the answer lies more in ethics and attitude than in economics or science based regulation." This may be true, but the political question on all environmental issues is what to do in the meantime.

107 *It is further.* Bandhua Mukti Morcha v. Union of India, A.I.R. 1984, S.C. 802 ("There is always the possibility, in public interest litigation, of succumbing to the temptation of crossing into the territory which properly pertains to the legislature or to the Executive Government. In contrast with policy making by legislation . . . no such viable impact can be perceived when judicial decrees are forged and fashioned by a few judicial personages in the confines of a court."). The more recent case of Balco Employees Union (Reg'd) v. Union of India, 2001, 4 LRI 957 (refusing to interject the Court into "policy" determinations).

107 *In a case.* M. C. Mehta v. Union of India (Oleum Gas Leak), A.I.R. 1987, S.C. 965.

107 *In another treating.* M. C. Mehta v. Kamal Nath, (1977) 1 S.C.C. 388.

107 *He went on.* Mehta presentation.

107 *In one of.* M. C. Mehta v. Union of India, Writ Petition No. 860 of 1991 (2003), http://www.downtoearth.org.in/html/sc-directive.htm.

107 *In furtherance, the.* M. C. Mehta v Union of India, A.I.R. 1992 SC 382.

107 *if the laws . . . consequences.* Id.

108 *We are in.* Id.

Chapter 6 Lenin's Trees

111 *ON A COLD.* Interview by Ilya Fedyaev with Vera Mischenko, President Ecojuris, in Moscow, Russia (January 13, 2005). The description that follows of the filing of the first Russian Forest case, Verkh. Sud RF Ruling of February 17, 1998 (Zlotnikova T. V., Lebedeva K. E. et al. v. Russian Federation) is taken from this interview.

112 *Russia is full.* Recalling Churchill's fine phrase: "[Russia] is a riddle wrapped in a mystery inside an enigma." Bartlett's Familiar Quotations, at 743.

112 *It has never.* Kevin Klose, RUSSIA AND THE RUSSIANS; INSIDE THE CLOSED SOCIETY (1984) (describing Russia's shifting attitudes vis-à-vis the West).

112 *Or what it.* USDA FOREIGN AGRI. SERV., REPORT NO. RS4007, RUSSIAN FEDERATION SOLID WOODS PRODUCTS ANNUAL REPORT 2004 3 (2004), available at http://www.fas.usda.gov/gainfiles/200402/146105502.pdf. The area of 850 million hectares covered with forest vegetation accounts for 22 percent of global forest area and 50 percent of the total area of Russia (1710 million ha).

113 *the spirits that.* V. O. Klyuchevsky, *The Course of Russian History,* in 1 WORKS IN 9 VOLUMES 1, 83 (1987), cited in V. K. Teplyakov et al., A HISTORY OF RUSSIAN FORESTRY AND ITS LEADERS. (1998), available at http://www.fs.fed.us/pnw/wenlab/pdf/394-Everett-2.pdf. "They built with pine and oak, they heated with birch splinters, they shod themselves with bast, and made household tools of linden. For centuries in the north, as in the earlier times in the south the forest fed the economy with the pelts of fur-bearing animals and the honey of forest bees. The forest served as a dependable refuge from external enemies who burdened the Russian people with sorrow and chains."

113 *a procession of.* Teplyakov, at 1.

113 *In the seventeenth.* Id., at 2. v. The description of his actions and those of Peter the Great that follows are taken from this text.

113 *It is true.* Id. at 14.

113 *merciless logging.* Id. at 5.

113 *precise relationship between.* Id. at 7. The description of pre- and postrevolutionary forest policies that follows is taken from this source.

114 *imperative . . . opportunistic . . . sustainability.* Klyuchevsky, at 10.

114 *liquidated altogether.* Teplyakov, at 11.

114 *THE STORY goes.* The author was told this story on two occasions, by two different Soviet officials, one in the Institute for State and Law and the other in the Kremlin, during an official US–Soviet Union science and environment exchange in 1977. Oliver A. Houck, Lenin's Trees, AUDUBON, March 1980, at 104, 107. Setting aside the unlikely possibility that this story was invented for the occasion, it clearly demonstrates something that Russians want to believe, true or not, which says something about values.

114 *In 1943, a.* V. K. Teplyakaov, at 10. The description of the first categories that follows is taken from this source.

115 *Group One forests.* In some *zapovedniki* (wilderness preserves), even fauna of the surrounding area are excluded. Elizabeth Barrett Ristroph, *Leave It to the Scientists! An Examination of Russian Environmental Policy-Making*, 10 ALB. L. ENVTL. OUT-LOOK 33, 57–61 (2205) (providing an overview of the history and present management of *zapovedniki* and discussing how in many such reserves human intrusion is limited to scientific study and measurements). "*Zapovedniki* were the brainchild of early Soviet scientists who sought to use these nature preserves as "reference points" (etalony) for pristine ecosystems, unspoiled by human encroachment." Id. at 57 (citations omitted).

115 *More particularly, it.* Id. at 56.

116 *State recognized Nature.* Leslie Powell, *Western and Russian Environmental NGOs: A Greener Russia?*, in THE POWER AND LIMITS OF NGOs: A CRITICAL LOOK AT BUILDING DEMOCRACY IN EASTERN EUROPE AND EURASIA 126, 149 n.5 (Sarah E. Mendelson and John K. Glenn eds., 2002).

116 *On the Radical.* Powell, at 130.

117 *The Effectiveness of.* Kathleen E. Watters, "Intial Environmental Examination" (1994) (unpublished manuscript, on file with author).

117 *In 1992, as.* Levin, at 711 n. 231; Zakon Rossiskoi Federatsii: Ob Okhrane Okrahaiushche Priirodnoi Sredi [Law of the Russian Federation: On the Protection of the Natural Environment]. December 19, 1991, 10 Vedomosti, S'ezda Narodnykh Deutatov RSFSR I Verkhovnogo Soveta RSFSR [Ved. RSFSR] [Bulletin of the Congress of People's Deputies of the Russian Soviet Federal Socialist Republic and Supreme Council of the RSFSR] 1992, No. 10, Item 457. President Boris Yeltsin signed Russia's first comprehensive environmental law *On Environmental Protection* in December 1991. In particular, the law required that government agencies prepare an expertise (similar to the environmental impact statement required for agency action in the United States) whenever the agencies' actions could adversely affect the environment. Levin, at 711.

117 *The following year.* Konstitutsiia Rossiiskoi Federatsii [hereinafter Konst. Rf. (1993)] [Constitution]. For an English translation of the Constitution, refer to G. DANI-

LENKO & W. BURNHAM, LAW AND LEGAL SYSTEM OF THE RUSSIAN FED-ERATION 591 (1999). Article 42 provides the constitutional right of each person to a healthy environment and covers the damage caused by environmental violations to health or property. Under Article 32, citizens have the right to participate in the governing of the state, either directly or via their representatives. In order to achieve goals of nature protection, and to efficiently participate in environmental decision making, citizens have the right to associate under Art. 30. They can also create and join trade unions in order to protect social, professional, and economic rights and interests. Denial of access to environmental information can be appealed to the court as a breach of the citizens' constitutional right, under the provisions of Articles 42, 24 29(4) 41(3), 46, and 52. Article 58 states that it is everyone's duty to preserve nature and the environment and to treat natural resources carefully.

117 *A new Civil.* Article 116 established citizen's rights to appeal in the Supreme Court against nonnormative acts of the RF president and the RF government, and against normative acts of ministries and agencies. Grazhdanskii Kodeks RF [GK] [Civil Code] art. 116 (Russ.) (1964) [hereinafter Civil Code].

117 *a new forest.* Lesnoi Kodeks [LK] [Forestry Code] art. 65 (1997), English translation available at http://www.forest.ru/eng/legislation /forestcode.html ("The sites for the building of facilities affecting the state and reproduction of forests shall be coordinated with the organ of state power of the RF subject and with the respective territorial agency of the Federal Forestry Agency, with mandatory performance of state ecological expert examination."); Lesnoi Kodeks [LK] [Forestry Code], Fed. Act. No. 22-FZ (adopted by the State Duma on January 22, 1997)(describing how conversion of forest lands into nonforestlands for purposes not related to forestry shall be allowed only in the presence of a positive conclusion of the state ecological expert examination).

117 *A 1995 statute.* On Ecological Examination, Russian Federation Federal Act No. 174-FZ, art. 11 (1995) (federal environmental expertise must be carried out for "the materials establishing transfer of the forest lands into non-forest lands.").

118 *If in the.* Memorandum from Ilya Feyaev on Russian Forest Research, to author (November 10, 2004) [hereinafter Fedyaev memorandum] (on file with author) (citing Natal'ia Evegen'evna Sidorkina, Natal'ia Evegen'evna Sidrkina, The Voluntary Nullification of an Illegal Decision of the Authorities—A Result of the Community's Legal Actions, [translation], available at http://webcenter.ru/~ecojuris/ RPUBLIC/B3/b3_4.htm [last visited April 1, 2007]). The description of this case is taken from this source.

119 *An active environmentalist.* Id. at 25 (translating and discussing V. Kolesnikova, *Forestry Summit*) [FOREST BULLETIN], August, 1999, available at http://www .forest.ru?rus/bulletin/11/6.html).

120 *Zlotnikova I, filed.* Fedyaev Memorandum, at 4; Verkh. Sud RF Ruling of February

17, 1998; Vera Mischenko and Ericka Rosenthal, Citizen Environmental Enforcement in Russia: The First Successful Nation-Wide Case, FIFTH INT'L CONF. ON ENVTL. COMPLIANCE & ENFORCEMENT 419, 419–421 (1998), available at http://www.inece.org/5thvoll/mischenko.pdf.

120 *The grounds of.* The complaint alleged: "The Government of the Russian Federation has issued decrees transferring land from 'first group' forests without conforming to the necessity that such transfers are to be made under exclusive circumstances, as stipulated by the law. Furthermore, plaintiffs believe that these government decrees should have been subject to a preliminary state ecological examination prior to their issuance, and in the opinion of petitioners, a requisite examination was not undertaken, despite the fact that such decrees can have a negative influence on the surrounding environment." Verkh, Sud RF Ruling of February 17, 1998. Because some of the challenged devrees predated 1977, the Court treated the case under forest law existing at the time, which retained "exclusivity." 993 Forest Law, art. 22.

120 *It refused to.* Mischenko and Rosenthal, at 419

120 *The first hearing.* Fedyaev memorandum, translating and discussing V. Kolesnikova, *Forestry Summit—New Round.*

121 *You women would.* Mischenko interview.

121 *smoldering discontent . . . overcome.* Fedyaev memorandum, translating V. Kolesnikova, *Forestry Summit—A New Round.* The government also argued that the lawsuit was premature because there was no harm to the plantiffs. ("Representatives of the Government of the Russian Federation believe that the transfer of 'first group' forests into forested land is not a violation of the ecological examination requirement, as the passing of decrees in and of themselves cannot have negative effects on the environment. They argue that the realization of decrees is possible only after acceptance by local authorities of the decision to transfer these 'first group' forests into non-forested land."), Verkh. Sud RF Ruling.

122 *I have just.* Fedyaev Memorandum, translating and discussing V. Kolesnikova, *Forestry Summit*; Mischenko.

122 *environmental harm.* Verkh. Sud RF February 17, 1998 ("[T]he Court cannot agree with a reason of representatives of the Government of the Russian Federation that challenged orders could not entail negative influence on a surrounding environment and that carrying out of the state ecological examination was not required.").

122 *no environmental review.* Id. ("[A] state ecological examination] must be carried out in each specific case transferring "first group" forests into non-forested land, taking into account the requirements of the law mentioned above and other circumstances.").

122 *and no showing.* Id. ("In none of challenged directions orders did the defendants justify 'exclusive' circumstances, or the necessity of transferring such forestlands. Representatives of the [Russian Government] also did not present during this judi-

cial session any materials proving the necessity of such transfer of forested land in 'first-group' forest to non-forested land.")

122 *And so, again.* Verkhovnyi Sud Rossiiskoi Federatsii [Verkh. Sud RF] [Supreme Court of the Russian Federation] Presidium Determination No. 48pv98 of September 23, 1998, available at http://infopravo.by.ru/fed1998/ch03/akt14637.shtm (reversing and remanding Verkh. Sud Ruling No. GKPI 97-249 of February 17, 1998).

122 *While the first.* Verkhovnyi Sud Rossiiskoi Federatsii [Verkh. Sud RF] [Supreme Court of the Russian Federation] Appellate Decision No. KAS98-121 of February 12, 1999.

122 *all current and.* Mischenko and Rosenthal, at 421.

123 *When the dust.* Verkh. Sud RF Ruling of May 12, 1999, translated ["The Court considers it necessary to inform the Government of the Russian Federation these facts establishing that the adoption of decrees must follow procedure; so that in the future transfer decrees whose realization can negatively be reflected in an environment are executed."]

123 *Western notions of.* Indeed, it can overthrow authoritarian society, as more than one Eastern Bloc country discovered during the breakup of the Soviet Union. For example, James Friedberg and Branimir Zaimov, Politics, Environment and the Rule of Law in Bulgaria, 4 DUKE J. COMP. & INT'L L. 225, 263 (1994) ("Environmental activism was central to the peaceful Bulgarian revolution that culminated in the ouster of Todor Zhivkov in November 1989. Terrible ecological degradation coalesced with a national desire for change to incubate political rebellion in the relatively protected atmosphere of environmental protest—an atmosphere safer than direct political challenge to the totalitarian reqime.").

123 *established an independent.* Powell, at 131 (describing the rise and fall of the Ministry of Protection of Environment and Natural Resources of the Russian Federation).

124 *vertical executive power.* Bill Nichols, *Putin's Victory Clear—Russia's Future Cloudy*, USA TODAY, March 15, 2004, at 09A.

124 *managed democracy.* Mark McDonald, *Russia: Watchers Say Putin Amassing Power—Economic, Democratic Reforms Giving Way to Authoritarian State*, CHARLOTTE OBSERVER (N.C.), January 8, 2005, at 14A.

124 *Putin is not.* Ernest Partridge, The Online Gadfly, *Notes from a Conference: Environment and Human Rights in the Russian Federation*, http://gadfly.igc.org/russia/report.htm (last visited August 12, 2006).

124 *The subsequent crackdown.* Tom Lantos, *Putting Democracy First in Relations with Russia*, FLETCHER F. WORLD AFF., Summer 2005, at 13 (describing the "reversals in human rights, the rule of law, and freedom of expression since Putin took power in 2000. The country has eliminated virtually all independent media, clamped down on political opposition, conducted seriously flawed parliamentary and

presidential elections, jailed business leaders who were perceived to be hostile to the state, used dubious excuses to nationalize the largest private oil company, and most recently eliminated direct elections of regional governors and representatives."); Nichols, Sullivan, Goldgeier.

125 *As soon as . . . problems. Russian Leader Blasts Environmentalists for Holding Back Development,* AGENCE FRANCE-PRESSE, July 20, 2005, available at http://www .terradaily.com/news/russia-05x.html (last visited August 12, 2006).

125 *Sadly," Putin declared . . . organizations".* Rory Cox, Putin Sets Back Ecological Clock, PAC. ENV'T, July 15, 2000, available at http://www.pacificenvironment.org .article.php?id=199 (last visited March 30, 2007).

125 *terrible, but better.* Powell, at 132.

125 *and abolished, yet again.* Id.; Danielle Knight, World Bank Slammed for Eco-Destruction of Russia, INTERPRESS SERV., September 6, 2006, available at http:// www.commondreams.org/headlines/090600-0.htm (last visited January 12, 2007). Putin's decree amounts to more than just another restructuring of Russian bureaucracy according to Dimitry Lisitsyn of Sakhalin Environmental Watch, an advocacy group on Sakhalin Island of the Russian Far East. "The abolished committee on environmental protection was one of the major achievements of the democratic movement in Russia following the collapse of the Soviet Union," said Lisitsyn.

125 *letting the cat.* Environment News Service, Court Asked to Reverse Putin's Purge of Russian Environment, Forest Agencies, E-LAW, August 22, 2000, available at http:// www.elaw.org/news /partners/text.asp?id=313 (last visited January 16, 2007).

125 *Following a referendum.* For discussion of the referendum, Farewell, Referendum, available at http://www.democracy.ru/english/article.php?id=166 (last visited January 11, 2007); for an overview of the new law see Valdimir Volkov, New Law on Russian Referendums: Crude Attack on Democratic Rights, World Socialist Website, June 8, 2004, available at http://www.wsws.org/articles/2004/jun2004/ refe-j09/shtml (last visited January 11, 2006).

125 *At first we.* Tomila Lankina, Karelians Denounce Federal Forestry Reforms, RUSS-IAN REGIONAL REPORT Vol. 11, No. 5 (Int'l Relations and Security Network), February 2006, available at http://sel.isn.Ch/serviceengine/FileContent?service ID=ISFPub&fileid=C6AA6cb9-7DF-B635-04C7-A911B7076405&Ing=en. (quoting Andrei Goromtsev, Senior Scholar the Forest Research Institute of the Karelian Research Center, Russian Academy of Sciences).

126 *Government actions against.* Cox, at 309; Powell, at 218, at 146. Since Putin's rise to power, "many advocacy groups have reported being harassed by police, security, and tax agents, some of whom have been known to barge unannounced into the NGO offices and confiscate files while dressed in ski masks and bearing assault weapons." Id.

126 *Not content with.* Rashi Alimov and Igor Kudrik, Bellona Foundation, NGO Bill Becomes Law (January 19, 2006), available at http://bellona.org/english_import_ area/international/russia/envirorights/info_access/41667; Josh Wilson, Russian

Bills on NGOs to Become Law, SRAS NEWSLETTER (The School of Russian and Asian Studies Newsletter), December 27, 2005, available at http://www.sras.org/news2.phtml?m=480. To be fair, President Putin did relax some of the most extreme provisions of the bill.

126 *The Kremlin is.* Alimov, at 325.

126 *You go there.* Sabrina Tavernise, *Siberian Oil Rush*, TIMES PICAYUNE, October 5, 2003, at A-36.

126 *In 1999, Ecojuris.* Id.; THE ROLE OF ENVIRONMENTAL NGOS, at 216, at 189.

126 *Five years later.* Two Lawsuits Against Sakhalin-2 in Moscow Courts, SAK= HALIN TIMES, March 26, 2004 ("'Ecojuris' Ecological Legal Institute and 50 non-governmental organisations filed the second lawsuit. The NGOs are protesting the results of the state ecological expertise report on the Sakhalin-2 project.").

127 *They garnered some.* Id.

127 *Putin won, but.* Levin, at 192, at 483 (noting that the Supreme Court of Russia dismissed the complaint without a court hearing, on the ground that it had no jurisdiction and that the decree did not violate citizens' rights). Ecojuris Institute then went before the European Court of Human Rights, asserting that Putin's decree violated the European Convention on the Protection of Human Rights and Fundamental Freedoms. The Court refused to consider the case, finding it had no jurisdiction to decide the question of legality of the presidential decree.

127 *While all this.* Pacific Environment: Siberia Pacific Pipeline: Putin's Pipedream, available at http://www.pacificenvironment.org/article.php?list=type&type=65 (last visited January 16, 2006). The description of the Lake Baikal pipeline controversy that follows is taken largely from this source.

127 *Putin took credit.* Steven Lee Meyers, *Putin Reverses Decision on Pipeline Path*, N.Y. TIMES, April 26, 2006.

127 *But he would.* Russian Leader Blasts Environmentalists for Holding Back Development, AGENCE FRANCE-PRESSE, July 20, 2005, available at http:// www.terra daily.com/news/russia-05x.html ("Putin gave as an example environmental objections that had caused the re-routing of an oil pipeline that is being built from western Siberia to Russia's Pacific coast in order to supply Asian markets.").

127 *What she and.* In addition to participating in the Network of Russian Public Interest Environmental Lawyers from 1997, Ecojuris has established the Eurasian Public Interest Environmental Law Network to work alongside colleagues from Azerbaijan, Moldova, Ukraine, Kazakhstan, Kyrgyztan, and Uzbekistan. Id. at 187–188.

Chapter 7 Acheloos

131 *ACHELOOS WAS the.* REX WARNER, THE STORIES OF THE GREEKS 102–104 (1976). The account of the struggle between Acheloos and Hercules that follows is taken from this source.

132 *The Acheloos today.* Ioannis Karakostas and Ioannis Vassilopoulos, ENVIRON-MENTAL LAW IN GREECE 9 (1999) (identifying the Acheloos as the second-largest river, at 220 km); Kimon Hadjibiros, The Acheloos Diversion Scheme 1 (n.d.) (unpublished manuscript, on file with the National Technical University of Athens, Faculty of Civil Engineering), available at http://www.itia.ntua.gr/~kimon/ACHELOOS_KH.doc.

132 *For the last twenty five.* Carol Reed, *Greece Bids Huge Irrigation Complex: Six Joint Ventures Are Expected to Compete for Project and Arrange Financing,* ENGINEER-ING NEWS-RECORD, August 18, 1988, at 59.

133 *sleeping giant.* Hadjibiros[0], at 1.

133 *Instead, a numbing.* Encyclopædia Britannica, Greece, History of (2008), available at http://search.eb.com/eb/article-26433 (last visited June 14, 2008). Germany invaded and occupied Greece in 1940. When it retreated in 1944 civil war broke out between royalist (Greece was a monarchy at the time) and anarchist resistance groups, ending around 1949. In 1956 a military coup against King Paul failed. In 1964, King Paul died and the government descended into chaos; new coalitions began taking hold. In 1967, a Greek military coup succeeded, followed by a failed counter-coup. A military junta ruled until 1974, when a parliamentary government was installed. Id.

133 *The enthusiasm of.* World Wildlife Fund, Pipedreams? Interbasin Water Transfers and Water Shortages 17–18, (June 2007) (available at http://assets.wwf.es/downloads/pipedreams_ibts_final_report_27_june_2007_1.pdf).

133 *a Testament.* Psaropoulos, Id. at 2.

133 *They had so.* Background and General Elements, at 20, at 1. "For decades the work of draining lakes went on in Thessaly without moderation . . ." with the result that the "most important hygrobiotype in Europe after the Danube delta was completely lost, together with a considerable fish production (a thousand tons annually, employing 1,300 fishermen)." Id.

134 *The cotton growers.* Kagkelidou, at 3.

134 *No one has . . . go.* Brown, at 2.

135 *We would not . . . rich.* Brown, at 2.

135 *By the late.* Id.; Kagkelidou, at 3.

135 *Seeing the hand.* Brown at 1.

135 *Meanwhile, sponsors back home.* Id.

135 *Compounding the project's.* Id.; Background and General Elements, at 2 (calling the deception "an organized confusion").

135 *descend[ed] into farce.* Brown, at 1.

135 *It was demanding.* Id.

135 *Cotton production would.* Id. (calling the irrigation benefits "purely imaginary").

135 *the thief of.* Id.; *The Diversion of the Acheloos River: The Last Study (August 1995),*

http://www.agrinio.net/ perivallon/enaxel21.html) (December 20, 1996) [herein-after *Last Study*].

136 *taking in mind.* Id.

136 *anyone who suggests.* Brown, at 1.

136 *water cannons . . . rain.* Psaropoulos, at 2.

136 *By the 1980s.* Psaropoulos, at 2. The Pieios River is "reduced to a poisonous trickle of agricultural runoff in the summer." Id.

137 *The member States.* Treaty Establishing the European Economic Community, March 25, 1957, 298 U.N.T.S. 11 (Cmd. 5179-II) [hereinafter EEC Treaty]; Rod Hunter and Koen Muylle, *European Community Environmental Law*, in ENVTL. LAW INST. ET AL., EUROPEAN COMMUNITY DESKBOOK 7, 7–11 (2d ed. 1999). The summary of European Community (EC) history and organization that follows is taken from these sources. The workings of the EC are, of course, far more complex and the role of its parliament, mentioned later in this story, of greater magnitude. Although the EC is now called the European Union, the term *European Community* is used here because it was in use at the time the Acheloos case arose.

137 *Commerce was the.* It was, after all, the European *Economic* Community and its pro-visions were designed to reduce trade barriers. *EEC Treaty* arts, 30–36.

138 *"harmonize" national laws.* LÜDWIGO KRAMER, EC TREATY AND ENVIRON-MENTAL LAW 1–3 (1990); Hunter and Muylle, at 19–21. Additional authority was found under EEC Treaty art. 235 a "Necessary and Proper"–like clause authorizing action to obtain Community "objectives."

138 *The theory worked.* KARAKOSTAS AND VASSILOPOULOS, at 29–30; KRAMER, at 2.

138 *It dropped the.* Single European Act, 1987 O.J. (L 169) 1 [hereinafter SEA] (amend-ing EEC Treaty). The United States, by contrast, still clings to the notion that envi-ronmental laws are justified as protecting interstate commerce, causing consider-able confusion where their objects, such as wetlands and endangered species, are not in commerce at all. For example, National Ass'n of Home Builders v. Babbitt, 130 F.3d 1041 (D.C. Cir. 1997), cert. denied, 524 U.S. 937 (1998); Rapanos v. United States, 547 U.S. 715 (2006).

138 *It would protect.* SEA, art. 100(A)(3) (defining environmental protection as a Com-munity legislative objective), and art. 130(r)(2) (reiterating environmental objec-tives of Community "action"). For rigors of the SEA's environmental policies, KRAMER, at 29–30.

138 *They dropped the.* Id. art. 130(s); for a discussion of Europe's odyssey over the leg-islative role of Parliament from debate club to full partner with the Council of Min-isters, Hunter and Muylle, at 1, 9–10.

138 *Pollution should be.* Id. art. 130(r)(2).

138 *the polluter should.* Id. A full discussion of Article 130(r) and (s) can be found in KRAMER, at 31–91.

· 138 *"sustainable" over time.* Id. at 11–12, art. 130(s). A full discussion of Article 130(r) and (s) can be found in Ludwig Krämer, *EC Treaty and Environmental Law 31-91* (2d ed., Sweet and Maxwell, 1995).

138 *Europe followed with.* Council Directive 85/337, On the Assent of the Effects of Certain Public and Private Projects on the Environment 1985 O.J. (L 175) 40, as amended by Council Directive 97/11, 1997 O.J. (L 73) 5.

139 *The year was.* Symboulion Epikrateias [SE] [Supreme Administrative Court] 2759/1994, (Greece) [hereinafter 2759/1994], available at http://www-penelope .drec.unilim.fr/Penelope/cases.htm.

139 *Minister of Environment.* Kagkelidou, at 1.

139 *The Council of.* Symboulion Epikrateias [SE] [Supreme Administrative Court] 2759/1994 (Greece) (available at http://www-enelope.drec.unilim.fr/Penelope/ cases.htm) [hereinafter SE, 2759/1994].

140 *fundamental principle . . . follow.* Id., at par. 10.

140 *exceptionally rich flora.* Id., at par. 12.

140 *The Ministry of.* Id., at par. 14.

140 *dynamic, not linear . . . composite.* Id.

140 *DR. MICHAEL DECLERIS.* Michael Decleris, *Global Judges: Sustainable Development and the Rule of Law* 26 (unpublished ms.) (available at http://www.unep.org/ Law/Symposium/Documents/Country_papers/MICHAEL_DECLARIS.doc); see also Michael Decleris, *The Law of Sustainable Development: General Principles* (European Communities 2000) (citing his work on systems analysis) [hereinafter Decleris, *General Principles*]. The description of Decleris's background that follows is taken from these sources.

141 *Greece did not.* See Greek Envtl. Legis. 86/1650/L, available at http://www.imbc.gr/ institute/idd/ Greek_Legislation4.doc (concerning the protection of the environment) (last visited March 13, 2009).

141 *obligation of the . . . measures.* 1975 Syntagma [SYN] [Constitution] 2:24(1) (Greece) (providing that "the protection of the physical and cultural environment constitutes an obligation to the State. The State must take special preventive or repressive measures in the conservation thereof.").

141 *It took the.* DECLERIS, at 10–11 (tracing development of law) 22–25 (summarizing council jurisprudence), 67–125 (analyzing application to environmental issues); KARAKOSTAS AND VASSILOPOULOS, at 10.

142 *The most heated.* KARAKOSTAS AND VASSILOPOULOS, at 16 (calling the Greek Council of State "the missing link between what is and what ought to be environmental law"); COMPARATIVE ENVIRONMENTAL LAW IN EUROPE 199 (René Seerden and Michiel Heldeweg, eds. 1996) (explaining that the Council of State was applying article 24 "in a very large and creative way").

142 *Like other scholars.* KARAKOSTAS AND VASSILOPOULOS, at 12; Id. at 13–14: "Private interests in Greece define policies and practices in the public sector in such a way as to evade any legal controls while, at the same time, managing to present themselves as representatives of the people. The way private interests escape legal control is through financial power and coordinated action at various levels. In many instances, they are also organized in associations, which, at least in name, represent the needs of larger parts of the citizenry (e.g., unions, agricultural and building associations). The reasons for the uncontrolled growth of private interests in Greece are historical and relate mainly to the undeveloped environmental consciousness of the people and the lack of respect for public goods, common spaces, and legal rules."

142 *in thrall . . . disorder.* Decleris, at 13.

142 *The governments of.* Id.

142 *The regulatory vacuum.* Id.; KARAKOSTAS AND VASSILOPOULOS, at 13. "Another particularly serious problem in Greece is the destruction of the natural environment by public works. The public works do not cause this destruction alone; rather it is caused by the low quality of planning and a vicious circle of corruption, which starts with the decision-making process and goes all the way to the selection of the contractor." Id.

142 *VASSILIS ANAGNOSTOPOULOS takes.* Kagkelidou, at 3. The description of Anagnostopoulos and quotations that follow are taken from this source.

143 *Anagnostopoulos finds an.* Interview by Alexander Marcopoulos with Dr. Glykeria Sioutis, Assistant Professor of Public Law and Environmental Law, Univ. of Athens, Greece (January 3, 2008). The quotations that follow are taken from this interview. Decleris's part of this conversation is extrapolated from his treatise, THE LAW OF SUSTAINABLE DEVELOPMENT, at 88.

143 *On the other.* For example, GLYKERIA SIOUTIS, DROIT MEDITERRANéEN DE L'ENVIRONNEMENT, LES INSTITUTIONS GRECQUES (Jean-Yves Cherot and André Roux, eds. 1988); Curriculum Vitae of Glykeria Sioutis (unpublished, on file with the European Public Law Center), available at http://www-penelope.drec .unilim.fr/Penelope/partners.htm.

144 *The village of.* Paul Brown, Greek Dam Project Drains EC's Funds Leaving Poor High and Dry; The Community Is Helping to Pay for New Dams and a Tunnel on the Acheloos River to Carry Water Away from Three Dams for Which It Also Footed Most of the Bill, GUARDIAN (London) 35 (June 26, 1993); Last Study, at 5.

144 *Shortly after the.* Aecheloos II.

144 *doomed anyway.* Sioutis Interview.

144 *Meanwhile, however, the.* Nantsou, at 4.

145 *Two years later.* Archeloos III.

145 *A new directive.* Council Directive 2000/60, EU Water Framework Directive O.J. (L 327) 22.

145 *One quarter of.* Hunter and Muylle, at 16–17.

145 *In recent years.* Note 38, Wild Birds, Habitats and Water Directives; *Treading Familiar Path to Court*, ATHENS NEWS, October 21, 2005, A07; *The European Commission.* Case C-166/04, Comm'n v. Hellenic Republic (2005) (failure to take measures to protect Messolongi Lagoon) (unpublished) [hereinafter Acheloos I], available at http://curia.europa.eu/en/content/juris/index_rep.htm; Clairie Papazoglou, The Acheloos River Case: The Diversion of Common Sense! (BirdLife Int'l, European Cmty Office eds.) (n.d.) (Nitrates Directive violations). See also Case C-334/04, Comm'n v. Hellenic Republic (2007) (manifestly insufficient classification of special protection areas for the purposes of Article 4[1] and [2] of Council Directive 79/409, On the Conservation of Wild Birds 1979 O.J. [L 103] 1, As Amended by Commission Directive 97/49, 1997 [L 223] 9) [hereinafter Acheloos II]. In October 2005, Greece was further condemned for noncompliance with the Waste Framework Directive at 1125 uncontrolled sites (citing Case C-502/03), available at http://www.europarl.europa.eu/meetdocs/2004_2009/documents/dt/608/608859/608859 en.pdf.

145 *Other European policies.* Council Directive 75/268, On Mountain and Hill Farming and Farming in Certain Less-Favoured Areas O.J. (L 222) 37, as last amended by Council Directive 87/786 art(2) (protecting mountain communities and promoting their agricultural livelihood).

145 *direct effect.* Direct effect is not mentioned in any of the EC treaties, and was established by the European Court of Justice in Van Gend en Loos v. Nederlandse Administratie der Belastingen (Case 26/62); [1963] ECR 1; [1970] C.M.L.R. 1, in which the court held that rights conferred on individuals by European Community legislation (treaties, regulations, directives, etc.) should be enforceable by those individuals in national courts. in Grad v. Finanzamt Traunstein (Case 9/70) [1970] ECR 825, a case involving VAT, the ECJ ruled that a directive could be directly effective, as they imposed an obligation to achieve a required result.

146 *overriding public interest.* For example, Council Directive 92/43 (natural habitats). "If, in spite of a negative assessment of the implications for the site and in the absence of alternative solutions, a plan or project must nevertheless be carried out for imperative reasons of overriding public interest, including those of a social or economic nature, the Member State shall take all compensatory measures necessary to ensure that the overall coherence of Natura 2000 is protected."

146 *Exploiting the opening.* Acheloos River Diversion Scheme. "In July 2006, the Environment Minister, George Souflias, successfully argued that the project was of national interest and after a lengthy debate, the Greek parliament voted through legal amendments to allow it to proceed." Id.

146 *it declared that.* Press Release, Parliamentary Questions, European Parliament, April 4, 2007.

147 *like the skeleton . . . framework.* Norman Davies, Europe: A History 99 (Oxford U.

Press, 1996) (from Plato, *Critias*, quoted by Clive Ponting, A Green History of the World 76–77 [London, 1991]).

147 *Man and Nature.* See George Perkins Marsh, *Man and Nature*, 7–52 (David Lowenthal, ed., U. Wash. Press, 2003).

147 *They have done.* Psaropoulos, at 2.

Chapter 8 Trillium

151 *I told David.* Wayne Crosby, *The Challenge of Developing Sustainability in Tierra del Fuego: Environmental Contestation of the Río Cóndor River Project in Chile*, at 94 (Spring 2006) (unpublished M.A. thesis, Simon Fraser University) (on file with author).

151 *IN THE WINTER.* BERGREEN, OVER THE EDGE OF THE WORLD: MAGELLAN'S TERRIFYING CIRCUMNAVIGATION OF THE GLOBE 34–39 (2003). The description of Magellan's voyage and that of Darwin later taken from this source.

152 *The few native . . . world.* Id., at 185.

152 *IN 1993, DAVID.* Bill Dietrich, *Chile's Tierra del Fuego—Harvest With Care—Washington Lumber Baron Backing Technique That Could Turn Logging On Its Ear*, SEATTLE TIMES, January 26, 1997, at A1, available at http://community.seattletimes .nwsource.com/archive/?date=19970126&slug=2520877. Trillium's original purchase of around 650,000 acres in Chile was augmented by a subsequent purchase in Argentina, bringing its total to 825,000 acres. Id.

152 *"terrific value," with.* Id.

153 *"aggressive" when speaking.* Crosby, at 51 (quoting Rand Jack, First Land Steward of Río Cóndor Project).

153 *Syre had fought.* Id. at 68; Trillium's original purchase of around 640,000 acres in Chile was augmented by a subsequent purchase in Argentina, bringing its total to 825,000 acres. Id.

153 *at fire sale.* Dietrich. For further information on Trillium's ventures, George Draffan, Public Information Network, Profile of the Trillium Corporation, December 2003, available at http://www.endgame.org/trillium.html.

153 *"blistering" letter of.* Detrich.

153 *group vomit.* Id.

153 *"savage" and "destructive".* Crosby, at 69 (quoting Pat Rasmussen, Forest-Americas Coordinator, America Lands Alliance). Crosby, at 51 (quoting e-mail from Pat Rasmussen, Forest-Americas Coord., Am. Lands Alliance, to Wayne Crosby, Graduate Student, Dept. Sociology and Anthropology, Simon Fraser U., Complaint about Trillium [June 9, 2004]).

154 *over mature.* Crosby, at 55 (quoting Gabriel Rodriguez, Trillium Operation Manager).

154 *We thought over.* Id. (quoting David Syre).

155 *Syre and company.* TED Case Studies: Chilean Forest Preservation and the Project River Condor, available at http://www.american.edu/TED/chilewd.htm (last visited May 12, 2008) [hereinafter TED Case Studies].

155 *Chilean authors since.* Crosby, at 41 ("[T]he generation following the Pinochet era are [sic] nearly oblivious of Chile's history between 1973 and 1990.") (citing CHILE, LA MEMORIA OBSTINADA [ARTE 1998]).

155 *dagger pointed straight.* Hitchens, *The Case against Henry Kissinger—Part One: The Making of a War Criminal*, HARPER'S MAGAZINE, February 2001, at 53.

155 *Its primary resources.* Crosby, at 29, 42–43; TED Case Studies.

155 *Most of the.* Crosby, at 69.

156 *new copper.* TED Case Studies. "If one was [sic] to travel to Puerto Montt, Chile, in the early 1990s, it was likely one would see mountains of wood chips awaiting transport to their distant destination of Japan."; Crosby, at 69.

156 *the Chicago Boys.* TED Case Studies.

156 *David Syre was.* Crosby, at 57. The Chilean government began selling forestlands from $.50 to $1.50 an acre; Cetec-Sel purchased at between $2.50 and $25 an acre. Id., at 57 n. 22 (citing Nathaniel C. Nash, For Tierra del Fuego, It's Time to Consider a Rain Forest's Worth, NEW YORK TIMES, June 4, 1991, at C4).

156 *He got his.* Dietrich. Comparable forestlands in the state of Washington were selling at up to $30,000 an acre. Id.

156 *In 1991, a.* Crosby, at 48.

157 *massive, slow burning.* Id.

157 *like using old.* Dietrich.

157 *A Chilean economist.* Memorandum from Bernardo Reyes, Dir. of Ecological Econ. Program, Inst. for Political Ecology, Trillium: Lessons Learned From a Conflict over Patagonian Forests in Southern Chile 8 (on file with author).

157 *Even today, following.* Chile, http://en.wikipedia.org/wiki/chile (last visited May 12, 2008) ("Chile . . . suffers from one of the most uneven distributions of wealth in the world, ahead only of Brazil in the Latin American region and lagging behind even of [sic] most developing sub-Saharan African nations.") [hereinafter Chile].

158 *It also spends.* Id.

158 *The mass killings.* For a summary of the methods used by the Pinochet regime, Crosby, at 39–42. See also Monte Reel and J. Y. Smith, "A Chilean Dictator's Dark Legacy," The Washington Post, Dec. 11, 2006, "According to a government report that included testimony from more than 30,000 people, his government killed at least 3,197 people and tortured about 29,000. Two-thirds of the cases listed in the report happened in 1973."

158 *While the Pinochet.* Crosby, at 43. The committee, called the National Commission of Ecology, remains largely intact today as a successor, the National Commission for the Environment, established in 1990. Id. at 43–44.

158 *Review of private.* Crosby, at 44–45; Memorandum from Maria Fernanda Carvajal. Ref.: Legal Aspects Concerning Projects Which Voluntarily Submitted to the Environmental Impact Evaluation System before the Enactment of the Relevant Regulations 1 (June 6, 1997) (on file with author), at 2–3. Memorandum from María Fernanda Carvajal, The new environmental provisions were to come into effect only after the regulations were published, at 3.

159 *A "naturally occurring . . . wheat".* Crosby, at 56 (quoting Rand Jack, First Land Steward of Río Cóndor Project).

160 *"shelterwood" cutting, a.* Crosby, at 64.

160 *Syre had confidence.* In Syre's words, "we made virtually everybody unhappy because they felt we set standards too high . . . we made the environmentalists unhappy because we had answers," quoted in Crosby, at 67.

160 *"young soil" . . . "miracle" . . . "very, very slow".* Id., at 67 (quoting Bedrich Magas, Director of Iniciativa de Defensa Ecológica Austral).

160 *Worse still, once.* Id., at 60 (citing Alan Rebertus et al., *Blowdown History and Landscape Patterns in the Andes of Tierra del Fuego, Argentina*, 78 ECOLOGY 678, 678–692 (1997).

160 *To some scientists.* Id. at 83 (quoting Dr. Jerry Franklin, Forest Ecologist and Professor, University of Washington) (citing Rebertus, at 678–692; Alan Rebertus and Thomas Veblen, *Structure and Tree-Fall Gap Dynamics of Old-Growth Nothofagus Forests in Tierra del Fuego, Argentina*, 4 J. OF VEGETATIVE SCI. 641, 641–654 (1993)); Id. at 125 (quoting Dr. Jerry Franklin) (advocating the use of group selection rather than shelterwood technique).

161 *In the beginning.* Id. at 84–85 (quoting Marta Soto Andrade, Community Leader of Porvenir, Chile).

161 *moderate . . bring in plants.* Id.

161 *"so hopes were".* Crosby, at 85 (quoting Marta Soto Andrade, Community Leader of Porvenir, Chile).

161 *analyzed better, . . . started.* Id.

161 *cold jungle.* Native southern Chilean forests are temperate rainforests, often referred to as "cold jungles" due to their subantarctic climates. TED Case Studies.

161 *sustainable management plan . . . harvest.* Crosby, at 51.

162 *positive environmental aspects.* TED Case Studies.

162 *extraction impacts.* Id.

162 *The heart of.* Memorandum from Bernardo Reyes, at 5–6.

162 *Accordingly, as might.* Memorandum from María Fernanda Carvajal, at 5.

162 *green bench.* The two Chilean senators backing the suit were Guido Girari and Alejandro Navarro. Memorandum from Bernardo Reyes, at 5.

163 *Back in 1972.* UN Conference on the Human Environment, GA Res. 2581 (XXIV), UN GAOR, 24th Sess., Supp. No. 30, UN Doc. A/RES/2581(XXIV) (1969)

(unanimously adopted on December 15, 1969); see UNEP, Brief Summary of the General Debate, http://www.unep.org/Documents.Multilingual/Default.asp? DocumentID=97&ArticleID=1497&l=en (last visited February 23, 2009) [hereinafter Stockholm Conference]. See also Lakshman D. Guruswamy, Sir Geoffrey W. R. Palmer, and Burns H. Weston, *International Environment Law and World Order: A Problem-Oriented Coursebook* 229 (W. Publishing. 1994); David Hunter, James Salzman, and Durwood Zaelke, *International Environmental Law and Policy* 173 (2d ed., Found. Press, 2002).

163 *A group of.* Personal conversation with Jacques Cousteau in New Orleans, La. (September 26, 1983).

163 *One of their more.* Declaration of the United Nations Conference on the Human Environment, Stockholm Conference princ. 1 (adopted June 16, 1972), available at http://www.unep.org/Documents.Multilingual/Default.asp?DocumentID=97& ArticleID=1503&l=en. Principle 1 states: "Man has the fundamental right to freedom, equality and adequate conditions of life, in an environment of a quality that permits a life of dignity and well-being, and he bears a solemn responsibility to protect and improve the environment for present and future generations." Id.

163 *The process is.* For a description of the development of these actions in Argentina, Brazil, Chile, Colombia, Mexico, and Venezuela in the 1990s, ISABEL MARTÍNEZ, EL ACCESO A LA JUSTICIA AMBIENTAL EN ARGENTINA, BRASIL, CHILE, COLOMBIA, MÉXICO Y VENEZUELA DURANTE LA DéCADA DE 1990 (2000).

163 *One story goes.* Personal conversation with Isabel Martínez in Havana, Cuba (August 1998).

164 *Chilean law required.* "Trillium Case," Decision No. 2.732-96, Sup. Ct. of Chile 6-7 (March 19, 1997) (majority opinion), available at http://www.elaw.org/resources/text.asp?ID=15698.

164 *the maintenance of . . . intrusion.* Id. at 12 (majority opinion).

165 *"vigilant" to secure.* Id. at 11 (majority opinion).

165 *Basically, said the . . . door.* Id. at 9 (majority opinion).

165 *The opinion had.* Id. at 12–13 (majority opinion). Chilean business leaders were said to be "fuming" over the ruling. Heather Walsh, Chile: Court Ruling Prompts New Environmental Regulation, PANOS, April 28, 1997, available at http://www.sunsonline.org/trade/areas/environm/05050197.htm. The President of Sofofa, a Chilean manufacturing association, stated that it created an atmosphere of "incredibility" on the part of the private sectors. Id.

166 *They agreed to.* Memorandum from Bernardo Reyes, at 8.

166 *At this point.* Press Release, Global Response, Protect Ancient Gondwana Forests/ Tierra del Fuego May–June 2001 (May 29, 2001), available at http://forests.org/archive/samerica/prangond.htm.

166 *That the Commission.* Memorandum from Bernardo Reyes, at 6.

166 *Trillium's annual cut.* Id.

166 *ecological insurance.* Crosby, at 80–81, 103–105; Memorandum from Bernardo Reyes, at 8, 10–11.

167 *We saw that . . . industry.* Crosby, at 81 (quoting Carlos Noton, Forest Engineer and Environmental Coordinator).

167 *A professor of.* Id. at 81–82.

167 *They could disappear.* Id.

167 *could probably have . . . selection.* Id. at 83 (quoting Dr. Jerry Franklin, Forest Ecologist and Professor, University of Washington).

168 *Months following the.* Id. at 79–81; Memorandum from Bernardo Reyes, at 7.

168 *The Chilean Forestry.* Press Release, Trillium Looks to Argentina, May Put Native Forest Project in Chile on Hold for Several Years (September 2, 1998), available at http://forests.org/archived_site/today/recent/1998/trilhome.htm.

168 *Suddenly, in the.* Id.

168 *except maybe give.* Id.

168 *clearcut, build roads.* Press Release, Trillium Looks to Argentina, May Put Native Forest Project in Chile on Hold for Several Years (September 2, 1998), available at http://forests.org/archived_site/today/recent/1998/trilhome.htm; Press Release, Leavenworth Audubon Adopt-a-Forest, Washington Company Backs Out of Chile Proposed Logging Project (September 24, 1998), available at http://forests.org/archived_site/today/recent/1998/trilhome.htm.

168 *They also turned.* Tim Johnson, *Is Trillium Solvent?*, EVERY OTHER WEEKLY (Bellingham, Wash.), May 3, 2001; Peter Sleeth, *Grand Jury Indicts Louisiana Pacific*, OREGONIAN (Portland, Or.), June 16, 1995, at A1.

168 *began crumbling and.* Jeff Manning, *Timber via Tierra del Fuego: Two Portland Executives Help a Bellingham Logging Company Launch a Huge, Controversial Project in South America*, OREGONIAN (Portland, Or.), February 16, 2000.

168 *In June 1998.* Johnson.

169 *laughing their heads.* Crosby, at 125 (citing personal interview with Maria Luisa Robleto, Forest Campaign Director, Greenpeace South Pacific, in Santiago, Chile [November 3, 2003]).

169 *I came down.* Id. at 70 (quoting Rick Klein, Executive Director, Ancient Forest International).

169 *most unique forests.* Scott Ayers, *Adopt-a-Tree Plan Targets Trillium Land*, BELLINGHAM HERALD (Wash.), April 24, 2001.

169 *For his part.* Corporación de Defensa de la Soberania, Proyecto Trillium de Depredación Transferencia de Terrenos, July 2005, available at http://www.soberaniachile.cl/patag3b.html (last visited Forestal y Venta de Bondos de Carbono en la Tierra del Fuego. Goldman Sachs y Su Oscura May 13, 2008).

169 *Always have a.* Global Inst. of Sustainable Forestry, Yale Sch. of Forestry and Envtl. Studies, Sustainable Development, Can It Work? An Entrepreneur's Experience in Tierra Del Fuego (October 17, 2002), available at http://research.yale.edu/gisf/

assets/pdf/yff/lunch_summaries/david_syre.pdf (last visited May 13, 2008) (summarizing talk given by David Syre).

169 *"hefty" interest rate.* Johnson, at 5.

169 *At that point.* Jeff Manning, *Good News Emerges from Local Scandal,* OREGONIAN (Portland, Or.), December 22, 2003.

169 *We work with.* Mauricio Rodriguez and Valeria Ibarra, Goldman Sachs Gives Ex-Trillium Property in Tierra Del Fuego to Environmental Organizations, La Tercera (December 13, 2003) (quoting Peter Rose, spokesperson for Goldman Sachs) (taken from an English translation made available by George Draffan, Pub. Info. Network, Profile of Trillium Corporation, ttp://www.endgame.org/trillium.html [last updated December 2003]).

170 *The idea took.* Id.

170 *Goldman also put.* Scott Ayers, *Trillium Logging Plan Trimmed,* BELLINGHAM HERALD (Wash.), December 16, 2003; Wildlife Conservation Society, Rhode Island-Sized Wilderness Given Away by U.S. Investment Firm (September 16, 2004), available at http://www.newswise.com/p/articles/view/507119/.

170 *and offered to. Saving the Ends of the Earth: Preserving Chile's Southern Forests,* THE ECONOMIST, March 11, 2006, at 74, available at http://www.economist.com/science/displaystory.cfm?story_id=E1_VGDTVVQ&CFID=5514812&CFTOKEN=71208242 (last visited May 13, 2008) [hereinafter Saving the Ends of the Earth].

170 *taken the project.* Id.

170 *at the highest.* Patrick Nixon, Goldman Sachs to Create Nature Reserve in South Chile, Reuters, (December 15, 2003), available at http://www.planetark.com/dailynewsstory.cfm/newsid/23112/newsDate/15-Dec-2003/story.htm.

170 *A Goldman spokesman.* Mauricio Rodriguez and Valeria Ibarra, *Goldman Sachs Gives Ex-Trillium Property in Tierra Del Fuego to Environmental Organizations,* LA TERCERA, December 13, 2003 (English translation).

170 *a very interesting.* Id.

170 *According to their.* Manning.

170 *it was always.* Press Release, Global Response, Protect Ancient Gondwana Forests/ Tierra Del Fuego May–June 2001 (May 29, 2001), available at http://forests.org/archive/samerica/prangond.htm.

170 *Then, in 1998.* David Haskel, *Argentina, Chile to Create Nature Preserve That Straddles Andean,* Patagonian Region, 29 INT'L ENV'T REPORTER 579, 579 (2006).

170 *This purchase set.* Native Forests Network, NFN—*Gondwana Forest Sanctuary,* available at http://www.nativeforest.org/campaigns/gondwana/index.htm (last visited May 13, 2008).

171 *In the early.* James Langman, *Thinking Big—Esprit Founder Doug Tomkins Invests in Chile Natural Reserve,* E/THE ENVIRONMENTAL MAGAZINE, September–

October, 1997, at 24, 24–25, available at http://findarticles.com/p/articles/mi_m1594/is_n5_v8/ai_19926794.

171 *Tomkins was in.* Langman, at 24–25.

171 *They inspired a. Saving the Ends of the Earth*, at 74; Triple Pundit, Sebastián Piñera: Chilean Businessman, Politician, and Environmental Philanthropist, May 1, 2008, http://www.triplepundit.com/pages/sebastian-piaera-chilean-busin-003071.php.

171 *On the other. Saving the Ends of the Earth*, at 74.

172 *The first Supreme.* Greg Brown, *Logging Gripes—Chile*, LATIN TRADE 31, September 1999, available at http://findarticles.com/p/articles/mi_m0BEK/is_9_7/ai_55548155.

172 *[w]e are, in.* Id.

172 *I think it.* Id.

173 *[Trillium] had answers.* Crosby, at 67.

173 *[T]he reality was, . . . preserved.* Id., at 74 (quoting Dr. Jerry Franklin, Forest Ecologist and Professor, University of Washington).

173 *[s]ome places are.* Ayers.

Index

About the Author

Oliver Houck lives in New Orleans with his wife and dog, a stone's throw from the Mississippi River. A graduate of Harvard College and Georgetown Law Center, he spent several years in military intelligence overseas, several more as a prosecutor in the District of Columbia, and ten years subsequent as general counsel to the National Wildlife Federation, just as the environmental movement was breaking.

He has been teaching law at Tulane University in New Orleans since 1981 and is deeply involved in river management, coastal protection, and wetlands and wildlife issues. He has served on the boards of several national environmental organizations and remains on the litigation review committees of the Environmental Defense Fund and Defenders of Wildlife. He has also served on the Army Corps of Engineers Advisory Board and several committees of the National Research Council of the Academy of Sciences. He has taught environmental courses in Europe, Mexico, Cuba, and New Zealand, which, in addition to his international students at Tulane, has sensitized him to the commonality of environmental issues and the role of environmental litigation in meeting them. It is a difficult role to play, rarely a definitive one, but indispensable for protecting the world we have inherited and, one way or another, are going to pass on.

Island Press | Board of Directors